'This highly significant book explores the work of Tearfund over its first 50 years, emerging in the 1960s as a "new kind of missionary organisation", becoming a major development NGO during the 1990s and then reorienting itself as a faith-based development organisation (FBDO) from the mid-2000s onwards. The insightful analysis unpacks the story of where "faith" sits in this history, telling us as much about shifting social attitudes towards the role of religion in the public sphere as the internal dynamics of this important evangelical relief and development organisation. Skillfully researched and highly readable, this book presents an essential addition to the growing literature on religion, development and humanitarianism, and is especially significant as it is one of the very first in-depth studies of an FBDO.'

Emma Tomalin, Professor of Religion and Public Life, University of Leeds, UK

'Dena Freeman's book about Tearfund, the UK's largest evangelical development organization, is a path-breaking and timely contribution to the burgeoning field of global development studies and the prominent role religion plays in development today. Freeman's privileged access enabled her to write a unique account, at once honest and empathetic, of Tearfund's institutional history and the fierce debates that preoccupy staff as they seek to reconcile the antinomy of faith and secularism. More than just the history of an evangelical development organization, this book offers a window onto a history of the contemporary.'

Charles Piot, Professor of Cultural Anthropology, Duke University, USA

'This is a gripping story of "development" and its relationship to mission and evangelism. Through detailed interviews and in-depth archive research, Freeman critically analyses how a Non-Governmental Organisation has come to new understandings of "doing development" over the course of its history, from giving grants to missionaries to carrying out development projects in the 1970s, to campaigning for structural policy change to address poverty and climate change today. The book's historico-conceptual analysis is peppered with interesting anecdotes about why things happened the way they did, such as how the Jubilee 2000 debt cancellation campaign started and how the Evangelical Alliance embraced social action and care for creation as part of its mission. Freeman shows in a captivating narrative style the creative tension between evangelism and social action. Both are intimately connected but, she argues, have an "almost entropic tendency to come apart". This book will be an invaluable resource for students, scholars and practitioners alike to better understand the connections between faith and development, and the role that faith plays in the work of a major faith-based development NGO.'

Séverine Deneulin, Associate Professor of International Development, University of Bath, UK

'This book opens up fascinating insights about "development" in the 20th century: the emergence of "faith-based" approaches, the plural continuities of missionary interventions, and the mainstreaming of development values and processes in the religious and secular sectors alike. Tracing the story of Tearfund, and the many twists and turns in the understanding of its mandate, Freeman adds a brilliant chapter to the story of how the dividing line between religion and secularity has been negotiated within and through Christianity all along. As such, the book pioneers a much-needed connection between the study of World Christianity and the burgeoning field of religion and development.'

Jörg Haustein, Lecturer in World Christianities, Cambridge University, UK

'Freeman has written one of the first books in what will hopefully become a trend – deep histories of faith-based humanitarian and development organizations that examine the role of faith in organizational culture. Faith-based organizations are not a neatly defined category and histories of this sort can demonstrate the internal debates and external pressures that lead organizations to define their own parameters. This book is significant not only for those interested in religion and development research (for whom it is a crucial read), but also for those wishing to understand more about non-profit organizations in general.'

Olivia Wilkinson, Director of Research, Joint Learning Initiative on Faith & Local Communities, Washington, DC, USA

Tearfund and the Quest for Faith-Based Development

This book gives an in-depth analysis of the role of faith in the work of Tearfund, a leading evangelical relief and development NGO that works in over 50 countries worldwide.

The study traces the changing ways that faith has shaped and influenced Tearfund's work over the organisation's 50-year history. It shows how Tearfund has consciously grappled with the role of faith in its work and has invested considerable time and energy in developing an intentionally faith-based approach to relief and development that in several ways is quite different to the approaches of secular relief and development NGOs. The book charts the different perspectives and possibilities that were not taken and the internal discussions about theology, development practices, and humanitarian standards that took place as Tearfund worked out for itself what it meant to be a faith-based relief and development organisation. There is a growing academic literature about religion and development, as well as increasing interest from development ministries of many Northern governments in understanding the role of religion in development and the specific challenges and benefits involved in working with faith-based organisations. However, there are very few studies of actual faith-based organisations and no book-length detailed studies showing how such an organisation operates in practice and how it integrates its faith into its work.

In documenting the story of Tearfund, the book provides important insights into the practice and ethos of faith-based organisations, which will be of interest to other FBOs and to researchers of religion and development.

Dena Freeman is a Senior Visiting Fellow in the Department of Anthropology, London School of Economics and Political Science, where she is also a member of the Laboratory for Advanced Research on the Global Economy and an Associate of the International Inequalities Institute. Her previous books include *Pentecostalism and Development: Churches, NGOs and Social Change in Africa* (2012), *Peripheral People: The Excluded Minorities of Ethiopia* (2003), and *Initiating Change in Highland Ethiopia: Causes and Consequences of Cultural Transformation* (2002).

Routledge Research in Religion and Development

The *Routledge Research in Religion and Development* series focuses on the diverse ways in which religious values, teachings and practices interact with international development.

While religious traditions and faith-based movements have long served as forces for social innovation, it has only been within the last ten years that researchers have begun to seriously explore the religious dimensions of international development. However, recognising and analysing the role of religion in the development domain is vital for a nuanced understanding of this field. This interdisciplinary series examines the intersection between these two areas, focusing on a range of contexts and religious traditions.

Series editors:

Matthew Clarke, *Deakin University, Australia*
Emma Tomalin, *University of Leeds, UK*
Nathan Loewen, *Vanier College, Canada*

Editorial board:

Carole Rakodi, *University of Birmingham, UK*
Gurharpal Singh, *School of Oriental and African Studies, University of London, UK*
Jörg Haustein, *School of Oriental and African Studies, University of London, UK*
Christopher Duncanson-Hales, *Saint Paul University, Canada*

Religion and Society in Sub-Saharan Africa and Southern Asia
Carole Rakodi

Negotiating Religion and Development
Identity Construction and Contention in Bolivia
Arnhild Leer-Helgesen

Tearfund and the Quest for Faith-Based Development
Dena Freeman

Tearfund and the Quest for Faith-Based Development

Dena Freeman

LONDON AND NEW YORK

First published 2019 by Routledge

2 Park Square, Milton Park, Abingdon, Oxon, OX14 4RN
605 Third Avenue, New York, NY 10017

Routledge is an imprint of the Taylor & Francis Group, an informa business

First issued in paperback 2020

Copyright © 2019 Dena Freeman

The right of Dena Freeman to be identified as author of this work has been asserted by her in accordance with sections 77 and 78 of the Copyright, Designs and Patents Act 1988.

All rights reserved. No part of this book may be reprinted or reproduced or utilised in any form or by any electronic, mechanical, or other means, now known or hereafter invented, including photocopying and recording, or in any information storage or retrieval system, without permission in writing from the publishers.

Notice:
Product or corporate names may be trademarks or registered trademarks, and are used only for identification and explanation without intent to infringe.

British Library Cataloguing-in-Publication Data
A catalogue record for this book is available from the British Library

Library of Congress Cataloging-in-Publication Data
A catalog record has been requested for this book

ISBN: 978-0-367-36021-4 (hbk)
ISBN: 978-0-367-77764-7 (pbk)

Typeset in Times New Roman
by Wearset Ltd, Boldon, Tyne and Wear

 Printed in the United Kingdom
by Henry Ling Limited

Contents

Acknowledgements ix

1 Introduction 1
2 Religious and secular actors in the emergence of humanitarianism and development 18

PART I
A new kind of missionary organisation 39

3 Tearfund's first 25 years, 1968–1993 41

PART II
Emerging as a development NGO 59

4 Tearfund joins the mainstream, 1990–2005 61
5 The religious revitalists and the quest for transformation 80
6 The globalists and the localists – the start of campaigning and advocacy 98

PART III
Becoming an FBO 111

7 Trying to institutionalise faith-based approaches, 2005–2015 113
8 Mainstreaming faith-based development, 2015 onwards 141

PART IV
Paradoxes of faith-based development   159

9   Conclusion   161

Appendix: Tearfund's work with supporters in the UK   168
Bibliography   177
Index   191

Acknowledgements

I am very grateful to the many people who have supported this research and made it possible.

I would like to thank the numerous staff at Tearfund, past and present, who gave their time to be interviewed, openly shared their experiences and reflections on their work, and in many cases responded patiently to my ongoing emails clarifying details and requesting documents. In particular, I would like to thank Catriona Dejean and Lydia Powell for their tremendous help and support throughout the research process. Lydia was fantastic at organising interviews, finding documents, unearthing crucial pieces of information, managing rounds of comments and feedback, and troubleshooting problems. Her efficiency, patience, and cheerful countenance helped to make this research an enjoyable, as well as an interesting, experience. Catriona was a marvellous sounding board throughout the research and during the writing process, and her wise countenance was much appreciated. I would also like to thank Mike Hollow, a former Tearfund staff member who wrote a book about Tearfund in 2008, for generously allowing me to see and quote from the transcripts of interviews that he carried out for that work in 2006. Most of all, I am grateful to Tearfund for letting me carry out this research and publish my analysis, even though at times my framing and perspective differs quite significantly from theirs.

I would also like to thank Tearfund's partner organisations in Africa and Asia for graciously showing me around their projects when I visited, facilitating and often translating conversations with beneficiaries, and sharing their views with me.

Initial phases of this research were carried out while I was a Senior Visiting Fellow at the Centre for Religion, Economy and Politics at the University of Basel, Switzerland, and I would like to extend my sincere gratitude to Professors Andreas Heuser and Jens Köhrsen for inviting me to participate in the Research Group on Religion, Development and Faith-Based Organisations. A few years later I was fortunate to be invited to the University of Sapienza, Rome, Italy as a Visiting Professor in the Department of History, Culture and Religion, and it was there that most of this manuscript was written. I would like to extend my thanks to the Department, and in particular to Professor Pino Schirripa, for hosting me so nicely. I would also like to thank the Department of Anthropology at the

London School of Economics, my academic home base, for encouraging me in this research.

Many people have commented on earlier drafts of the manuscript. The full list is too long to include here, but particular gratitude goes to Catriona Dejean, Jörg Haustein, Paul Gifford, Joanna Sadgrove, Hannah Swithinbank, Emma Tomalin, Olivia Wilkinson, and the anonymous reviewers from Routledge. The final analysis and conclusions in this book remain, of course, my own.

And finally, I must thank my wonderful husband, who has followed me around the world, supported me in so many ways, and quietly accepted the countless working evenings and weekends. Thank you, my dear; this book would not have been possible without you.

1 Introduction

This book examines the changing role of faith in Tearfund's work over 50 years, from its formation in 1968 up to 2018. It is not an 'authorised history', recounting stories of heroic work overseas in various projects and programmes in the fashion of Maggie Black's book about Oxfam (Black 1992), Mark Luetchford and Peter Burns's book about War on Want (Luetchford and Burns 2003), or indeed Mike Hollow's earlier book about Tearfund (Hollow 2008). Instead, the aim is more specific – to explore the role of faith in Tearfund's work and to trace how its identity has changed over the years and how its development, humanitarian relief, and advocacy work has adapted as a result. At the book's centre is an analysis of Tearfund's attempt to develop a distinctly Christian faith-based approach to its relief, development, and advocacy work.

During the past 15 years there has been an increase in scholarly work about so-called 'faith-based organisations' (FBOs) and particularly about those FBOs which are involved in relief and development activities overseas ('faith-based development organisations', FBDOs). While there is now a rather large literature about 'religion and development' and 'faith-based development', much of it has remained at the level of generality, seeking to delineate differences between FBDOs and secular NGOs, and to make generalised claims about their comparative advantages or disadvantages. However, there is a huge diversity within the category of 'FBDO', and the term bundles together hugely different types of organisation – from different faiths and denominations, with different aims and purposes, and in which religion is embedded and operationalised in vastly different ways. Much of the scholarly literature has centred on forming typologies of such organisations with the aim of setting an analytic order and framework with which to understand this vast diversity (e.g. Bradley 2009, Clarke and Ware 2015, Jeavons 1998, Sider and Unruh 2004, Thaut 2009, Tvedt 2006; for a good overview of FBO typologies, see Smith 2017).

What has been sorely missing, however, has been in-depth studies of particular FBDOs – how they operate in practice, how they understand and frame what it is that they do, and how they negotiate the contestations and tensions that occur as they seek to engage with both secular and religious practices and discourses about 'good change'. While there have been a small number of book-length field-level studies of faith-based development organisations working in particular contexts, such as Bornstein's study of Protestant NGOs in rural Zimbabwe (Bornstein 2003), Occhipinti's study of Catholic NGOs in rural northwest Argentina (Occhipinti 2005), and Halvorson's study of American Lutheran NGOs in Madagascar (Halvorson 2018), there has been no book-length organisational study of a single FBDO. Several scholars have highlighted the need for such work. Elizabeth Ferris has argued that 'further research is needed on the faith-based organizations themselves, including research on their development and history ... in order to deepen our understanding of the ways in which they operate' (Ferris 2011: 622). Likewise, Jonathan Smith has called for 'in-depth organizational case studies [that] would add richness to the complex interaction between material and sacred dimensions, and longitudinal studies [that] could reveal how organizations adapt their beliefs and practices over time' (Smith 2017: 73).

This book seeks to respond to these calls by looking in depth at one particular FBDO, Tearfund, and exploring in some detail the role that faith has played in Tearfund's work over the years. This role has not been static: it has evolved as it has been influenced by changes in Christian ideas about evangelism and social change, secular theories of development, and mainstream ideas about the role of religion in society, as well as broader socio-political–economic transformations. By tracing this history, we can look inside one particular FBDO and get a deeper sense of how it works in practice and the role of faith in that. And, at the same time, we can begin to understand some of the key elements that differentiate Tearfund from secular NGOs, and indeed from many other Christian FBDOs, and in this way develop a more contextualised understanding of some of the lines of variation between different FBDOs.

Tearfund was chosen for this study as it is the UK's largest and most influential evangelical development NGO. Evangelical development NGOs have increased in size and number since the 1990s and currently represent the fastest-growing category of FBDOs. It has been estimated that evangelical NGOs account for almost 80 per cent of all US faith-based humanitarian and development agencies (Barnett and Stein 2012: 5, McCleary and Barro 2008). In the UK the numbers are much smaller, but evangelical development NGOs still have a considerable, and growing, presence within the British international humanitarian and development sectors. As the UK's largest evangelical development NGO, Tearfund occupies a significant position of influence within this growing sector of evangelical relief and development organisations, and among British evangelicals more widely. As such, the story of Tearfund also allows insights about some of the dynamics within the UK evangelical relief and development sector more broadly.

Academic book-length studies of specific NGOs are surprisingly few and far between. There is Forsythe's study of the Red Cross (Forsythe 2005), Hopgood's study of Amnesty International (Hopgood 2006), and Redfield's study of Médecins Sans Frontières (Redfield 2013). These in-depth studies of major humanitarian and human rights NGOs show the value of an approach that combines institutional history and ethnography to give a detailed understanding of how these organisations carry out their work and how this has changed over time as they have grown, institutionalised, and dealt with dilemmas around whether and how they should modify their original mission in order to respond to external changes. The long-term historical view enables a dynamic analysis of the internal moral and political debates that arise as organisations negotiate changes in their fundamental understanding of what they do and why, and the best ways to manifest these changed understandings in their evolving mission, strategy, and practice. To date, there are no similar book-length studies of major development NGOs, or indeed of major FBDOs. This book thus fills an important gap by looking in depth at Tearfund. It is more institutional history than ethnography, focussing less on Tearfund's internal workplace culture and more on the debates about how best to integrate faith into the various areas of its overseas work as it sought to conceptualise and carry out a distinctly Christian kind of development.

The research for this book was mainly carried out between October 2017 and March 2019 and was based on interviews, ethnography, archival research, and field visits. Over 60 in-depth interviews were carried out with present and past Tearfund staff and a further 15 interviews were conducted with a small selection of partner organisations and other Christian NGOs and mission agencies. The research also draws on 14 interviews with partner organisations carried out by Lydia Powell, a Tearfund research analyst, in March 2018. Transcripts of 34 interviews carried out by Mike Hollow, an independent consultant and former Head of Creative Services at Tearfund, for previous research in 2006, were also drawn upon, and quotes from these interviews are marked in the text with an asterisk (*). Two months of ethnographic research were carried out in Tearfund's headquarters in Teddington, UK, including attendance at staff prayers, team meetings, new staff inductions, information briefings, and one of the year's special 'jubilee days' of prayer and reflection. In addition, two field trips were made to visit partner projects in Africa and Asia, and insights from a third field trip by Lydia Powell to visit partners in Latin America were also drawn upon. These field trips included visits to projects, interviews with local partner staff at national- and field level, and focus group discussions with beneficiaries. Finally, well over 500 Tearfund project proposals, reports, evaluations, policy papers, strategy documents, and internal memos from over a 50-year period, in both digital and paper archives, were reviewed. While Tearfund allowed and facilitated this research, it should be stressed that this book does not present an official Tearfund perspective and that the analysis and conclusions are very much my own.

Theoretical discussions

The academic literature on religion and development is diverse and interdisciplinary, drawing on scholarship from development studies, international relations, religious studies, sociology, and anthropology. Nonetheless it is possible to discern three interconnected research themes that dominate much of the literature. The first, as mentioned above, is defining and categorising FBOs in order to try to understand their variety and their relation to secular development NGOs. The second focusses on analysing the role of faith in FBDOs and on discerning whether and how FBDOs do development differently from secular development NGOs. And the third looks more broadly at the role of religion in development and asks more general questions about the role of ideas, values, and worldviews in societal change. This book touches on issues across all these three research themes and thus some of the main lines of discussion will be reviewed here.[1]

From typologies to historical and contextual analysis

There are literally dozens of different typologies seeking to make sense of the variety of FBOs. Many seek to categorise FBOs according to the degree to which faith affects their activities. Sider and Unruh (2004), for example, suggest that faith-based organisations exist along a spectrum from 'faith background', in which the organisation may have a historical tie to a faith tradition and some staff may be motivated by faith, but in which there is no religious content in their activities or programming, through to 'faith permeated', where the connection with religious faith is evident at all levels of mission, staffing, governance, programming, and support. Thaut (2009) proposes distinguishing among FBOs according to their 'theologies of humanitarian engagement' as evidenced in their mission (how they conceptualise the change they want to bring about), their institutional affiliations (for example, with a particular religious denomination), their staff policies (for example, whether they require staff to sign up to a statement of faith), and where they get their funding from (individual donors or government grants). Paras (2014) seeks to distinguish between those that are 'proselytising' and those that are not. And so on and so on.

Typologies such as these seek to provide an analytic framework in which all kinds of FBOs can be placed, including for example places of worship, religious schools, and community centres, as well as small and large NGOs, across the full range of different religions. In attempting to bring together such a wide variety of actors within one framework these typologies necessarily become rather vague and abstract. An alternative approach, I suggest, is to narrow the focus to one particular faith tradition and then to map out some of the different actors through an understanding of their histories, theologies, and objectives. Thus, in seeking to understand Tearfund, this book aims to contextualise the organisation within the setting of Protestant development actors. As will be shown, primarily in Chapter 2 but also throughout the text, there is considerable variety even within this one sector, and an understanding of the missionary past (and present) theological differences between various camps within the broader Protestant church, and the history of the emergence of secular development NGOs is necessary to appreciate the differences and distinctiveness of the various Protestant development actors and therefore to position Tearfund within this field. Thus this book does not discuss FBDOs from Muslim, Hindu, Buddhist, or other faith traditions, and only mentions Catholicism and Catholic

FBDOs in passing. This is not because these actors are not important, or not prolific, but rather because I seek to develop an understanding of a particular FBDO within the fields in which it most often operates and through which it defines and understands itself.

Having narrowed the field of enquiry in this way, it is then instructive to try to locate Tearfund between the secular development sector and the evangelical missionary sector. Some scholars refer to evangelical development NGOs as missionaries (e.g. Hofer 2003, Pelkmans 2009, Hearn 2002), while others see them as a particular kind of development NGO (e.g. Berger 2003, Clarke and Ware 2015). And indeed, it can be difficult, for both staff of Christian FBDOs and the scholars who study them, to clearly demarcate the boundaries between 'mission' and 'development' (Paras 2014, Hovland 2008). A lot of the debate hinges on the definition and understanding of both 'mission' and 'development', both of which are contested terms with multiple meanings that have changed and evolved over time (Bosch 2011, Rist 1997). The detailed historical analysis in the following pages allows us to understand how Tearfund has positioned itself with regard to these two fields and how it has variously worked to differentiate itself from both mission agencies and secular development NGOs at different points in its history.[2]

The role of faith in FBDOs

A second research theme seeks to identify and clarify the role of faith in FBDOs. It is undisputed that faith provides a strong motivational force for many people to become involved in projects of charity and 'betterment' and is a source of inspiration for many FBDOs. It is also clear that faith can significantly shape the workplace culture of FBDOs, many of which institute times for reflection and devotion and seek to integrate prayer into team and strategy meetings. However, the question that is most pervasive in the literature, and which is much less clear, is whether faith influences the way FBDOs actually carry out relief and development.

Underlying many studies in this strand of research is an interest in religion as a worldview or a set of beliefs, ideas, and values. The guiding question is, how do these different beliefs affect the practice of FBDOs? Scholars in this area are drawn to the presumed potential of FBDOs to offer alternative approaches to development (e.g. Kim 2007, Lunn 2009, Ter Haar 2011, Tyndale 2006). Ter Haar, for example, argues that religious ideas can present 'a new vision of what development means' (Ter Haar 2011: 24), while Lunn suggests that religious approaches have the potential to envision a 'more holistic' development that takes into account non-economic matters such as emotions and spirituality (Lunn 2009).

However, for many Protestant Christian FBDOs it has not been the case that an 'alternative vision' of development has emerged directly from their different beliefs and worldview. Most of them are firmly rooted in secular thinking about development, which they have then sought to combine with some of their religious ideas, practices, and motivations. Thus the role of faith in relief and development work has become a subject of intense and complex discussion within many FBDOs themselves (e.g. Hovland 2012, Lynch and Schwarz 2016, Paras 2014). Far from being immediately apparent, FBDOs are actively and self-consciously thinking about how their faith could or should shape their work. This is certainly the case for Tearfund, and much of this book focusses on these internal debates and discussion as Tearfund has self-consciously sought to *integrate* faith into its development work.

For many evangelical organisations the major question has been how to combine evangelism and social action. This has been the subject of discussions at large international evangelical conferences and consultations, and FBDOs such as Tearfund, World Vision, and Compassion have played important roles in putting these ideas into practice in their practical work. As this book will show, for many years Tearfund lived with a dichotomy that it carried out both evangelism and social action but for the most part these were two separate activities that were carried out in parallel. It was only from the mid-1990s onwards that it consciously thought about how to combine these two activities into one integrated type of action – a distinctly Christian, faith-based, form of development.

While scholars and FBDOs have been discussing the role of faith-as-worldview, donors, on the other hand, have recently become interested in FBDOs less because of their beliefs and more because of their institutions and networks. In the 1990s and early 2000s a number of national governments began to start thinking about the potential role of religion in development and how they could work with FBOs as development partners. In 1995 the Canadian government developed a policy framework for how it could engage with FBOs. In 2002 a new Center for Faith-Based and Community Initiatives was created within the United States Agency for International Development (USAID) and in 2004 USAID started to support faith-based NGOs through its funding schemes. A few years later the Australian government launched its Church Partnership Program in Papua New Guinea. At the same time several European governments began to fund research looking at the existing and potential roles for religion in development. In 2005 the UK's Department for International Development (DFID) funded a £3.5 million research project about 'Religions and Development' that was carried out by scholars at the University of Birmingham. In subsequent years further research studies were initiated by the Dutch Ministry of Foreign Affairs, the Swiss Agency for Development and Cooperation, the German Federal Ministry for Economic Cooperation and Development, and others.

These studies highlighted both the potential benefits and the challenges for governments in working with faith-based organisations. While several studies noted a number of downsides of working with faith-based organisations, namely that they sometimes had exclusionary approaches and worked only with people of their own faith, sometimes exacerbated local religious tensions, were often small and unprofessional, and had a tendency to engage in forms of evangelism and proselytism, they also highlighted a number of presumed strengths of FBOs that could nonetheless offer advantages for development interventions. Most importantly, religious organisations were connected in large national and international networks that led from offices in the cities of the North to churches in the smallest and most distant village in the global South. It was this possibility of working through existing grassroots networks of trusted local organisations embedded in local communities that made partnership with FBOs so enticing for DFID and other government donors. Furthermore, in Southern contexts where trust in governments is often low, it seemed likely that many people would be more likely to listen to development messages if they came from local faith leaders.

In other words, these secular government agencies sought to instrumentalise religious institutions and to use their networks to deliver (secular) development services (Jones and Peterson 2011). Thus, despite their newfound interest in working with FBOs, most government donors sought to rigorously separate 'development' and 'evangelism' by stipulating that their funds could only be used to pay for material development work and not to spread faith. DFID's Civil Society Challenge Fund states that projects containing any element of proselytising or evangelising will not be considered and its Global Poverty Action Fund will not consider applications from organisations 'actively involved in proselytising'. AusAID's partnership programme with NGOs similarly excludes evangelistic activities. The Canadian International Development Agency (CIDA) stipulates that its funding must not be used to support programmes designed to convert people to a different religion, and USAID states that its funds cannot be used for religious or evangelistic purposes although it allows its grantees to carry out such activities as long as they are separated in time and space from the USAID-funded elements (Bradbury 2013: 423, Paras 2014: 446).

These rules have posed a number of challenges for many Christian FBDOs, often leading to their setting up special 'secular' workstreams that can receive government funding, while more 'faith-based' work, which includes evangelism, is funded from individual donations (Bradley 2009: 102). It has also led to what Ingie Hovland has called a kind of 'schizophrenia' as FBOs use different language and discourse to speak to different audiences (Hovland 2008). As one FBO worker interviewed by Clarke observed, staff were forced to 'leave their faith at the door' when they sought DFID funding (Clarke 2007: 84). As this book will show, the donor desire to separate development from evangelism has been particularly challenging for evangelical FBDOs, who have been working hard for years specifically to find ways to combine development and evangelism into one integrated activity.

The detailed historical analysis in this book offers a more nuanced and contextualised understanding of how these dynamics have played out in a particular evangelical FBDO as it has sought to devise a distinctly faith-based approach to development while also engaging fully in the mainstream development world.

The role of religion in development

A third strand of research has asked the more general question of what role is played by religion in development itself, rather than just in FBDOs. This is a much larger question about the role of ideas, values, and worldviews in societal change.[3] Work in this vein argues that, since most people in the world hold religious beliefs and are part of religious communities, it must be important to engage with their religion when trying to bring about development (Ager and Ager 2011, Ellis and Ter Haar 1998, Noy 2009, Rakodi 2012, Ter Haar 2011). As Deneulin puts it, 'for its adherents, religion infuses all aspects (and decisions) of their lives, and this has implications for the way they understand what development processes and outcomes ought to be' (Deneulin 2009: 6). In contrast to Western notions of privatised religion centred on individual beliefs, religion in much of the global South is very much present in the public sphere, shaping politics, economics, and social discourses. Thus Deneulin and Rakodi argue that 'the task for development research is to understand how religious discourses are embodied in certain social practices, how social and historical processes have led to that particular embodiment, and how the religion itself redefines its discourses, and practices' (Deneulin and Rakodi 2011: 51). According to this view development practitioners should not project the Western separation of church and state, secular and profane, onto the Southern contexts in which they work. Rather they should take into account people's different beliefs and worldviews and engage with them as religious subjects.

Some scholars and FBDO practitioners argue that, because religion is so important in much of the world, FBDOs are uniquely positioned to work with people to bring about development. The 'cultural proximity' thesis argues that, because FBDOs share the same religious beliefs and are part of the same greater religious community as their target beneficiaries, they will understand local contexts better than secular actors (Benthall 2012). However, a more detailed analysis suggests some problems with the 'cultural proximity' thesis. With regard to Christianity, a large body of anthropological writing has shown that there are huge variations in local instantiations of Christianity around the world, with local variants often existing in complex hybrid forms with local pre-Christian spiritual beliefs and practices (e.g. Cannell 2006, Canessa 2000, Freeman 2017, Hirsch 2008, Robbins 2004, Vilaça and Wright 2009). Local versions of Christianity might include practices such as exorcisms, finding witches, rubbing butter onto church doors, and numerous other practices that are largely unintelligible to Western Christians. International Christian FBDOs working from a particular, Northern, understanding of Christianity and staff in their European and American headquarters are unlikely to have much understanding of these grounded localised forms.

Indeed, in many of the poorer parts of the global South where FBDOs tend to work, it is often these local non-Christian spirit beliefs that are particularly important in shaping people's understandings of development and social change. To take one example, there is a large body of literature showing how economic development often intersects with traditional beliefs about witchcraft and occult forces (e.g. Englund 1996, Eves and Forsyth 2015, Fisiy and Geschiere 1991, Geschiere 1997, Smith 2008, Taussig 1980, Weller 1994). These studies show how wealth accumulation, one of the major aims of economic development, is an intensely morally charged activity, often conflicting with local ideas about equality and egalitarianism. In much of Africa, Oceania, and elsewhere individuals who succeed in accumulating wealth are often accused of being witches or of having used occult forces to bring about their development. Or conversely individuals avoid accumulating wealth in the first place, fearing that it might elicit envy and recourse to witchcraft against them. In many places the discourse of witchcraft provides a 'moral framework within which people evaluate economic behaviour' (Hickel 2014: 108). This can have severe effects on local attempts to promote development, and it has been argued that witchcraft accusations can 'act as a brake on the pace of economic and social differentiation' (Golooba-Mutebi 2005: 943).

Would an FBDO be better positioned to deal with this type of situation than a secular NGO? This context is far removed from the type of situation generally under discussion in the mainstream religion and development literature and the answer is not immediately apparent. However, some insights can be drawn from Erica Bornstein's anthropological analysis of field-level staff from Protestant FBDOs in Zimbabwe who indeed came across such situations in their work (Bornstein 2003: 141–68). Bornstein recounts how local staff were well aware of traditional beliefs in witchcraft and demons and in the moral and spiritual dangers enmeshed with development. More senior staff in the office headquarters in the capital city did their best to ignore these issues, while field-level staff struggled to find a way to negotiate them as part of their development work. They did not deny the reality of these forces, but claimed that Christianity and sincere prayer had the power to combat them. Thus when a community member employed by World Vision as a project bookkeeper got 'attacked by a demon' or when community members refused to take on leadership positions for fear of similar spiritual attack, they were not afraid to discuss these matters during committee meetings and project coordinator site visits where they prayed, read the Bible, and tried to convince people that a firm belief in Jesus would protect them from attack by evil forces. For field-level World Vision staff the moral struggle between God/Christianity/good and Satan/witchcraft/evil framed the organisation's more prosaic work of drilling boreholes and building schools. Their main strategy for engagement was evangelism. (For a similar discussion from a World Vision International staff member see Myers 2015: 119.[4])

This type of scenario raises complex issues about the connection between spiritual beliefs and economic development and links in to a set of questions raised in a related body of research that looks at the role of religious conversion in development. As Ter Haar has noted, 'many religions believe that transforming individuals is the first step to transforming the world' (Ter Haar 2011: 5). Can the deep individual transformation brought about by new religious belief empower people to cast away 'harmful traditional beliefs' such as witchcraft, and to improve their lives? This is an uncomfortable question that many in the FBO community are wary to address in public due to Western antipathy towards evangelism and proselytism. However, it reaches to the very heart of serious questions about the very nature of development. As the previous example highlights, 'development' is often fundamentally about societal and value change, replacing traditional values of community and equality with Western neoliberal values of individualism and accumulation – a type of 'proselytism' if you will (cf. Lynch and Schwarz 2016). If traditional values 'act as a brake' on development, surely these values will have to be changed or replaced if development is to occur. This takes us deep into difficult questions about cultural imperialism, the goodness or badness of capitalism, and the nature of the good society. My intention here is certainly not to set up 'development' as good and 'tradition' as bad, but merely to show that the two do not sit well together. If you want to bring about 'development' in its contemporary neoliberal form (and you may not) then changing traditional beliefs, practices, and values is likely to be necessary. Economic change and ideational change tend to go hand in hand (Freeman 2017).

Scholarship on the development impacts of Pentecostal Christianity in Africa highlights how Pentecostalism's emphasis on making a 'break with the past' can enable people to disentangle themselves from complex community interdependencies and traditional spiritualities and formulate a new morality and subjectivity in which individual accumulation and 'development' is not only morally acceptable, but morally desirable (Freeman 2012a, 2013, 2015, Hasu 2012, Piot 2012). Other forms of Christianity can also have similar effects, although Pentecostalism is perhaps the most effective at making this kind of 'break'. Evangelicalism and other forms of Protestantism, with their focus on the individual and their antipathy to traditional spirits, also afford similar types of transformation, while Catholicism and Orthodoxy tend to be more accommodating to local traditional beliefs and practices (Freeman 2017).

As the studies in *Pentecostalism and Development* (Freeman 2012a) show, Pentecostal churches tend to bring about this kind of transformation through their regular religious work. By far the greatest impact that Pentecostals have on development comes from the changes instilled in 'believers' by the religious activities of the churches themselves. There can be seen to be a 'Pentecostal ethic and spirit of development', to paraphrase Weber and his pioneering work on the role of Protestantism in the emergence of capitalism in Europe (Freeman 2012b, Weber 2008 [1904]). Pentecostalism tends to bring about three key interlinked processes of change: a major embodied personal transformation and empowerment of the individual; a shift in values that provides moral legitimacy for a set of behaviour changes that would otherwise clash with local sensibilities; and a radical reconstructing of the social and economic relationships in families and communities (Freeman 2015). Thus their developmental impact is not brought about through 'development projects' for material improvement, but rather through their conventional religious activities that focus on belief and ritual practice. However, as discussed above, many Northern donors and

Christian FBDOs seek to engage local churches in explicitly development activities. A question thus arises – how does encouraging local churches to carry out development projects or communicate development messages affect the developmental impact of these churches? And moreover, if it is the religious activities of these churches that have significant development impacts, does it make sense for Northern donors and NGOs to try to separate development from evangelism? The cultural politics of seeking to bring about social and economic change elsewhere are perhaps rather more complicated than is generally acknowledged in the mainstream development world.

To further complicate the claim that FBDOs are more effective than secular NGOs because they share 'cultural proximity' with those with whom they work, it should be remembered that international FBDOs often work in dozens of countries. And they often seek to create one centralised and unified approach that they can apply everywhere. How, then, can they be sensitive to particular local cultures and contexts? Thus blanket claims about FBDOs' 'inherent ability' to understand local contexts and work more closely with local communities need to be unpacked and subjected to scrutiny in particular situations and contexts. A far more nuanced discussion is necessary, looking both at field-level dynamics and international strategy.

This book engages with issues raised across all three of these strands of literature. It seeks to position Tearfund within the broader field of secular NGOs and Protestant FBDOs; to analyse the role that faith plays in Tearfund and to consider whether Tearfund carries out development differently from secular NGOs; and to see if and how it mediates a contextually sensitive form of development that takes into account local religious sensibilities. The preceding discussion thus provides a useful framing for the in-depth story of one particular FBDO that follows. We will return to these theoretical discussions in the conclusion, while the main body of the book tells the story of Tearfund largely in its own terms, foregrounding the voices of past and present staff and their own self-understanding of their work.

Tearfund

Tearfund[5] was formed in 1968 as a small evangelical[6] organisation that made grants to overseas missionaries to alleviate material poverty and physical suffering. Today it is one of the ten largest relief and development NGOs in the UK with around 400 UK-based staff and an annual income of some £75 million (Tearfund 2018a). It is a well-respected and recognised actor in mainstream development circles, being an active member of British Overseas NGOs for Development (BOND), the Disasters Emergency Committee (DEC), and the Active Learning Network for Accountability and Performance (ALNAP), as well as many other mainstream networks of relief and development NGOs. At the same time it is also a member of many networks of specifically evangelical relief and development NGOs, such as the Micah Network and Integral Alliance, both of which it helped to found, as well as networks of evangelical mission agencies, such as Global Connections (formerly the Evangelical Missionary Alliance). It is also a founding member of the Joint Learning Initiative on Local Faith Communities, an inter-faith network of FBOs that carries out research on faith-based development.

As this study will show in some detail, Tearfund is located fairly close to the 'faith-permeated' end of the spectrum of FBDOs. There is a faith element at all levels of its mission, staffing, governance, and support. It was founded by the Evangelical Alliance and remains strongly connected with the UK evangelical community through funding sources and affiliation. It is known by around 52 per cent of UK evangelicals and counts some 20 per cent as its supporters (Ashworth 2017). There are Tearfund church representatives in about 3,000 UK churches, out of a total of approximately 25,000 evangelical churches (and 50,000 churches in total), meaning that around 12 per cent of UK evangelical churches support Tearfund in one way or another. While it seeks to reach out to all evangelicals, its core constituency of supporters is predominantly white, middle-class, evangelical Anglicans, Baptists, Charismatics, Independents, Methodists, and Presbyterians.

The Board and most staff are required to share Tearfund's religious commitments and to sign up to its statement of faith. Faith provides the driving motivation for the majority of staff and for the organisation as a whole. Tearfund has elaborated a list of key Christian values, which it asks its staff to live out in their work and particularly in their interpersonal conduct with others. Faith shapes the working culture in the head office in Teddington, a leafy suburb just outside London, where prayer and devotion form part of the regular activities.

Every Wednesday morning the cafeteria is transformed into a place of worship as weekly staff prayer meetings are held, with all UK staff attending and many of the international staff participating virtually over live stream. These sessions typically start with joyful worship, often accompanied by keyboard and guitar played by some staff members, with staff praising the Lord in a mainly charismatic Anglican style. After that there will usually be updates about certain projects or campaigns, a sermon or teaching from the Bible, and a period of quiet prayer carried out either individually or in small groups.

Prayer is not limited to these once-weekly meetings. All team meetings start and/or end with prayer, staff induction sessions include periods of prayer, and special prayer sessions may be initiated to pray for particular events or situations, such as the Nepal earthquake or the Haiti hurricane. Team leaders regularly pray for their team members. The Executive Team and the Board regularly pray at the beginning and end of their meetings and also after each item that is discussed. When individuals or teams present their work at these meetings they will be prayed for at the end of their section. There will be prayer when funding applications are submitted, when new methodologies are developed, and when new campaigns are launched. Prayer always precedes major strategic decisions and the Executive Team go away on regular quarterly retreat days to 'pray into' the issues of the organisation and seek to discern 'God's voice'. Tearfund's overseas partners also share the same faith commitments and typically start each day with prayer and devotion and work according to Tearfund's values. Thus faith permeates the whole organisation and its network of partners, shapes the interrelationships between colleagues, and forms an essential part of the experience of working at Tearfund.

As part of the celebrations for its 50th anniversary Tearfund offices around the world were encouraged to plant a cross in their grounds as a symbol of their commitment to put Christ at the centre of all they do and to consecrate the year to him. In the Teddington headquarters a large wooden cross was erected in the central courtyard early in 2018 and stood there for all to see and reflect on as they looked through the large office windows while going about their work. Throughout the year Tearfund also organised five special 'jubilee days', building on the biblical concept of the fiftieth year being a 'jubilee', a time for restoration and rebalance. These were days of prayer and reflection on key themes, such as relationship with God, or relationship with others. No work was carried out on these days and instead the Teddington offices were transformed into a kind of spiritual retreat centre where staff moved between different 'stations' where they were encouraged to reflect on key biblical passages, to pray in silence, to write poetry expressing their relationship to God, or to partake in musical worship, among other things. The atmosphere was special, perhaps sacred. Staff in international offices also marked these days, setting aside work and using the special resources produced by Tearfund UK to reflect, pray, and worship together.

Thus there is no doubt that faith 'matters' to Tearfund. It is central to how it understands itself and to everything it does. What this book seeks to explore is whether and how this high degree of faith permeation makes a difference to the way that Tearfund and its partners actually carry out their relief and development work on the ground.

Outline of the chapters

The book follows an approximate chronological structure as it looks at Tearfund's work in different historical periods. The main body of the book focusses on Tearfund's international work with partners and beneficiaries, while a short appendix gives an overview of Tearfund's work with supporters in the UK. The aim is not to write a complete history of Tearfund, but rather to focus on pulling out the key events and activities that have shaped Tearfund's evolution and to explore the internal struggles and debates as Tearfund strove to develop a distinctly faith-based approach to development.

Chapter 2 gives a historical sketch of the evolution of secular and faith-based humanitarian and development organisations from the nineteenth century up until the time of Tearfund's formation in 1968. It reviews nineteenth-century (mainly religious) voluntary associations that provided charity for the poor, sent missionaries to the colonies, and provided medical care to the soldiers on Europe's battlefields, and then traces the twentieth-century emergence of secular development and humanitarian actors. It looks at what happened to the missionaries after the rise of 'development' as a supposedly secular field, charting the different paths taken by the classical mission agencies that adopted a more liberal theology and the evangelical mission agencies that held true to a more conservative theology. Understanding this entangled history of religious and secular actors sheds light on why Tearfund was formed and helps to position it within the field of British Protestant and mainstream humanitarian and development organisations.

In Part I, Chapter 3 explores Tearfund's formation and its work in its first 25 years. It discusses the way in which Tearfund's identity as an evangelical organisation developed and changed during this period. From the beginning Tearfund sat somewhere between two different worlds – the evangelical missionary world and the new world of 'international development' – as it sought to encourage evangelical missionaries to carry out relief and development projects. Many of its founders considered Tearfund itself to be a 'new kind of missionary organisation' as ideas about mission started to change in the post-colonial context, while others saw it more as a new evangelical relief and development NGO, the 'Christian Aid' of the evangelical community. As Tearfund got established, determined its working modality, and gained more practical experience, these questions about its purpose and identity began to gain increasing salience. At the core of the issue was how Tearfund would combine evangelism with development. Initially Tearfund was primarily an organisation that supported evangelical missionaries to carry out relief and development projects, assuming that they would evangelise as they did so. After ten years it was decided that this approach was too one sided and thus Tearfund also started to give grants to directly support evangelism and Christian education. The chapter discusses how a conceptual and practical division between the 'material' and the 'spiritual' permeated the entire organisation such that there was no specifically 'faith-based' approach to relief and development. By the end of this period many were feeling that things needed to change.

The three chapters in Part II discuss the period between roughly 1990 and 2005, when Tearfund emerged as a major relief and development NGO. This was a time of major change within the organisation, when it was completely restructured, several new areas of activity were developed, and major internal discussions and struggles took place about how Tearfund should operate and what type of change it should try to bring about. Chapters 4 and 5 chart the debate between two broadly defined groups within the organisation – those I call the 'mainstreamers', who saw their faith as their motivation and thought that the best way for Tearfund to serve Jesus was to carry out the highest quality development work to help the poor in much the same way as their secular peers, and those I call the 'transformationalists', the passionate religious revitalists who wanted to make their faith more central to their work and to combine development and evangelism in order to bring about a specifically Christian form of change. Chapter 6 then looks at another set of debates that was important at this time – around whether or not Tearfund should start engaging in campaigning and advocacy, and the associated discussions as to whether change was best brought about at the local level or the global level, by changing individuals or by changing the system.

Chapter 4 charts the course of some of the fundamental changes that Tearfund went through in this period as it changed from a small, quasi-missionary organisation into a major relief and development NGO. The chapter shows how the new leadership restructured the organisation and brought it out of the 'Christian ghetto' and into the mainstream development and humanitarian worlds where it could sit around the table with the likes of Oxfam and Save the Children. These 'mainstreamers' wanted Tearfund to grow and professionalise, to sign up to international standards and codes of conduct, and to attract government funding. Alongside these changes the chapter discusses the tensions and angst that accompanied this process as several staff began to feel that the changes were leading to Tearfund beginning to secularise and become just like any other relief and development NGO. They argued that Tearfund should remain a firmly evangelical organisation and should carry out a distinctly faith-based, more 'transformational' type of development.

Chapter 5 looks more closely at the arguments of the 'transformationalists'. It discusses Tearfund's efforts to clarify the Christian nature of its work and to get over the dichotomy between the material and the spiritual that had characterised the previous years. It charts the appointment of Tearfund's first theological adviser and his work, alongside colleagues, to develop a theology of development that combined spiritual and material development into one integrated, 'transformational', Christian whole. This in itself did not prove too difficult, but the challenge came when Tearfund's 'transformationalist' theologians sat down with their practitioner colleagues and tried to think through how to put this theology into practice in their relief and development work. Meanwhile, as all this theoretical debate was taking place, two young female, more junior staff members from the global South pushed ahead with creating two specifically faith-based types of development interventions – Gladys Wathanga from Kenya created the early formulation of Church and Community Mobilisation (CCM) and Veena O'Sullivan, originally from India, began to develop early work with churches around HIV and AIDS. As more and more Tearfund staff began to hear about these novel 'transformationalist' approaches, many began to think that they offered a better way forward than the route being taken by the leadership and the 'mainstreamers'.

Chapter 6 looks at the beginning of Tearfund's campaigning and advocacy work, which only started at this time, and was another source of contention during this period. It outlines the tensions between the evangelical emphasis on individual change and their antipathy towards engaging in politics, on the one hand, and broader understandings of structural injustice and systemic change, on the other. It shows how the massive Jubilee 2000 debt campaign, partly initiated by a Tearfund part-time staff member, and with its biblical framing, drew Tearfund into campaigning activity alongside religious and secular peers. The chapter then discusses how Tearfund went about establishing dedicated advocacy and campaigns teams and how it thought about ways to carry out this work in a particularly Christian, faith-based manner.

These three chapters show the different directions in which different parts of the organisation were travelling in the 1990s and early 2000s, and the increasingly fierce internal debates between the 'mainstreamers' and the 'transformationalists' about what kind of organisation Tearfund should be and how faith should be integrated into its work. Being both a major relief and development NGO *and* a truly evangelical organisation was proving to be rather difficult. By 2005 these tensions were threatening to pull the organisation apart. A new leadership and some major decisions were required.

Part III shows how these internal tensions were resolved after 2005, as a way forward was chosen and Tearfund shifted its identity again – this time from NGO to FBO. Chapter 7 focusses on the period between 2005 and 2015 when Tearfund tried to institutionalise a new faith-based and church-centred form of development, while Chapter 8 looks at the period after 2015 when Tearfund sought to expand its faith-based work and tried to bring some of it into the mainstream.

Chapter 7 shows how a new CEO came in and, in the context of a resurgence in religion in wider society and a huge wave of interest in FBOs, decided to foreground the faith-based, church-centred approach and particularly CCM. This decision had major implications for all of Tearfund's work in the areas of development, humanitarian relief, and advocacy as it was decided to try to put the local church explicitly at the centre of all practical work. This chapter outlines the ways that the different departments changed their work and sought to institutionalise the new approach. Despite a number of significant changes, it shows that in practice Tearfund staff found it rather difficult to shift their work to a faith-based, church-centred approach. Thus by the end of this period only a small proportion of Tearfund's development, relief, and advocacy work was being carried out in a distinctly faith-based way, while most of Tearfund's work continued to be mainstream, 'secular' work carried out by professional NGO partners in accordance with international standards and best practice.

Chapter 8 looks at the post-2015 period, taking the story up to 2018. It shows how the next CEO sought to consolidate Tearfund as an FBO by trying to expand the proportion of work that was carried out in a faith-based manner and, most importantly, by seeking to mainstream CCM. In order to turn CCM from being a small, niche-area type of project in which Tearfund works with local churches into a serious development modality that could be accepted, respected, and possibly even funded by mainstream development actors, Tearfund put considerable effort into formalising its approach and making it fit with the interests of the wider development sector. The chapter discusses how Tearfund staff came to clarify the type of change that they were seeking to bring about with CCM and to depict what successful change would look like. They called this 'flourishing' and began to develop a set of holistic indicators of how this could be measured in their project sites. Nonetheless, despite these attempts to make CCM mainstreamable, a number of issues emerged around the spiritual aspects of this work. The chapter looks at some of the dynamics and challenges in trying to mainstream faith-based approaches to development.

Chapter 9, the conclusion, summarises the main argument of the book and reflects on Tearfund's overall 50-year journey. It then returns to some of the theoretical questions raised in this chapter and discusses how this analysis of Tearfund's history and work contributes to our understanding of some of these broader questions and gives an insight into some of the paradoxes of faith-based development.

Notes

1 The academic literature on religion and development tends to use the term 'religion' somewhat more than 'faith'. However, Tearfund staff and partners speak almost exclusively about 'faith' and sometimes place faith in polar opposition to 'organised religion'. Many would argue that 'religion' is entirely irrelevant for their work, although 'faith' is central. Throughout this book the term 'faith' is used frequently, especially when discussing Tearfund's internal perspective and when the element being highlighted is the role of specific beliefs or worldviews. The term 'religion' is mainly used in more analytical sections and when the element being highlighted is some aspect of the practical or organisational nature of the religious community, such as the existence of a network of local churches or the establishment of annual theological conferences. However, it is extremely difficult to separate out these elements in all contexts and thus there will be instances in which either term could have been used.
2 Missionaries have been surprisingly understudied in the literature on religion and development. For some exceptions see Hearn 2002, Hovland 2008, 2012, Pelkmans 2009.
3 For earlier studies exploring how various religions affected orientations to economic development, with the aim of understanding why some countries modernised more rapidly than others, see Bellah 1957, 1963, Geertz 1956, 1962, Nash 1965, Spiro 1966, and Stone 1974.
4 Bryant Myers of World Vision reports that, when he led a 'Christian Witness Commission' for World Vision, he came across similar situations. In one country, he recalls, the national leadership affirmed the need to examine the organisation's Christian integrity since they claimed that some of the field personnel working in their front-line programmes were 'out of control' and might not really be Christian. Myers found that 'out of control' turned out to mean that they were Pentecostals using all the gifts of the Holy Spirit as part of their development work. Field staff, for their part, complained that there was a lack of Christianness in the head office because staff there 'did not pray expecting change, did not believe that the Holy Spirit could heal, and were not convinced that demons could be banished' (Myers 2015: 119).
5 The organisation was known as 'Tear Fund' until 1988, when it officially changed its name to 'Tearfund'. For the sake of simplicity and coherence I use the name 'Tearfund' throughout.
6 Tearfund was born out of the UK Evangelical Alliance and has a strong identification with evangelical Christianity. Although there is no single way of defining evangelicalism or an evangelical there are four key elements of the faith that have tended to be common and pivotal and which are central to Tearfund's understanding of the term: (1) the belief in the importance of the Bible as the highest authority for knowledge of and about God, against which all other sources of knowledge are to be tested; (2) the belief that the cross is the heart of the Christian faith and that Jesus' death and resurrection are the essential factors in making salvation possible; (3) the belief that people are called to respond to the cross and to accept the salvation that Jesus offers for them; and (4) the belief that accepting salvation has an impact on people's lives and that Christians are called to share the good news of salvation with others. Tearfund holds these positions and describes itself as an evangelical organisation.

2 Religious and secular actors in the emergence of humanitarianism and development

Introduction

The origins of humanitarian and development organisations can be traced to the late eighteenth and early nineteenth centuries. This was a time of huge social change in many European countries, with industrialisation changing the shape of people's domestic and working lives, colonial expansion bringing much of the world into the European orbit, and competition between increasingly nationalistic European countries leading to frequent wars across the continent. These changes brought with them new social ills – increasing poverty and inequality at home, slavery and poor treatment of the 'others' in the colonies, and increasing numbers of men wounded on the battlefields of Europe. It was in seeking solutions to these new social problems that new ideas about 'cosmopolitanism' and 'humanitarianism' were born and that the seeds of contemporary NGOs were sown (Barnett 2011, Paulmann 2013).

The nineteenth century was also a time of new ideas and worldviews. Enlightenment ideas about science and evolution were gaining ground, leading to a 'crisis of faith' among many British and European Christians (Helmstadter and Lightman 1990, Watts 2015). While Christianity was still intimately tied up with family, morality, and social life, growing numbers of people were struggling with belief and unbelief. At the same time there were a number of evangelical 'awakenings', in which significant numbers of people came afresh to the Christian faith and demanded a more deeply passionate engagement with it in their own lives and a stronger manifestation of its values in society (Bebbington 1989). Thus many of the social reform movements of the time were initiated by evangelical Christians and inspired by Christian values. However, over the course of the nineteenth and twentieth centuries many religious organisations began to downplay their interest in evangelism in favour of improving the lives of others, leading some observers to claim that 'religion might have been instrumental in the establishment of humanitarianism, but it passed the torch to secularism' (Barnett and Stein 2012: 5). While there is much truth to this statement, it does not portray the full complexities of the relationship between religion and humanitarianism and development that evolved through the nineteenth and twentieth centuries, and which continues to evolve now in the twenty-first century.

In order to set a backdrop to the emergence of Tearfund that will allow a clearer understanding of the reasons for its formation and of the field, or fields, into which it emerged, this chapter will trace out a more detailed history of the entwined and entangled areas of Christian social engagement, overseas missionary activity, and the growth of secular humanitarianism from the early nineteenth century up to the time that Tearfund was established, in 1968. Many of the issues that Tearfund was to face in later years, as a faith-based development organisation, were prefigured in this period. While it is not a simple case of history repeating itself, understanding this broader history helps to cast a particular light on the contemporary story of Tearfund, and indeed on the Protestant faith-based development sector in general.

The formation of voluntary societies in the UK

During the nineteenth century industrialisation and urbanisation were leading to increasing poverty and growing inequality throughout the UK. Factory workers were beginning to organise and to protest about their poor living and working conditions, more people were demanding a vote in parliamentary elections, and social unrest was simmering. At the same time the middle classes were expanding and setting up a huge array of voluntary societies to promote associational life in the new towns. These societies carried out activities ranging from the diffusion of science and culture and the organisation of leisure to moral reform, education and thrift, and radical discussion groups (Hilton *et al.* 2012). There were also several religious societies, such as the Bible Societies, which collected money, organised sermons and meetings, distributed Bibles, and arranged local evangelising (Morris 1983: 103). Several voluntary societies were established with the particular aim of carrying out charitable activities, mainly directed towards devising and operating solutions to the 'poverty problem' in order to alleviate suffering and to retain social order (Morris 1983).

While there were some secular charitable voluntary societies, the vast majority of them were started by Christian individuals and institutions, in particular by nonconformists and evangelicals[1] (Morris 1983). Many of the upwardly mobile urban middle classes of the nineteenth century were indeed nonconformists and evangelicals, particularly in the large manufacturing towns, and many of their chapels supported a varied structure of voluntary societies. For example, in 1800 Norfolk Street Chapel in Sheffield supported a Wesleyan Library, a poor fund for its own congregation, and a non-sectarian Benevolent Society. By 1830 there was also a Wesleyan Home and Foreign Mission Society and a Sunday School, and later still a Band of Hope (Morris 1983: 105).

It has been widely noted that the practice of the voluntary provision of poor relief by charitable societies rather than by the state enabled the delivery of welfare to be closely aligned with other objectives, such as evangelism or the advancement of political ideas (e.g. Gorsky 1999: 19). In many cases volunteers from the voluntary societies would visit the poor to ascertain whether or not they were deservingly needy and, if appropriate, give them charitable donations. This mode of operation led to the societies becoming increasingly involved in influencing the lifestyle of those they helped. For the Christian societies this often meant seeking to turn them into good Christians. Morris reports that, in one early nineteenth-century Edinburgh society, the visitor was

> required earnestly to recommend cleanliness to those he visits ...[,] exhort them to attend a place of worship, to send their children to Sunday School, and to ascertain whether or not they possess a copy of the Holy Scripture that they may be supplied.
>
> (Morris 1983: 108)

This mode of operation created considerable tensions between the different Christian denominations and also with those who believed that charity should be given in a non-sectarian manner (Morris 1983: 108, Gorsky 1999).

By the 1850s most of the charitable voluntary societies were finding that their funds were too small to deal with the widespread poverty that was evident. They began to turn to the state for funds and in the second part of the nineteenth century they increasingly received government grants, particularly in the field of education. Eventually the state began to take over these social actions, providing a more uniform, consistent, and effective service. The voluntary societies continued to function and indeed grow, but now within the shadow of the state (Morris 1983: 118). The subsequent emergence of the modern welfare state after the Second World War displaced much of this Christian-inspired voluntary action with the detached authority of secular experts and the disinterested provision of welfare (Prochaska 2006). Nonetheless, voluntary activity continues up to the present and several contemporary UK-oriented charitable NGOs can trace their origins back to associations formed at this time (Hilton *et al.* 2012: 13).

The growth and development of missionary societies

While voluntary societies were forming at home, significant changes were also happening overseas. The nineteenth century was a time of major expansion of colonial empire. As colonial regimes expanded in Africa, Asia, and Latin America, European entrepreneurs and adventurers began to travel all over the world and to send home news of exotic lands and peoples. One result of this was that people's 'mental map' of the world began to change and Europeans became increasingly aware of the existence and exotic lifestyles of 'distant others'. This of course influenced many areas of European society in a great number of ways. For our purposes here it is instructive to look at how it influenced thinking among Protestant Christians.

In the late eighteenth century Protestant revival movements had swept across Europe in what has since become known as the 'Great Awakening' (Bebbington 1989). In these circles there was a renewed emphasis on personal spiritual experience and transformation. Many 'awakened' Christians felt a strong desire to share their experience with others and began to believe that it could bring them salvation. This experience, alongside increasing awareness of 'distant others' overseas, started a theological debate within the Protestant world. Up until then mainstream Christian thinking had been that the 'Great Mandate' to spread the gospel had ended with the apostles and that salvation depended on election by God and was not something that could be influenced by worldly activity or personal faith. But in 1792 William Carey, widely known as the father of Protestant missions, wrote a small booklet called *An Enquiry into the Obligations of Christians, to Use Means for the Conversion of the Heathens*, which argued that the Great Mandate had not ended with the apostles and that new methods had to be discovered in order to fulfil it in the present (Catalano 2014: 112).

Carey's booklet led to the founding of the Baptist Missionary Society (BMS) later that year, and to the founding of many other missionary societies in the subsequent years.[2] The London Missionary Society (LMS) was formed in 1795, the Edinburgh and Glasgow Missionary Society in 1796, the Church Missionary Society (CMS) in 1797, the British and Foreign Bible Society (BFBS) in 1804, the Wesleyan Methodist Missionary Society in 1813, the Basel Evangelical Missionary Society in 1815, and the South American Missionary Society (SAMS) in 1844, among many others. The birth of these missionary societies represented an unexpected and unprecedented development in the Protestant world. As the nineteenth-century American missionary Rufus Anderson noted, 'It was not until the present century that the evangelical churches of Christendom were ever really organised with a view to the conversion of the world' (cited in Catalano 2014: 108).

It is worth noting that the task of evangelising the world was initiated by voluntary missionary societies, and not by local churches. Such societies can thus be seen as one sector of the broader field of voluntary associations that was expanding at this time, and indeed operated according to similar principles based on member subscriptions. It was generally lay people, not ordained clergy, who ran these societies, raised funds, and went as missionaries. During the nineteenth century they sought to raise funds and to educate people by publishing information bulletins, with letters and diaries from the different missions. In this way they mobilised a mass movement in Britain, Switzerland, the German states, and elsewhere, in which people felt called to be involved in the mission enterprise by financially and spiritually supporting their missionaries overseas (Catalano 2014: 118). As we will see, this mode of operation was widely adopted by humanitarian and development NGOs in the twentieth century.

The sole aim of these missionary societies at this time was to spread the gospel and to convert the heathens of the world to Christianity. Preaching alone was unlikely to achieve these goals and thus from the beginning the missionaries used other techniques. One of their most important activities was translating the Bible into local languages and teaching the natives literacy so that they could study the Bible themselves. Thus education was a key tool of the early missionaries. And, as Catalano writes, education served as a means to an end – evangelism – and was not the end itself:

> It has been always clear in ... the BMS that schools were to be considered as one of the most effective means of evangelization, instrumental for taking the light of the Gospel to the world. It is clear that the educational enterprise was never an end in itself. Education and cultural formation aimed ever at evangelization.
>
> (Catalano 2014: 120)

Medical work was also used by the missionaries as a means to secure access to places and people resistant to the missionaries and their message. While the LMS missionaries heading to the Pacific islands already had a medical surgeon among them, it was not until the mid-nineteenth-century missionary approaches into China that medical missions truly started to flourish, and since then they were used particularly in countries where there was a strong anti-foreign sentiment as a means to open access (Catalano 2014: 124).

Social involvement beyond education and medicine was extremely limited at this time and focussed mainly on trying to stop traditional practices that the missionaries considered to be anti-Christian and inhuman, such as *sutti* in India (which was understood as the practice whereby widows throw themselves on their husband's funeral pyre), child marriage, the caste system, and the opium trade. Most of the mission societies' social attention at this time was focussed on the anti-Christian and inhuman behaviour of their fellow countrymen, particularly their degrading treatment of local peoples and the practice of slavery.

In the early nineteenth century many missionaries had been radicalised by what they saw in the colonies. While most of them had not intended to get involved in any kind of political activity, many felt impelled to do so after witnessing plantation slavery close up. These Christian missionaries, and their associates back home, were among the first to start advocating for the abolition of slavery (Stamatov 2010, Ward 2000). Missionary and Christian groups drove much of the abolitionist movement throughout the nineteenth century and they formed voluntary societies back in Europe for this purpose. Several contemporary anti-slavery NGOs, such as Anti-Slavery International, can trace their origins to these early societies (Hilton *et al.* 2012: 13).[3] In the process they developed the rudimentary institutional forms of what we know today as 'transnational activism' (Stamatov 2010).

In these early years the relationship between missionaries and the colonial administration was thus often fraught. Colonial officers and trading companies were initially hostile towards the missionaries and tried to keep them away. Missionaries were often imprisoned or expelled, or limited to work only with the expatriate community (Porter 2004). The core of the tension was that missionaries saw the local people in a fundamentally different way from the colonial officers. While the colonialists saw local people as a source of cheap labour and as little more than commodities, missionaries saw them as potential or actual Christians and thus as fellow human beings entitled to dignity and rights. They thus called for the humane treatment of imperial 'others', if only to facilitate their evangelisation and conversion to Christianity (Stamatov 2010: 615). In this way the logic of their evangelical and universalist religion, placed in the context of colonial empire, led to many missionaries beginning to develop a growing sense of 'cosmopolitanism' – a sense of the common nature and value of every person, irrespective of race, religion, or kinship (Turner 2019).

The relationship between missionaries and the colonial administration began to change when the colonialists saw the educational work being carried out by the missionaries and began to think that missionaries could be a useful force for maintaining the social balance in the colonies. From then on relations warmed and missionaries were given freer contact with the local population. This new collaboration between the missionaries and the colonialists was even codified in India in the so-called Pious Clause, an important modification introduced into the Charter of the East Indian Company in 1813 that required the Company to support, from its revenues, a bishopric and three archdeaconries to superintend the British settlements (Catalano 2014: 123).

From then on, and particularly after the 1830s, the missionaries were effectively co-opted into the colonial project and their work expanded. As their calls to end the slave trade increased, the new idea of 'commerce and Christianity' arose, in which a supposedly 'legitimate trade', not dependent on slavery, could be established in Africa and Asia through a combination of entrepreneurial and missionary effort (Stanley 1983: 76, Haustein and Tomalin 2017: 78). Infused with the Calvinist work ethic and inspired by Livingstone's injunction that 'we ought to encourage the Africans to cultivate for our markets as the most effectual means next to the Gospel for their elevation' (cited in Faught 1944: 122), most evangelicals at this time considered their capitalist economic interests to be fully in line with their Christian faith. Put another way, it seemed quite natural to them that religious change and economic development should go hand in hand.

However, during the course of the 1860s the alliance between commerce and Christianity began to fall apart and many missionaries lost confidence in the redemptive function of commerce. They observed that engaging 'the natives' in commerce often failed to support their spiritual development as Christians. Instead it seemed that many people were converting simply to gain improved access to trading possibilities and as a result the quality of their faith was poor and superficial. Thus a growing body of Christian opinion in the later part of the nineteenth century began to repudiate the association with such material matters as commerce, and to reconceive of the missionary task as purely spiritual and focussed solely on evangelism (Faught 1994: 122, Stanley 1983: 92).

The most adamant in this approach were the 'faith missions', a new wave of mission societies that had emerged in the latter half of the nineteenth century and which will be discussed in more detail below. For most of the classical missions it meant disentangling themselves from commercial activities but continuing with other activities that might be seen as 'developmental', such as education and medicine. They remained a central and complementary part of the colonial enterprise well into the twentieth century due to the many developmental services they delivered in the colonies. Mission stations regularly provided vocational training, employment opportunities, and medical care. Most importantly, they had an unchallenged monopoly on education, as colonial governments only established very few schools in the colonies (Haustein and Tomalin 2017). For many of the classical missions at this time education came to be seen as a lofty goal in its own right, and not just as a means to evangelism.

By the early twentieth century these classical missionary societies had grown hugely in scale and resources. In 1906 the CMS, for example, had an annual income of £300,000, and was responsible for 975 missionaries and 8,850 'native agents', 37 theological and training colleges, 92 boarding schools, 12 industrial institutions, 2,400 elementary schools, 40 hospitals, 73 dispensaries, 21 leprosaria, six homes for the blind, 18 orphanages, six other homes and refuges, and 17 presses or publishing houses (Stanley 2003: 42). This increase in scale led to the voluntarist model of mission being somewhat taken over by an institutional business culture as the mission societies used the methods of secular corporations to manage the whole complex enterprise. Business efficiency and specialist technical expertise became increasingly important, leading to the growth in the power of the home boards over field policy and the professionalisation and bureaucratisation of the whole enterprise (Stanley 2003: 42). These dynamics would later replay themselves in the development NGOs in the second part of the twentieth century.

The faith missions

In 1858 there was a second evangelical awakening (the 'Second Great Awakening') and this gave birth to a new missionary movement, initially known as the faith missions, and later more commonly called the evangelical missions (Fiedler 1994). These faith missions were a new wave of mission agencies, with their own, separate revival roots, their own spirituality, and their own missionary concepts. Their efforts were based on the belief emanating from a premillennial dispensationalist theology that those who do not believe in Christ are eternally lost and that Christ would return when everyone had had the opportunity to hear the gospel. Thus for the faith missions evangelism and conversion were urgent and they were driven to bring the gospel to the 'unreached peoples' (Fiedler 1994).

The first faith mission was the China Inland Mission (CIM) started by Hudson Taylor in 1865, and subsequent faith missions were established in the following years, including the Regions Beyond Mission Union (1873), the Livingstone Inland Mission (1878), the Sudan Interior Mission (1893), the Africa Inland Mission (1895), and the Sudan United Mission (1904). They typically had a single geographical focus, were non-denominational, and their central tenet was individual conversion. As their names suggest, many of these missions focussed their efforts on Africa and sought to reach the third of the continent that had been unreached by missionaries by this time (Fiedler 2010: 67).

While the faith missions engaged in some educational and medical activities, they were much clearer than the classical missionary societies at this time that these were a means to an end and that the end was evangelism. Gehman, for example, explains that, for the Africa Inland Mission in the late nineteenth and early twentieth centuries,

> Education was always conceived ... as a means toward evangelism, an auxiliary in helping them to produce a literate church which could read the Bible. Higher education was never their contemplated goal.
>
> (Gehman 2004: 135)

And indeed, if human history was about to end, what was the point of the traditional missionary concerns of civilisation, education, and commerce (Faught 1994: 122–3)? Thus in the late nineteenth century, as the classical missions were placing more emphasis on education and medical care in their own right, the faith missions focussed purely on evangelism and only used education and medical care in instrumental ways as a means to this end. They had no interest in commerce and found the idea that 'commerce and Christianity' somehow went together totally repugnant.

Early twentieth-century split between conservatives and liberals

During the first part of the twentieth century a major split emerged between conservative and liberal Protestants, and accordingly between the classical and the faith missions. While the conservatives insisted on a literal reading of the Bible as God's word, the liberals developed a new theology that took into account the claims of biblical criticism and placed more emphasis on the role of the church in social life (Bebbington 1989: 181–228). These theological differences ultimately led to the separation of conservative and liberal Protestant churches and mission societies into two more or less clearly defined groupings. Following the Edinburgh Missionary Conference in 1910, probably the first and last formal missionary conference in which all the missionary societies participated, the liberals, including most of the classical mission societies, began to focus more on working together across the different Christian denominations, to bring the mission societies closer to the churches, and, significantly for our story here, to place a greater emphasis on social action. This was the birth of the 'ecumenical movement' that by 1942 had given rise to the British Council of Churches (BCC) and to Christian Aid, and in 1948 gave rise to the World Council of Churches (WCC).

The conservatives, including the faith missions, disagreed with this approach and decided to take a different route.[4] They took issue with the more liberal theology and growing emphasis on social issues and maintained that strict adherence to scripture was important and that evangelism was urgent and primary. They also strongly believed that mission societies should remain separate from the organisational structure of churches. Most conservative evangelical churches decided not to join the BCC or the WCC and the faith missions, now more commonly known as the evangelical missions, remained separate. At this time they had no umbrella organisation of their own – the Evangelical Alliance, which had existed since 1846, was then an alliance of individuals rather than churches – and for many years they were fragmented and isolated from wider secular or Christian society. Nonetheless, while their position was weak within the UK, their missionary work continued overseas with great zeal, and with a markedly different approach from the increasingly liberal classical missions.

Throughout the first part of the twentieth century and into the 1940s and 1950s missionaries from the classical mission societies became more and more involved in social matters and worked closely with colonial administrations to carry out what was coming to be called 'development'. A report by the Colonial Office's Advisory Committee on Education in the Colonies entitled *Education for Citizenship in Africa* set out a vision in which missions were to be instrumental in the continuing provision of both primary and secondary education to children in Africa (Stuart 2008: 530). And following the 1940 Colonial Development and Welfare Act, which set out a vision and funding mechanism for the provision of education and welfare in the colonies, the classical missionaries shifted their activities from a narrow focus on education and health to work more broadly on 'developmental' activities, such as agriculture and welfare, in order to capitalise on the government grants that were made available by the Act. And as they sought to win these grants they claimed that their work was modern, progressive, and superior to that of colonial officials. They claimed that, as religious actors, they dealt with the 'whole person', body and soul, and thus had what we would now call a 'comparative advantage' over secular development actors (Hughes 2013: 824). This claim would later be echoed by many faith-based development organisations in the twenty-first century.

Throughout the 1950s classical missions such as the LMS and the CMS championed humanitarian development work as an integral part of mission. In 1953, for example, the CMS issued a call for 'doctors, health workers, teachers and agricultural specialists to enlist as "Christian revolutionaries" in Africa' (Hughes 2013: 823). At the same time, however, they wrestled with the degree to which missions should be evangelistic or humanitarian. They reflected on Christ's interactions with humans and concluded that Christ cared for both souls and bodies as he promised 'abundant life'. Thus they developed an 'incarnational theology' in which they looked to Christ's example as a 'servant' and his ministry of care to the 'whole man', both body and soul (Hughes 2013: 824–30).

The classical mission societies also expanded their promotional work in the UK in order to raise funds, recruit missionaries, and garner spiritual support through prayer. Each society maintained its own publishing arm and distributed a primary journal to keep its supporters informed. Both the LMS *Chronicle* and the CMS *Outlook* had monthly circulations of around 30,000 each during the 1950s (Hughes 2013: 837 fn20). Additionally, they disseminated pamphlets, promoted films of their work, and hosted meetings and exhibitions that were designed to stimulate involvement with missions. They also encouraged their supporters to stay apprised of British involvement in Africa and urged them to express Christian opinions on colonial politics by writing to their MP or contacting the BBC or the press (Hughes 2013: 827). This basic mode of operation was to be followed by many development NGOs in the coming years.

As the classical missions became more and more involved in humanitarian development activities and began to see this as a lofty goal in its own right, the evangelical missions moved in the opposite direction. As the premillennialist theology spread more widely, the belief grew that 'the holy spirit ... was opening the world to Christianity in preparation for the second coming of Christ' (Robert 1990: 31). Therefore the evangelicals focussed their energies on the proclamation of the gospel, and placed much less emphasis on activities such as the provision of education and health care, which they nonetheless continued to do to some extent in order to facilitate evangelism. Their discourse was one of 'bringing the gospel to the unreached peoples' and there was a sense of passion and urgency in this endeavour. Their focus was not on 'development', but on saving souls.

One of Tearfund's first board members emerged out of this environment. Ernest Oliver, who later went on to have several senior roles in Tearfund, studied at All Nations Bible College and in the 1930s went to Bihar, India as a missionary with the Regions Beyond Missionary Union (RBMU), an evangelical missionary society that had been established in 1873 'to preach the gospel in the regions beyond you'. He recalls, 'there was an urgency abroad in those days: we should not spend too much time in preparation, we must get out to the place of God's calling as quickly as possible, for the Lord's return was imminent' (quoted in Tiplady 2005: 38). In 1954 he was a founding member of the United Mission to Nepal and was one of the first foreign missionaries to enter that country (Tiplady 2005). In 1958 the Evangelical Missionary Alliance (EMA) was formed and Ernest Oliver became its first General Secretary (Hylson-Smith 2011).

In the post-war years there was another wave of evangelical mission expansion and many new mission agencies were formed. Many of these initially formed in the US and then later opened branches also in the UK. Several, such as Wycliffe Bible Translators, Open Doors, Youth with a Mission, and Youth for Christ quickly grew to become large agencies, representing a new and exuberant generation of evangelical mission.

The emergence of humanitarian and development NGOs

Another set of developments was also taking place in parallel to these activities during the nineteenth century. Competition surrounding industrialisation and colonial expansion was leading to more frequent and more ferocious wars in Europe. There was mass conscription in many countries, and as news of the large number of battle wounded spread from the battlefields to the cities, concern grew. Peace societies were established throughout Europe and the associated demilitarisation movements flourished. At the same time voluntary associations formed to treat the injured on the battlefields. Up until the mid-nineteenth century, similar to the situation with charitable societies working in the UK, most of these voluntary associations were run by religious groups.[5] Examples include the Order of St. John of Jerusalem, Quaker associations, various Sisters of Charity, and the Committee for the Wounded of the Evangelical Society of Geneva (Dromi 2016: 202, Reid and Gemie 2013: 226). The religious groups sought to bring inner peace and salvation to the wounded, as well as providing medical care when there was hope of recovery.

In the second half of the nineteenth century this association of humanitarianism with religion began to change. And interestingly, it was evangelical Christians who sought to bring about this separation. In 1863 Jean-Henri Dunant, formerly a member of the Committee for the Wounded of the Evangelical Society of Geneva, and four other Swiss Calvinist philanthropists established the International Committee of the Red Cross (ICRC). In contrast to the other voluntary aid societies that treated the battle wounded alongside providing religious counsel, and which tended to emerge when a war broke out and were disbanded once the war ended, the early Red Cross advocated for humanitarian activities to be recognised as independent and organised in permanent volunteer professional institutions. Moreover, even though Dunant and his fellow founders were all strict Calvinists, influenced by the *réveil* (awakening) movement, they argued that humanitarian care should be separated from religious organisations and provided in a secular manner (Dromi 2016: 198).[6] This marked the start of the progressive de-linking of Christian missionary activity and humanitarian aid and the beginning of the formation of humanitarian relief as a distinct and secular field (Benthall and Bellion-Jourdan 2003, Krause 2014). From then on 'humanitarian action' came to be seen as a unique endeavour that followed its own independent logic and that should be pursued for its own sake, rather than as an outworking of Christian faith. The modern humanitarian system, and indeed the modern human rights system, can thus trace their origins to these events (Ferris 2011: 608).

During the twentieth century the codification of humanitarian principles and law, accompanied by the institutionalisation of humanitarian actors and accountabilities, saw the growth and formalisation of the distinctively secular humanitarian regime (Ager and Ager 2011, Calhoun 2008). In the early twentieth century a host of new humanitarian associations were formed, particularly in the aftermath of the First World War. Relief work became more professionalised, more secular, and organised around transnational networks of experts, such as physicians, engineers, and social workers. Nonetheless, despite the self-conscious secularisation of the humanitarian field, religious organisations, of course, continued to provide humanitarian relief.

The war gave rise to a renewed sense of internationalism, which led to the creation of the League of Nations and to a new generation of international humanitarian NGOs larger in scale and more geared for practical action than their predecessors. The International Federation of Red Cross and Red Crescent Societies was established in 1919 as the League of Red Cross Societies, with the intention of bringing together the existing national Red Cross entities and expanding their activities beyond strictly wartime assistance to include public health and disaster relief (Cabanes 2014: 4). In the same year the Save the Children Fund (SCF) was established by sisters Eglantyne Jebb and Dorothy Buxton. Both were devout Christians, but like the founders of the Red Cross movement they set up SCF as an explicitly secular organisation, appealing to universalist discourses of 'humanity' rather than religious inspiration (Jones 2014: 42, Wilson 1967). Like the other 'war charities' that formed at the time, they started by focussing on alleviating wartime suffering, particularly of children, and then later on reconstruction efforts (Freeman 1965: 27, Mulley 2009: 98). In 1937 Plan International was founded, initially as Foster Parents Plan for Children in Spain, to help children affected by the Spanish Civil War.

The Second World War acted as a further catalyst for the growth of humanitarian NGOs and led to further transformations of the humanitarian sector. In the immediate post-war years, until the US Marshall Plan started in 1948, it was voluntary agencies that sought to provide relief to the destroyed communities of Europe. Many British humanitarians at this time were seriously concerned with famine and suffering in post-war Europe. In 1942 the Council of British Societies for Relief Abroad (COBSRA) was established, initially as the Council of Voluntary Societies for the Relief of Suffering and for Aiding Social Recovery. It was a consultative committee designed to facilitate closer coordination between aid agencies and the state, and at this time some 40 humanitarian organisations joined, including the Red Cross, Save the Children, and others. Despite the secular rhetoric it is interesting to note that a significant number of the member organisations as this time were religious organisations, including the Friends Relief Service (Quaker), the Salvation Army, and Catholic and Jewish relief organisations (Black 1992: 26, Jones 2014: 49).

Many of the major contemporary aid agencies were founded during this period in response to the Second World War, including Oxfam, Christian Aid, and War on Want. All three had some connection to Christianity, but in quite different ways.

Oxfam was founded in 1942 as the Oxford Committee for Famine Relief, one of several such committees that had been formed in towns around the UK with the aim of providing famine relief to victims of the UK's war-time blockade in Europe. Although it is an avowedly secular organisation now, the two principal organisers of the first meeting of Oxfam in October 1942 were the Anglican cleric Canon Richard Milford and the Quaker-inspired philanthropist Cecil Jackson-Cole. Many of its early staff were Quakers and for many their humanitarian and pacifist motivations came from their Christian values. However, the Oxford Committee could not be described as a 'religious organisation' as such (Black 1992: 23).

Christian Aid was also formed in 1942, initially as a committee of the British Council of Churches (BCC), called the Christian Reconstruction in Europe Committee. In 1949 this committee was combined with another BCC committee – the Ecumenical Refugee Committee – to form the Inter-Church Aid and Refugee Service, which then became a permanent department of the BCC. The stated objective of this new body was to 'provide succour to churches, church institutions, and individuals overseas or from overseas, who are in want'. The organisation initially raised funds in Britain through church networks and sent them via the World Council of Churches to aid refugees in Germany, Austria, Italy, and Greece. This marked the beginning of a shift in the ecumenical world from humanitarianism being carried out by mission agencies to it being carried out by church agencies.

War on Want, which was founded in 1952, also grew out of this post-war reconstruction movement. Its founder, Jewish socialist Victor Gollancz, had initiated the 'Save Europe Now' campaign in 1945 and founded the Association for World Peace in 1951. Even though it was strongly connected to the Labour movement and had a more overtly secular and political ethos, War on Want also initially relied extensively on Christian support and assistance. One of its founders was the Anglican clergyman Canon John Collins and its grassroots network of local support groups relied strongly on Quakers and other churches (Hilton 2012: 452, Luetchford and Burns 2003).

In 1948 the United Nations was established and the Universal Declaration of Human Rights launched to present a new globalist and universalist view of the world. However, according to Hilton, the inspiration for most of the new humanitarian organisations to relieve human suffering 'owed more to Christian fellow-feeling than it did to the secular recognition of people's universal and inalienable rights' (Hilton 2012: 449). And indeed, the language of rights was almost entirely absent from the publications and policies of Oxfam, Christian Aid, and War on Want at this time.[7]

In the 1950s these three organisations, and others like them, began to expand their focus beyond post-war relief in Europe, to first provide aid to refugees in other parts of the world and then to start providing aid to the poor in the newly decolonised countries of Africa and Asia. They thus began to shift from engaging primarily in humanitarian relief to beginning to work in the newly emergent area of 'development'. They ran adverts in national and local newspapers and organised appeals on BBC radio, in these ways making the British public aware of overseas suffering and raising funds. President Truman's speech in 1949 had widely publicised the notion of 'development' as the idea that the richer or 'developed' countries would help the poorer or 'under-developed' countries in the post-war and post-colonial era. By the late 1950s the new field of 'development' was in place and many of the 'war charities' had now repositioned themselves as 'development NGOs' (Rist 1997: 70–9).

The new field of development that emerged after the Second World War was, like the humanitarian relief field, self-consciously secular.[8] However, many of its main actors had links in one way or another to Christian ideas, institutions, or individuals. Most of the organisations that were working on the ground oversees continued to be missionaries. And thus Oxfam, Christian Aid, War on Want, and many other organisations, initially operated by raising funds in the UK and making grants primarily to missionaries or church organisations overseas to do development work (Black 1992, Luetchford and Burns 2003, Manji 2002). As they began to send funds for relief and development work in Africa and Asia, the classical missionaries repositioned themselves again, this time as providers of (secular) development services, and began to downplay their religious nature in order to conform to mainstream development paradigms (Salemink 2015: 51). Thus by the late 1950s many classical missions had been subsumed into the provision of overseas aid and relief and had adopted an approach and discourse that rendered it difficult to distinguish them from secular agencies (Ager and Ager 2011: 457, Stuart 2008: 537, Thaut 2009).

There were mixed feelings about this in many of the mission societies. While many saw development and the alleviation of poverty as ways of living out Christian values of charity and justice, others saw this path of travel as harmful to mission. 'What need would there be for missionaries,' asked Max Warren of the CMS, 'if the West's engagement with Africa emphasised aid and development rather than spirituality?' (cited in Stuart 2008: 537). The evangelical missions were clearer that they did not want to become 'development agents' and they largely kept to their own separate world (Agensky 2013). Thus, while a self-consciously secular development regime developed, organisations with varying connections to faith traditions remained strongly active in the field, both at home and overseas, and classical and evangelical missionary agencies positioned themselves quite differently in relation to this emerging field.

Mission, humanitarianism, and development in the 1960s

By the 1960s colonial empire had given way and a host of new countries had gained independence. As Maggie Black writes,

> The rapid pace of change took most people by surprise. Africa was suddenly full of nation states demanding an equal place at the international table.... For those in Britain for whom the imperial sway and the responsibilities of the civilising mission had been cornerstones of a worldview and a lifetime of service, the changes were greeted with misgiving. For others, they were intoxicating in their promise of renewal, of a world casting off its chains to find new paths of cooperation on terms which respected the dignity of all.
>
> (Black 1992: 67)

The British mental map of the world was changing and 'distant others' who had been seen primarily as 'natives', 'primitives', or 'heathens' in the nineteenth and early twentieth centuries, were now recast as 'people living in poverty'.

The 1950s had witnessed a rapid spread of television ownership, especially after the Queen's coronation in 1953 and the introduction of commercial television (ITV) in 1955. By 1960 over 70 per cent of the British population had access to both channels, as television firmly supplanted radio as the leading medium. And in the 1960s the institutional and technological development of television helped fuel the growth of humanitarian and development NGOs in the UK. News footage of overseas emergencies publicised distant suffering to large audiences, and this in turn encouraged donations to aid agencies (Ogrizek 2008: 65). It was during the 1960s that the stereotypical image of a starving African child was elevated into a 'universal icon of human suffering' (Jones 2014: 27). The establishment of the welfare state and the increased post-war affluence precipitated a shift in values for many people, leading to greater concern about issues such as the environment, human rights, and development (Byrne 1997).

In 1960 the United Nations launched the Decade of Development and the Freedom from Hunger (FFH) campaign. These two campaigns had profound effects on the development NGOs and on British society more broadly. The NGOs embraced the new discourse of development with much enthusiasm and Oxfam, Christian Aid, and War on Want grew to become household names in these years. A huge array of activities connected to the FFH campaign took place across the UK. FFH committees were set up in over 1,000 towns and villages across the country, raising money and sending it to one of the FFH's selected projects (Black 1992: 75). Teaching materials were produced to be used in schools to teach schoolchildren about world hunger (Black 1992: 72). Large numbers of ordinary people were engaged and involved. In 1965 the United Nations Food and Agriculture Organisation (FAO) launched the Young World Mobilization Appeal (YWMA) to involve youth in educational and operational activities associated with the FFH campaign. Like its adult counterpart, the YWMA aimed to build financial and political support for long-term agricultural development projects in order to 'help the hungry to help themselves'. In the UK, this took the form of Youth Against Hunger (YAH) (Bocking-Welch 2016: 154).

Development NGOs such as Christian Aid and Oxfam ran YAH activities alongside their own educational and promotional work, and non-humanitarian associations, such as the Boy Scouts and church groups, found ways to introduce YAH into their broader remit of social activities (Bocking-Welch 2016: 155). British adolescents supporting YAH attended 'teach-ins' on aid and development, organised fasting demonstrations, signed petitions, sent out letters to MPs, trade unions, and industry, and protested with placards in Trafalgar Square. In 1968, YAH sponsored an all-party letter-writing campaign in which the youth movements of the Labour, Liberal, and Conservative parties pressed for more equitable trading terms, an increase in government aid to £300 million per year by 1970, and for industry to preserve the career prospects of qualified volunteers serving overseas (Bocking-Welch 2016: 162). As these events illustrate, during the 1960s there was a huge popular interest in development and great support and engagement from the public.

During the 1960s a new 'development infrastructure' was put in place in the UK. In 1963 the Disasters Emergency Committee (DEC) was set up as an umbrella body for the 'big five' aid agencies – the British Red Cross, Christian Aid, Oxfam, Save the Children, and War on Want. It was intended to facilitate closer coordination between its members by making joint emergency appeals to the public on television after major disasters. The Committee was granted special arrangements with the BBC to make these appeals, the proceeds of which would then be shared between the members (Jones 2014: 22). In 1964 the Labour Government created a Ministry of Overseas Development, and in 1965 the Voluntary Committee on Overseas Aid and Development was set up, including all the relevant aid agencies. In 1962 the Catholic Agency for Overseas Development (CAFOD) was set up, in 1964 Inter-Church Aid changed its name to Christian Aid, and in 1965 the Oxford Committee became Oxfam.

The liberal end of the Protestant church, the ecumenical Christians, also spent much of the 1960s thinking about 'development', as part of a broader process of trying to rethink the place of the church in society, both in Britain and overseas. By this time the idea of overseas mission was proving more and more difficult for them to justify and it was being subjected to criticism from within the classical missions as well as from without. With the end of colonialism and the increasing secularisation of British society, the classical missions started a major decline, finding it harder to raise funds and harder still to find people willing to serve as missionaries. Missionary confidence fell dramatically and the image of the 'heroic' missionary collapsed (Hughes 2013: 826). However, these mission societies did not die out. While some did indeed close doors, others combined or merged with larger agencies in order to overcome funding challenges, and many of them set up new departments for relief and development as their focus shifted away from evangelism towards this more material type of work. The 1960s and 1970s can thus be described as a period of the NGO-isation of many of the classical missionary societies (Paras 2014: 443).

In 1965 the British Council of Churches set up a Working Group to look at the issue of 'world poverty and British responsibility'. The Working Group was a collaboration between two departments in the BCC – the International Department and the Christian Aid Department. Its members consisted of the Director of Christian Aid, a number of missionaries and heads of mission societies, academics, development professionals, and former colonial officials (British Council of Churches 1966: 74). The resulting report discussed how the world economic system needed to be structured in order to better serve the interests of the 'underdeveloped countries' and it focussed its suggestions on changes to British government policy regarding aid, trade, and debt. It suggested that individual Christians could help in three ways: they could vote, campaign, and seek to influence government policy; they could do voluntary service overseas and help with skills transfer; and they could make donations to secular or Christian voluntary agencies. Throughout the report the reason why Christians should care about development is because of Christian notions of justice and the command to 'love your neighbour', and at this time people in distant lands were being reconceived of as 'neighbours' and often as 'fellow members of the world church'. Bringing about 'development' was now seen as a matter of justice and morality, and not as a means to an end. Indeed, evangelism was rarely mentioned in the report.

Theological discourse within the WCC at this time similarly focussed almost exclusively on rethinking the role of the church in a post-colonial secularising society and putting more emphasis on social action and speaking out against injustice. It established a Commission of the Churches on International Affairs and in 1966 the World Conference on Church and Society 'concentrated on such concrete human issues as the problems of development and the relations between the affluent nations and the nations engaged in a desperate struggle against poverty' (Visser t'Hooft 2004: 12).

However, while both secular development NGOs and ecumenical Christian organisations were thinking about the huge material disparities in the new post-colonial world order and pondering what a more just world could look like, evangelical Christians were mainly thinking about entirely different matters. Since the end of the Second World War they had seen the peoples of the world as ripe for evangelising and their overseas missionary efforts had expanded with new energy and vigour. Dozens of new evangelical mission agencies were established and the number of Northern missionaries serving overseas in the global South grew rapidly. Their focus was evangelism and the verbal proclamation of the gospel. Relief work, when carried out at all, was a secondary activity that was thought to help 'gain access' to more closed areas.

Nonetheless, as the 1960s progressed, there were some early signs of change as some evangelicals began, tentatively, to reconsider their single-minded focus on evangelism and their isolation from worldly matters. The impetus for this change in thinking came mainly from Latin America. There, evangelical theologians such as René Padilla and Samuel Escobar, influenced by the burgeoning liberation theology of the Catholics and the context of increasing inequality and poverty, began to develop a new theology of mission that sought to integrate both evangelism and socio-political involvement on behalf of the poor and oppressed into a holistic version of the Church's mission. They wanted to respond to the same realities addressed by liberationists while still upholding their evangelical commitments to the authority of scripture, the divinity of Christ, and the necessity of evangelism. Their solution, which they called 'misión integral' or integral mission, emphasised an incarnational and kingdom-centred theology claiming that, because Jesus was Lord over all of creation and all spheres of life, there was no real distinction between serving spiritual needs and serving physical needs. From this perspective the mission of the church could not simply be reduced to winning converts but must also include action on behalf of the poor and for social justice (Carpenter 2014: 274, Clawson 2012: 792). In the 1960s they began to increasingly participate in international evangelical conferences, and they started to push for their vision of a more holistic understanding of the gospel that included social engagement.

Thus in 1966, for example, the outcome document of a major evangelical congress held in Wheaton, Illinois under the title of 'The Church's Worldwide Mission', with around 1,000 participants from over 70 countries, recognised that evangelicals 'are guilty of an unscriptural isolation from the world that too often keeps us from honestly facing and coping with its concerns' and that there has been a 'failure to apply scriptural principles to such problems as racism, war, population explosion, poverty, family disintegration, social revolution, and communism'. It urged 'all evangelicals to stand openly and firmly for racial equality, human freedom, and all forms of social justice throughout the world' (cited in Padilla 2002).

Nonetheless, this was not an easy discussion and many remained unconvinced. Several conservative evangelicals pushed back and argued that their one and only focus should be evangelism. In the same year, 1966, British theologian John Stott spoke at the World Congress on Evangelism in Berlin and forcefully argued that the task of evangelicals was 'not to reform society, but to preach the

Gospel ...[. T]he primary task of the members of Christ's church is to be Gospel heralds not social reformers' (quoted in Stanley 2013: 155).

While these debates certainly rippled into the UK, during the 1960s British evangelicals were largely focussed on an entirely different discussion – they were locked in a fierce internal debate about whether they should stay within the increasingly liberal mainline denominations, which were taking doctrinal positions that many evangelicals found problematic, or whether they should leave and set up their own separate churches. In 1966 tensions came to a head in the National Assembly of Evangelicals conference, where there was a charged public discussion about this issue. Morgan Derham, General Secretary of the Evangelical Alliance, and John Stott, two people later to be strongly associated with Tearfund, argued that evangelicals should stay in the denominations. Martyn Lloyd-Jones from the British Evangelical Council (BEC) took a more fundamentalist stance and argued for separatism. This led to a major rift, and many evangelicals left the Evangelical Alliance and moved to the BEC (Randall 2004: 66).

During the next few years those evangelicals who had decided to stay with the Evangelical Alliance focussed on fashioning for themselves a new identity and position as distinctly evangelical yet part of broader denominations, particularly in the Church of England. At that time evangelicals had a very poor image among their fellow Anglicans, being associated with narrow partisanship, obstructionism and a tendency to be irresponsibly inward looking. But this began to change. In 1967 the first National Evangelical Anglican Congress met at Keele University for three days of intense debate. Almost 1,000 delegates from evangelical parishes, mission societies, and theological colleges formulated a new strategy for engaging with the Church of England. Many saw this event as a major turning point in the history of Anglican Evangelicalism. The Congress chairman, John Stott, declared that 'nothing comparable has been attempted within living memory, if ever before' (cited in Atherstone 2017). One observer likened the Keele Congress to the Second Vatican Council, breathing a spirit of *aggiornamento*[9] through the Anglican Evangelical movement (Atherstone 2017). Stanley remarks that the conference

> was evidence of a decisive mood shift among younger evangelicals in the Church of England towards an unprecedented degree of commitment to full participation in a theologically plural church. Conservative evangelicals had emerged from the fundamentalist ghetto and were about to enter an era of predominant influence unparalleled in Anglican history.
>
> (Stanley 2013: 44)

Thus in the late 1960s, just before the establishment of Tearfund, young evangelicals in the Church of England were feeling energised and outward looking – keen to 'exit their ghetto' and demonstrate that they, too, could move with the times and engage with real-world problems. At this particular point in time, that meant engaging with social issues and, of course, with 'development'. Many of them were already giving money to Oxfam, Christian Aid, and War on Want. The time was ripe for the birth of a new evangelical NGO through which they could support development 'as evangelicals' or in a distinctively evangelical manner.[10] This organisation, of course, would be Tearfund.

Conclusion

It can be seen that, by the time Tearfund came into being, the fields of 'development' and 'humanitarian relief' were already well established. And while they were portrayed as fundamentally secular, they were in fact crowded with a wide variety of organisations with different relations to Christianity. In the UK there were secular NGOs that had been founded by Christians and whose thinking was inspired by Christianity. There were secular NGOs with no faith connection at all. There was Christian Aid, which was an agency of the British Council of Churches and associated with the liberal ecumenical movement. And there was CAFOD, which was an agency of the Catholic Bishops' Conference of England and Wales. Overseas, most of the development work was in practice being carried out by missionaries from the classical mission societies (and also large numbers of Catholic missionaries). Evangelical mission societies were carrying out some education and medical work, but they did not consider this to be 'development' as such and did not want to partake in the 'development sector'. Thus the field was rather more complex than has generally been recognised, and, at this point in time, was far from fully secularised.

It can also be seen that not all 'faith-based organisations' are the same, even when just looking at Protestant Christian organisations. Christian Aid and Tearfund grew out of very different parts of the Protestant world, and thus brought with them different priorities, different theologies, and different institutional networks. Indeed, it is possible to see the birth of Tearfund as a response to the existence of Christian Aid. The split within the evangelical movement and the decision of the Evangelical Alliance and its supporters to remain within the Church of England, to retain their distinctiveness, and yet to also engage more in the outside world, can be seen in the context of the 1960s to almost create the need for an evangelical development agency – if the liberal wing of the Church of England had its own relief and development NGO (Christian Aid), then surely the evangelical wing should have its own too (Tearfund)?

And of course, this historical sketch helps us to understand how Tearfund would try to differentiate itself from Christian Aid. As an evangelical organisation it would surely seek to combine evangelism and social action. And yet this history also shows that there had been many previous attempts to combine evangelism and social action in the preceding 150 years, both in activities in the UK and overseas. And by and large they had all failed in this endeavour, with the majority of them secularising over time. Would Tearfund simply repeat this history or would it be able to find a way to hold together these two dimensions of change that seem to have an almost entropic tendency to come apart?

Notes

1 Nonconformist referred to Presbyterians, Congregationalists, Baptists, Calvinists, Methodists, Unitarians, Quakers, Brethren, the English Moravians and other 'reformed' groups and less organised sects who were not part of the Church of England, and later became known as the Free Churches. It also includes the evangelicals or 'Low Church' element in the Church of England. A religious census in 1851 revealed that, of the 40 per cent of the population that attended church services on Sundays, approximately half were Church of England and half were Nonconformist (Floyd 2008: 5).
2 The Society for the Propagation of the Gospel in Foreign Parts (SPG) had been formed at the start of the eighteenth century, but its initial focus was on providing Christian services to colonial settlers in North America rather than on evangelising the 'heathens' (O'Connor 2000, Tennant 2013). It later went on to carry out more typical missionary work. It has changed much over the years and still exists today as the Union Society for the Propagation of the Gospel (USPG).
3 Anti-Slavery International can trace its origins to 1787 when the Society for Effecting the Abolition of the Slave Trade was formed (by Quakers and Anglicans), which later in 1839 morphed into the British and Foreign Anti-Slavery Society, and which after several other mergers and name changes finally took on its current form in 1995 (Hilton *et al.* 2012: 13).
4 In some cases the rift between conservatives and liberals led to mission societies splitting apart. For example, the CMS split in 1922 when its more conservative members left and established the Bible Churchmen's Missionary Society (BCMS), while CMS developed for several decades along a more liberal route.
5 A significant amount of battlefield medical care was also provided by military medical facilities.
6 Indeed, Dromi argues that it was Calvinist beliefs – about warfare, charity, and the relations between state and society – that convinced the founders of the Red Cross that humanitarianism should be waged as an autonomous field, rather than being proffered under the auspices of church or state (Dromi 2016: 198).
7 Several scholars have argued that 'development' itself can be seen as a kind of religion, with its faith in progress and human betterment and its utopian vision of a future fair and just world (Rist 1997, Van Ufford and Schoffeleers 1988).
8 At this time these two fields were widely overlapping, with many organisations carrying out both types of activity, now called 'relief' and 'development'.
9 *Aggiornamento*, 'bringing up to date', was one of the key words used during the Second Vatican Council both by bishops and the clergy attending the sessions, and by the media and Vaticanologists covering it. It was used to mean throwing open the doors of the Church in a desire to dialogue with the outside world.
10 Several evangelical relief and development NGOs had been established in the USA after the Second World War. The National Association of Evangelicals had established World Relief in 1944, World Vision was founded in 1950, and Compassion came into being in 1952.

Part I
A new kind of missionary organisation

3 Tearfund's first 25 years, 1968–1993

Introduction

Tearfund was officially launched in 1968. This chapter outlines its work in its first 25 years and discusses the way that its identity as a Christian organisation developed and changed during that period. From the beginning Tearfund sat somewhere between two different worlds – the evangelical missionary world and the new world of 'international development' – as it sought to encourage evangelical missionaries to carry out relief and development projects. Many of its founders considered Tearfund itself to be a 'new kind of missionary organisation' as ideas about mission started to change in the post-colonial context, while others saw it more as a new evangelical relief and development NGO, the 'Christian Aid' of the evangelical community. As Tearfund got established, determined its working modality, and gained more practical experience, these questions about its purpose and identity began to gain increasing salience.

At the core of the issue was how Tearfund would combine evangelism with development.

For the first ten years or so Tearfund sent out 'overseas personnel' (OPs) and made grants to evangelical organisations for work to alleviate people's material suffering – digging wells, distributing food, running clinics, etc. – and it envisaged that these organisations would do this work alongside their regular spiritual activities of preaching and evangelism. After about ten years it was felt that Tearfund was tipping the balance too far towards the material side of things and that it should support the whole church in all its work. So a new department was formed that would make grants for more spiritual matters such as evangelism and Christian education. During this time Tearfund thus supported work on both material and spiritual matters but kept them completely separate in different sections of the organisation. There was no specifically 'faith-based' approach to relief and development. By the end of this period many in Tearfund were struggling with questions about how Tearfund should work, how evangelism and development should be combined, and what kind of organisation Tearfund should be going forward.

The formation of Tearfund

While Tearfund was officially launched in 1968 its history stretches back a few more years. The UN's World Refugee Year was 1959–60 and fundraising campaigns were being run by various organisations in the UK, such as Oxfam, Christian Aid, and War on Want. Evangelicals heard about these campaigns on the radio, on TV, and in the mainstream newspapers, and many made donations to these organisations. As public awareness of the refugee crisis grew, some evangelicals started to send cheques into the Evangelical Alliance (EA) and asked them to disburse them to evangelical organisations working with refugees around the world. In response the EA set up the Evangelical Alliance Refugee Fund, through which it collected the donations and then sent out grants to missionaries working with refugees.

The first grant was made in 1960, to a former missionary couple who were working to set up a refugee work-centre in Hong Kong (Endersbee 1973: 20). Even as World Refugee Year came to an end, donations continued to trickle in. Throughout the 1960s evangelicals sent in money to the EA whenever there was a disaster or crisis. And the EA Refugee Fund continued to make modest donations to missionaries working with refugees in what was then the Republic of Congo, in Vietnam, and in other places. In 1966 Morgan Derham took over as the new General Secretary of the Evangelical Alliance. He was a big thinker and visionary, less conservative than many evangelicals of this time, and he had two ideas – to set up a Scholarship Fund for Africans to come to study at theological college, and to establish a Relief Fund to help the poor overseas. He hired 22-year-old Mary-Jean Duffield as his assistant and together they tested the waters regarding these two ideas, speaking informally to some missionaries and young evangelicals. Cautiously optimistic, they decided to give them both a try. The Scholarship Fund never really caught on, as there were few applicants and very little money was raised. However, the Relief Fund did. Fitting well with the prevailing mood in both the secular and the evangelical worlds, it was an immediate success.

In 1967 Derham widened the remit of the small fund and renamed it the EA Relief Fund. Later that year George Hoffman joined the staff of the EA and took over responsibility for the EAR Fund, as it was then called. While Derham was the thinker and visionary, Hoffman was the entrepreneur and people person that would make the Fund grow. He had grown up in a secular family from a modest background and had come to faith a few years earlier during one of Billy Graham's crusades at Earl's Court in London. He was a charismatic and energetic character and a great communicator. He relaunched the Fund and sought to give it its own identity.

One of the first things he did was to set up a committee to oversee the work of the Fund. Hoffman thought that it was important to have Ernest Oliver on this committee, as he was then General Secretary of the Evangelical Missionary Alliance (EMA), and Hoffman saw the potential of working closely with the EMA and its 80 or so member societies who had a network of contacts around the world (Tiplady 2005: 40). Oliver's initial role was to advise Tearfund on its overseas work, as it was recognised that he was the only person on the Committee with experience of managing change overseas.

The Committee had its first meeting on 29 May 1968 and this is generally taken as the birth date of Tearfund. At this meeting Hoffman announced the first ten grants that the EAR Fund had made. The very first official grant of this new fund had been to the South American Missionary Society (SAMS) for its medical and welfare work with indigenous Indians in the Chaco area of Northern Argentina (Endersbee 1973: 120). This was influenced by the fact that Hoffman was on the Board of SAMS and thus had contacts with the Anglican Church in South America. Other grants that year included support for famine relief in India, refugee work in Hong Kong and in Jordan, agricultural work in Nigeria, medical work in Paraguay, and rehabilitation work in Vietnam (Endersbee 1973: 40).

At its second meeting a few months later the Committee decided to add 'the' to the name of the Fund so that it became 'The Evangelical Alliance Relief Fund' and would be known as TEAR Fund, rather than EAR Fund. Committee members also began to think about how to advertise the new Fund to UK evangelicals. They decided on bold tactics to jolt evangelicals into action. The slogan for their first exhibition stand later that year was, 'They Can't Eat Prayer', and the first poster mailing sent out to evangelical churches similarly featured the face of a Vietnamese refugee boy above the caption, 'I can't eat prayer'. This was self-consciously provocative, challenging evangelicals to help the poor rather than just pray for them. The fact that Tearfund pulled this slogan just a few months later after receiving letters of complaint tells us much about the attitude of UK evangelicals at the time. Many were committed to prayer and evangelism and did not think that the evangelical church should be involved in social action.

Thus from the beginning Tearfund saw changing the mindset of the UK evangelical church to be a fundamental part of its remit (see Appendix). To this end George Hoffman spoke at the second National Assembly of Evangelicals in 1968 and gave an address titled, 'World Poverty and Christian Responsibility', arguing that evangelicals should get involved in social action. His speech was well received and the Assembly went on to adopt a resolution affirming that 'as evangelicals we have, to a large extent, failed to recognise our social responsibilities and acknowledge our corporate involvement in meeting the physical, as well as the spiritual, needs of men'. They went on to pledge 'to address the imbalance in our total ministry' (cited in Hollow 2008: 41).

In November 1968, as the Fund was growing, Tearfund produced its first policy statement to clarify what kind of work it would and would not support. This document made it very clear that Tearfund would only support work to alleviate physical suffering and that it would not fund educational or purely spiritual work. It stated:

> Tear Fund exists to relieve suffering. It operates in the name of Christ, in obedience to His command, taking into account spiritual needs as well as physical ones.... Urgent requests for immediate help to relieve extreme

suffering and famine will always be carefully considered ... [as well as] longer term economic 'pump-priming' projects such as agricultural education, well-digging, the construction of simple irrigation schemes, the provision of farm tools and seed, and long term medical care projects.

(Quoted in Hollow 2008: 46, 48)

That same month Tearfund also held its first press conference, serving up famine rations of puffed rice and powdered milk on silver banquet plates in order to highlight the difference in what the rich and the poor got to eat. In early January 1969 it organised two large gospel concerts at the Royal Albert Hall with Cliff Richard, named *Help! Hope! and Hallelujah!* The aim was to raise money in order to send a Land Rover out to the SAMS missionaries to help with their medical work in the Chaco, Argentina. A new Land Rover was displayed outside the Royal Albert Hall under spotlights.

These events announced the entrance of this new Fund into both the missionary and the development worlds. During the following months George Hoffman was invited to meetings with both Oxfam and Christian Aid, who were keen to know more about this new initiative (Endersbee 1973: 65).

At this time Tearfund was mainly giving grants to missionaries to carry out relief and development projects and some people were questioning why Tearfund was raising money from evangelicals in order to give it to missionaries, instead of evangelicals just continuing to give directly to missionaries. In 1969 donations to missionary societies were down and many were concerned about their financial situation. Some were criticising the new Fund for attracting money away from the missionary societies (Endersbee 1973: 78). There was also some confusion over what Tearfund's money could be used for and what was beyond its remit. Thus, in November of that year, Tearfund invited the leaders of several mission societies to a meeting. The invitation letter read:

Tear Fund has been channelling a substantial amount of aid through what are traditionally recognised as 'standard missionary projects'. And it is for this reason in particular that we welcome the opportunity to confer with representatives from a number of missionary societies, in order to think through Tear Fund's future role....

(Quoted in Endersbee 1973: 78)

The meeting was attended by representatives from many of the evangelical mission societies, including the South American Missionary Society, the Bible Churchmen's Missionary Society, the Sudan United Mission, the Africa Inland Mission, the Bible and Medical Missionary Fellowship, the Evangelical Union of South America, the Unevangelised Fields Mission, the Worldwide Evangelization Crusade, and the Regions Beyond Missionary Union (Endersbee 1973: 79).

At the meeting Tearfund sought again to clarify that it only supported material relief and development work. John Boxhall, one of the members of the Tearfund Committee, suggested:

Couldn't the distinction between Tearfund's work and that of the [missionary] societies be outlined as follows: if the emphasis is on economics and physical development, then it is a matter for consideration for Tearfund support; and if the work has an evangelistic emphasis then the responsibility for it lies with the missionary societies?

(Quoted in Endersbee 1973: 79)

The mission agencies were divided in their reception to the new Fund. Ernest Oliver, the missionary on Tearfund's Board, sought to convince them that Tearfund would be able to help them by taking a load off their shoulders – when faced with a disaster in the field, they would not have to simply pray that money would somehow arrive, as they would now be able to request financial assistance from Tearfund, which had money ready for exactly those kinds of emergencies (Endersbee 1973: 81). Some agreed. For example, in the press release after the meeting, Alan Neech of the Bible Churchmen's Missionary Society (BCMS) welcomed the distinctive emphasis of Tearfund and said he believed that Tearfund could play a valuable role in 'coming alongside the missionary society and sharing in its social relief programme, thus enabling the society to fulfil its primary evangelistic task' (quoted in Endersbee 1973: 79). The General Secretary of the South American Missionary Society (SAMS), Harry Sutton, was also an early supporter. However, some of the mission agencies were more reticent. They were still not sure about the theological basis for engaging in social action and thought that this would be a distraction from their main focus on the verbal proclamation of the gospel. This group left the meeting unconvinced and did not start immediately start applying to Tearfund for grants for relief and development work.

For Morgan Derham, Tearfund's initial founder, there was no dilemma. In his vision Tearfund was simply a new type of mission agency that fit better with the times. Speaking in the early 1970s, he said, 'I think Tear Fund represents the kind of specialist agency which is the shape of things to come in missions abroad' (quoted in Endersbee 1973: 160). Not only would Tearfund appeal to a new generation of supporters, it would be able to carry out mission more effectively in the new post-colonial world, where he noticed that 'Tear Fund can serve overseas [in some places] where missionaries cannot' (Endersbee 1973: 160).

Nonetheless, the Fund continued to grow as supporters responded to the appeals and sent in more cheques. Discussions began to take place about separating the Fund from the EA, which at this time was in a poor situation, financially and otherwise. In 1969 the Fund set up its own bank account and in 1970 it was incorporated as a company under the name of Tearfund Limited. Later that year its memorandum and articles of association as a charity were incorporated. In 1971 George Hoffman left the EA and became the full-time Director of Tearfund and in 1973 Tearfund was officially registered as a charity (Hollow 2008: 53).

The 1970s: getting established

During the 1970s Tearfund's work continued to grow. Tearfund found new people and projects to support through its contacts in missionary networks. Missionaries returning from the field might introduce Tearfund to a new organisation or George Hoffman might meet people running projects when he attended Christian conferences around the world. In 1969 Hoffman had been appointed coordinator of the World Evangelical Fellowship's newly launched International Christian Assistance programme, and this was a further avenue through which he developed contacts with overseas churches and evangelical social action programs (Endersbee 1973: 89). Thus the expanding group of organisations that Tearfund supported was very much rooted in the missionary world.

Tearfund's initial mode of operation was to raise funds from British supporters and to send them to missionaries working overseas in response to grant requests. This was not so different to the mode of operation of many of the secular development NGOs at this time. They also raised money and gave it mainly to overseas missionaries to carry out development work, quite simply because missionaries were the only Westerners on the ground out in Africa and Asia. The main difference between Tearfund and the other NGOs was that the secular NGOs and the mainline Christian NGOs sent funds to organisations associated with the liberal, classical missionaries, while Tearfund mainly sent funds to evangelical missionaries. There was of course a small overlap, as Tearfund also supported missionaries associated with the Anglican Church, such as SAMS and the CMS, who were also supported by Oxfam, Christian Aid, and others.

Being well plugged into this ready-made network of missionaries enabled Tearfund to quickly and easily know what was happening on the ground in many places around the world. For example, when Tearfund learnt of a disaster its staff would contact evangelical groups in the area to find out what was needed. The group would visit the affected area and write back with suggestions of what was required and what to do. Tearfund's Overseas Grants Committee would consider the request and, if it was accepted, send out money to the local organisation (Symonds 1993: 59). Other than responding to disasters, most of the early grant requests were for medical work, construction, and agriculture. For example, in 1969 the Overseas Missionary Fellowship (previously the China Inland Mission) requested a grant for rehabilitation work in Thailand; in 1973 a missionary from the Africa Inland Mission working in the Central African Republic submitted a grant request for a vehicle to transport building materials needed to construct a training centre for carpentry and agriculture; in 1974 the Worldwide Evangelization Crusade applied for a grant to build a new maternity block and dispensary for one of their hospitals in Zaire; and in 1975 the International Fellowship of Evangelical Students in Peru requested a grant to build a new building with a church and community centre in Lima.

In parallel to the grant-giving work, in 1971 Tearfund started to send personnel overseas. This idea drew on both the growing wave of volunteerism that was inspiring young people in the UK to volunteer overseas with organisations such as Voluntary Services Overseas (VSO) (Stuart 2008: 538), and the new idea of 'short-term mission' that was beginning to emerge in the evangelical world (Offutt 2011: 798). The first people it sent were agricultural missionaries Kevin and Denise McKemey and Peter and Frances Tyson, who went to work with SAMS in the Chaco, Argentina, to set up an irrigation project to help local farmers (Hollow 2008: 89–90). This went on to become one of Tearfund's largest projects, a ten-year programme of agricultural and medical development known as Iniciativa Cristiana. For Sutton, General Secretary of SAMS, receiving these agricultural missionaries was a great boost. Interviewed in the early 1970s, he explained:

> If we as a missionary society appealed to send out four agriculturalists, I think the response would be limited ... because people would say: 'Your job is to go and preach the gospel'. This is one of the misconceptions about the role of mission. Now, if Tearfund appeal for this project, they get a colossal response, and are able to share this money with the Church in Northern Argentina, providing them with four young qualified people ... through SAMS.
>
> (Quoted in Endersbee 1973: 121)

In 1972 Tearfund started to send nurses to Bangladesh, under the supervision of the Bible and Medical Missionary Fellowship (now called Interserve), which was at the time seeking to support short-term mission work, and in 1973 it started to send people out to work with the Sudan Interior Mission (now called Serving in Mission, or SIM) in Ethiopia.

In 1973 Tearfund decided to send out staff directly, rather than through UK-based mission agencies. The Overseas Personnel Department was set up, which arranged for Christian technical experts – physiotherapists, agronomists, foresters – to go overseas and spend up to four years working with a church or mission agency. Posts were advertised in *Tear Times* (see Appendix) and Tearfund supporters applied. This side of Tearfund's work grew quickly in the 1970s and 1980s and was in many respects its major focus. Many thought of these OPs as missionaries, while others considered them to be development workers. At this point the distinction was not clear. Graham Fairbairn, who worked for Tearfund from 1979 to 2008, reflects:

> We had Christian workers who had to have an evangelising heart. They had to be prepared to go into communities and make a difference for Christ.... I would say they were missionaries, others would say they were doing social work.

In 1974 Tearfund started two new initiatives, which would continue to run for many years alongside the organisation's more mainstream relief and development work. The first of these was a child sponsorship programme, known as the

48 *A new kind of missionary organisation*

Partners in Childcare scheme, whereby UK evangelicals could give money on a regular basis to support an individual child in a poor country. Tearfund initially started a child sponsorship scheme in partnership with World Vision Canada sponsoring children in orphanages in India and Bangladesh. However, in 1975 it pulled out of this partnership because of doubts about the benefits of institutional care and because it found out that often the orphanages were not being run by evangelical Christians and there was little Christian content in the scheme. Instead, Tearfund started to work with Compassion International, which preferred to work with families rather than orphanages and ensured that Christian education and evangelism were part of the scheme (Hollow 2008: 143).

The second initiative was a craft trading scheme called Tearcraft. This grew out of some of the work that Tearfund was supporting in Bangladesh, in which a New Zealand missionary was training local women to make jute handicrafts that they could sell to make an income. In 1974 he contacted Tearfund about the possibility of helping these women to sell their handicrafts overseas. Tearfund put him in touch with Richard Adams, who at the time was trying to set up a company importing craft items from the developing world on a fair basis (Hollow 2008: 133). Richard placed an order for £1,000 of goods. A short time later, following the huge floods in Bangladesh, Tearfund sent a plane packed with blankets, powdered milk, and basic medical supplies. It had the idea of filling up the plane with handicrafts for the return flight. The result was that in December 1974 Tearcraft was registered as a business and its first catalogue went out in February 1975, containing jute sikas, bags, baskets, and table mats made by the women in Bangladesh. It was run by Richard Adams for its first five years (Symonds 1993: 124).

Throughout the 1970s Tearcraft bought from more and more producer groups and began to expand its range of products. Tearcraft was run as a profit-making business, paying producers a fair price for their products, and the profits were ploughed back into Tearfund to support its work. The Tearcraft catalogue would be sent out to supporters each year, and they could then buy products from developing world producers. Tearcraft was firm that it only marketed goods that were made by groups linked with evangelical Christians who saw handicraft production as an outworking of the mission of the church (Symonds 1993: 124). Eventually this led to the parting of ways with Richard Adams, who in 1979 left Tearfund and Tearcraft to set up Traidcraft, a similar kind of trading organisation but one that would work with a broader range of producer groups coming from any faith or none.

While both these initiatives drew on ideas that were mainstream in the secular development world at the time (Save the Children, Plan International, and others had been doing child sponsorship for decades; Oxfam and War on Want had likewise been trading handicrafts from overseas supplier groups for many years), the issues that cropped up in both the programmes highlight some of the assumptions in Tearfund's working model regarding the interconnection between religion and development. While Tearfund's work would only support the material side of things, it was considered crucial that some other organisation was also caring for the spiritual side and if this was not the case then Tearfund did not consider it the appropriate way for them to work. For example, the original model of child sponsorship with World Vision Canada was stopped when Tearfund realised that the children were not being supplied with Christian education alongside the material support that Tearfund was offering, and a new arrangement was made with an organisation that would ensure Christian education and evangelism were fundamental parts of the programme. Likewise, in Tearcraft, the Tearfund leadership said that it would only work with producer groups who were connected with evangelical agencies and thus receiving Christian input as well as training on craft production.

As Tearfund began to grapple with the question of how to integrate evangelism and development in its work, broader discussions about evangelism and social action were taking place in the wider evangelical work. The calls for evangelicals to combine evangelism and social action into a form of 'integral mission' that had been started by Latin American theologians in the 1960s had come to a head at the International Conference on World Evangelization that had been held in Lausanne in 1974. This was a major conference, attended by some 2,500 evangelicals from 150 countries, and it led to a major change in evangelical thinking about mission, at least in some sections of the evangelical world. René Padilla and Samuel Escobar both gave provocative plenary addresses presenting their theology of 'misión integral', and calling on evangelicals to get involved in social action. Their addresses generated a lot of discussion and in the resulting Lausanne Covenant there was an entire section on Christian social responsibility, which stated, 'we affirm that evangelism and socio-political involvement are both part of our Christian duty ...[. T]he salvation we claim should be transforming us in the totality of our personal and social responsibilities' (cited in Clawson 2012: 796).

Anecdote has it that the UK's John Stott shared a room with René Padilla during the conference and that they argued about the importance of social action for hours into the night. By the end of the conference Stott had changed his position. He then played an important role in bringing ideas about integral mission back to the UK and promoting them within the evangelical constituency through the late 1970s and 1980s. In his formulation evangelism and social action went together 'like two blades of a pair of scissors or two wings of a bird.' In 1983 he became Tearfund's first President and his thinking influenced the organisation throughout the 1980s. Stephen Rand, who worked with Tearfund from 1979 to 2004, reflects:

> I think for George Hoffman ... the overwhelmingly dominant model was the ... thing about two blades of a pair of scissors.... Therefore to George initially it was very simple. If we worked through missionaries, missionaries were doing the proclamation bit, and we were enabling them to do the social action bit.*

But as Tearfund's work continued to expand into the 1980s many began to feel that it was actually rather more complicated than that. Three main drivers emerged that began to lead Tearfund to reconsider the relationship between evangelism and development – the decision that Tearfund would also start to directly support evangelism, developments in broader evangelical thinking about 'integral mission', and growing experience with some of the practical dilemmas involved in carrying out 'development'.

The 1980s: dilemmas of integrating evangelism and development

The Evangelism and Christian Education Department

By 1979 Tearfund had been established for ten years and had grown into an organisation with an income of over £2 million, providing grants and sending personnel to over 130 missionary and church organisations worldwide. Though still fairly small in comparison to major development NGOs, such as Christian Aid and Oxfam, which at this time had annual incomes of around £5.5 million and £9 million respectively (Black 1992: 208), Tearfund had become established and was growing. However, some in the leadership were beginning to feel that their approach was not completely right. Tearfund's leaders were not concerned by size, but rather by the role of faith. And they were particularly concerned that Tearfund, as an organisation, was only concerned with the material. Morgan Derham, the initial visionary behind Tearfund and a long-serving member of the Tearfund Board, recalls:

> It was capturing the imagination and interest of the younger generation in a way that I felt was tilting the balance too far in the direction of material relief and development programs. In the 60s, when Tearfund was gestating, the task was to persuade evangelicals that relief and development work was biblically acceptable – the 'You can't eat prayer' era. But that battle had been largely won, and I felt that the pendulum was swinging too far.
>
> (Quoted in Symonds 1993: 25)

At the same time Tearfund's success in fostering evangelical involvement in relief and development had led to numerous requests from overseas churches to the Evangelical Alliance for similar financial support for *all* their work, including evangelism and leadership training programmes. Derham thus suggested setting up another organisation under the Evangelical Alliance that would focus on spiritual ministries by supporting training for overseas church leaders in evangelism and leadership. Graham Fairbairn recalls:

> The EA were wondering about doing a HEAR Fund…. We suggested instead that it should be built into Tear Fund and that Tear Fund should give a percentage of its income to this new entity.*

Ernest Oliver argued against setting up a separate fund and said that it should be part of Tearfund 'since the overall objectives were the same and separating them would deny the fullness of mission' (quoted in Tiplady 2005: 41). While Derham had become concerned that Tearfund was not acting enough as a missionary organisation because it had become too focussed on the material, Oliver retained the original view that this material work was a fundamental part of a new kind of holistic mission best suited to post-colonial realities. His understanding of Tearfund's work can be seen in an article that he wrote for the *Christian Brethren Review* in 1985 called 'The challenge of mission today':

> There is an increasing resistance on the part of governments ... to the entry of an expatriate Christian evangelist. At the same time, those very governments are struggling with immense problems of providing an adequate educational, medical and social service to their people.... I believe, therefore, that it is consonant with the scriptural revelation of God's concern for the total state of all men, for individuals and international teams of Christian professional men and women to enter into contracts with such governments ... to fulfil a role within that country's development plans and thus be able in a very effective way to exercise thoroughly holistic Christian ministry today. The United Mission to Nepal, HEED in Bangladesh and ACROSS in the Sudan [Tearfund partners] are all current examples of this 'new' concept of mission today.
>
> (Oliver 1985: 28)

Eventually, following long discussions between Tearfund and the Evangelical Alliance, Oliver's view prevailed and it was decided to set up a new department within Tearfund, which would focus entirely on spiritual matters. Thus in 1979 the Evangelism and Christian Education Department was established. And the first Director of this new Department was none other than Ernest Oliver himself, one of the original members of the Tearfund Committee, and still Secretary of the Evangelical Missionary Alliance.

Tearfund initially allocated 5 per cent of its income to this Department, which later increased to 10 per cent (Symonds 1993: 26). Roughly a third of this was spent on providing scholarships for overseas students to study theology for Bachelors, Masters, or Doctoral degrees; a third went to grants for buildings and vehicles for missionaries, Bible colleges, and seminaries; and a third went to grants supporting the production and distribution of Christian literature, radio communications, and other activities to support church growth (Rogers 1989). Graham Fairbairn explains the motivation for this new Department:

> There was a need for leadership training, a need for support in evangelism and outreach, and a need for support in Christian education. We agreed that as an evangelical organisation we should also be an evangelistic organisation and that this should be given expression to in our ministry.*

In many cases Tearfund was giving grants to the same organisation for both spiritual work and material work, but there was a division between them built into the system. If, for example, a missionary organisation wanted funding to dig boreholes, it had to apply to the Overseas Relief and Development Department, while if it wanted bicycles for its evangelists it had to apply to the Evangelism and Christian Education Department.

Thus throughout the 1980s a fundamental separation of the material and the spiritual ran throughout the organisation. While Tearfund was now dealing with both material and spiritual matters the two were kept clearly separate. One side of the organisation made grants for scholarships, evangelism, and church growth, while the other side made grants for running clinics, setting up agricultural projects, and digging wells. The two sides of the organisation even felt very different from each other, with different styles and cultures. Graham Fairbairn recalls:

> The Evangelism and Christian Education department had a very different culture. It had more of a missionary society feel, quite different to the other departments.*

'Spiritual' work and 'practical' work were funded in different ways, by different teams, with little or no overall integration. As Stephen Rand recalls:

> In some cases Tearfund was working with Christian NGOs that were specifically social action organisations, so they were doing the relief work while another part of their denomination was doing the evangelism. I think there were some people who would even have argued that if Tearfund was supporting a development project in a country and there were Christians doing 'spiritual' work elsewhere in the same country, that was still integral because the 'two blades of the scissors' were seen on a national basis rather than on an individual project basis.
> (Stephen Rand, quoted in Hollow 2008: 197)

And he continues:

> What seemed to be missing was the idea that Christians would do relief and development work in a distinctively different way than non-Christian organisations.
> (Stephen Rand, quoted in Hollow 2008: 197)

Broader evangelical thinking about integral mission

During the 1980s the broader worldwide evangelical community had begun to devote more time and energy to thinking about social engagement. Following the Lausanne Conference, the first important steps towards formulating a distinctly Christian approach to social action had been taken during the World Evangelical Fellowship consultation in Wheaton, Illinois in 1983. This consultation culminated in the 'Wheaton Statement', which set out the outlines of a specifically Christian theology of development. The Statement did not use the term 'development', with its connotations of modernity, materiality, and sole focus on economic growth, but instead adopted the term 'transformation'. The Wheaton Statement describes transformation in the following way:

> Transformation is the change from a condition of human existence contrary to God's purpose to one in which people are able to enjoy fullness of life in harmony with God.... This transformation can only take place through the obedience of individuals and communities to the Gospel of Jesus Christ, whose power changes the lives of men and women by releasing them from the guilt, power, and consequences of sin, enabling them to respond with love toward God and toward others.... The goal of transformation is best described by the biblical vision of the Kingdom of God.
> (World Evangelical Fellowship 1983)

This thinking is based on a particular theology known as kingdom theology, which foregrounds Jesus' teaching about the Kingdom of God, particularly the Sermon on the Mount, and situates his teachings with the social concerns of first-century Galilee. Unlike premillennial dispensationalist theology, which emphasised the urgent nature of saving souls and the hopelessness of social reform, kingdom theology called for Christians to work towards a better world today, prefiguring the perfection to come with Christ's return (Steensland and Goff 2014: 13). This theology had much in common with the incarnational theology developed by the ecumenical missionaries in the 1940s and 1950s, similarly focussing on combining material and spiritual care in the nurturance of 'the whole person' (see Chapter 2).

By the late 1980s this thinking was beginning to influence many evangelical thinkers and activists, including those at Tearfund. An awareness was growing that Tearfund was not really doing 'transformation' – there was little integration of material and spiritual concerns in its work and no specifically Christian approach to development. Instead, as one staff member from the time recalls:

> There was a very strong tendency to ... import into the organization all sorts of theories and ideas and practices which were found in the so-called secular development world, and then to baptize them with a few texts, scratching through the Bible to find some Biblical passage that could be vaguely linked to this particular practice which you are adopting from the secular world, and then to put a text in brackets at the end of your statement and think that you were doing Christian development.*

Increasing experience of doing 'development'

The 1980s also saw many changes in the way that Tearfund carried out the practical, development part of its work. At this time most relief and development

NGOs had begun to shift away from making grants to missionaries and were instead beginning to make grants to indigenous local development NGOs that were springing up in Africa, Asia, and Latin America. Christian Aid had stopped sending its money through the WCC and was now mainly making grants directly to overseas churches and some other local organisations.[1] In this context Tearfund had also begun to rethink its mode of operation and started to work less with mission agencies and instead to develop more direct links with indigenous evangelical churches.[2] It began to seek out new organisations to fund through national Evangelical Alliances and the World Evangelical Fellowship. And its grants, along with those of other evangelical NGOs, were influencing these national EAs and indigenous churches to begin to set up separate development organisations or to establish development wings. So Tearfund's partners on the ground were beginning to change.

During this period Tearfund mainly supported emergency responses to floods, earthquakes, and other natural disasters and service-provision types of projects with professional agronomists, health experts, new infrastructure, and so on, as was general practice in the development sector at the time. In the mid-1980s Tearfund brought in more technical expertise, hiring three technical consultants, known as 'the three wise men', to add more technical rigour to the project selection and monitoring processes. A few years later it recruited a humanitarian specialist to oversee the relief work and then three regional managers to oversee the work in different regions of the world.

As project experience mounted up Tearfund began to realise that welfare provision was not addressing the root causes of poverty and it began to think more critically about how to bring about long-term developmental change. Organisations such as Oxfam and Christian Aid had already been thinking about these issues for many years, but at this time Tearfund was not integrated into the mainstream development world and did not participate in the rounds of conferences and seminars that discussed the value of integrated programmes, focussed on the importance of trying to reach the very poorest, and worried about local elites capturing development benefits for their own ends. While Tearfund often drew on the latest fads in development theory, it failed to engage with them deeply or to develop their own comprehensive approach. Many were beginning to feel that this was now necessary.

Thus several different factors were causing Tearfund to think more deeply about exactly what kind of long-term change it actually wanted to bring about and how it should go about doing this. What did it actually mean to do Christian development? Was that the same as 'transformation'? How should Tearfund better integrate evangelism and development? Jennie Collins, who came in as International Director in 1992, recalls:

> By the time I came there was the realization that Tearfund itself was living with this dichotomy, theologically and practically.... I think it was portrayed by us having these two departments.... We knew what we meant by holistic development but we weren't sure quite how to do it.*

As Tearfund entered the 1990s it thus felt that it was necessary to rethink the relation between evangelism and social action, and to reconsider its approach to both doing mission and doing development. As Graham Fairbairn explains:

> I felt at that stage that we really wanted to see evangelism as part of what we were doing in social action. We had actually made a false dichotomy again. We had done what we said we didn't do. And so we began to push for greater integration.*

And, related to this, were rather fundamental questions about Tearfund's identity. What kind of an organisation was Tearfund, and what kind of organisation did it want to be going forward? Was Tearfund a mission agency that focussed on material improvement, or a development agency that worked with a Christian ethos? At this point in time Tearfund staff had various different views. In an internal document about how to widen Tearfund's profile among British Evangelicals Stephen Rand had written:

> We have grown more into being recognised as primarily a relief agency rather than an evangelical organisation, a trend encouraged by the tendency to the assumption that relief and development is not really a 'spiritual activity' and therefore is not something done in any specifically evangelical way.... If we want to widen our profile in the evangelical constituency then ... we need to demonstrate that we really are an evangelical organisation.
>
> (Rand 1991: 1)

On the other hand, David Adeney wrote in an internal memo a few years later:

> The more we talk about holistic mission, as opposed to development, the more we appear as one of many missions rather than a unique evangelical relief and development agency.
>
> (Adeney 1994: 1)

So thinking through these issues and clarifying the fundamental nature of the organisation and its work became a major priority.

Case study: challenges of religion and development in Ethiopia

Tearfund had been funding the relief and development work of the Sudan Interior Mission (SIM) in Ethiopia and sending out Overseas Personnel to volunteer with them since the early 1970s, and some years later it also started to work with the indigenous evangelical church that had developed with the SIM's support – the Kale Heywet church. While social work, particularly in the field of education and health, had always been central to the missionaries' work in Ethiopia, it was only after the famine of 1973 that the Kale Heywet church had considered getting involved in donor-funded relief and development. Following discussions between the church and the SIM, the Kale Heywet Development Program (KHDP) was established in 1977 and started carrying out its first projects. Following the requirements of Ethiopian law that religious work and development work had to be kept separate, it became a separate organisation, changed its name to the Ethiopian Kale Heywet Church Development Program (EKHCDP), and was officially registered with the government as a development agency in 1984 (Dalelo 2003: 36).

Tearfund's work in Ethiopia during this period was much the same as that being done by secular development agencies. During the 1970s and 1980s the major focus in Ethiopia was providing emergency relief during periods of drought. Tearfund helped the EKHCDP to distribute food, seeds, and oxen to drought-stricken communities (Dalelo 2003: 41, Hollow 2008: 65). In the early 1990s the focus shifted away from relief and more towards development, and typical projects included income-generating projects such as grain mills and greenhouses, environmental protection such as soil and water conservation, cattle breeding, supply of water and electricity, and medical services (Dalelo 2003: 41–50). All these were very much the same as what secular NGOs were doing at the time.

By the 1990s both Tearfund and the Kale Heywet church were growing unhappy with this approach to development and the Kale Heywet church was experiencing a number of problems being a church carrying out development projects through its development wing (Freeman 2018). A review of the church's development work was carried out at this time by an Ethiopian academic, and in a survey of 90 church leaders and project officers two-thirds of them said they thought that there were unfavourable impacts related to the church's involvement in development work. Some church members went as far to say that the development projects were a 'curse' (Dalelo 2003: 82–3). The review goes on to state that the money and resources that were coming through the development projects were leading to competition and rivalry among the member churches and that in many cases church leaders were using the funds in inappropriate ways. The author of the review summed up the situation in this colourful way:

> Following the exotic ideas and practices encapsulated under what were called 'projects', almost all churches where the projects operated turned into a battleground. Love and concern for one another was replaced by competition and rivalry. One of the most respected church fathers [said it was like] the behaviour of pack animals. Such animals graze on a field peacefully with minor indications of rivalry. But when grain like barley is spread on the field, their behaviour changes automatically and they become mad, kicking and biting one another. This applies to many churches where grain and some money have been injected from somewhere. People began literally beating if not biting one another.
>
> (Dalelo 2003: 83)

His conclusion was that the underlying cause of all these problems, alongside some managerial and accountability shortcomings, was the separation between the spiritual and development work of the church. The link between the church's overall mission and its development work was unclear to many in the church, and the tension between the two sections was seen to be at the core of the problem (Dalelo 2003: 82, 85, Freeman 2018: 283–4).

Conclusion

This chapter has outlined the evolution of Tearfund in its first 25 years. During this period Tearfund was clearly steeped in religion – it was birthed by the Evangelical Alliance, it worked with overseas missionaries and later indigenous churches, it found new organisations and projects to fund through Christian networks, and from 1979 onwards it was actively funding evangelism and Christian education overseas. Tearfund only employed evangelical Christians and staff had to sign up to Tearfund's statement of faith. Tearfund did not engage much with the broader humanitarian or development sectors and instead largely kept itself to the Christian world of missionaries, churches, and theological conferences. And yet, in all this, it is not possible to discern any significant way that religion influenced the manner in which Tearfund and the organisations it funded actually carried out the relief and development part of their work. Tearfund gave grants to missionaries and churches to dig wells, set up clinics, train farmers in new agricultural techniques, distribute relief supplies after disasters, and so on.

The only thing that differentiated the work of Tearfund partners from that of secular organisations was that they also carried out evangelism. For Tearfund, evangelism and sharing the gospel was a fundamental aspect of its work. As Graham Fairbairn explains:

> Throughout the years I was part of Tearfund the spiritual impact of our relief and development projects was always considered. The objective of working through evangelical partners who shared our desire for people to know Christ was fundamental. The Overseas Personnel Department was operated on the premise that the individuals sent overseas would live and share their faith among those they served. The Child Care programme wanted to provide education and material assistance but also wanted to enable the individual children to come to know Christ. Evangelical theology permeated every aspect of Tearfund's work.

In this respect Tearfund was significantly different from many other Christian NGOs, particularly those from liberal Protestant backgrounds and those linked with the Catholic church. Much like the secular NGOs, these Christian NGOs felt that evangelism and development work should be kept clearly separated. An article in the evangelical magazine *Third Way*, written around this time, went to great lengths to emphasise how Tearfund was completely different from Christian Aid and CAFOD[3] because it sought to combine aid with evangelism. While Michael Taylor, then Director of Christian Aid, is quoted as saying that Christian Aid's work reflects a 'disinterested concern for helping' and Mark Topping, then Press Officer for CAFOD said that 'Catholicism is our motivation rather than our objective', the article emphasised how Tearfund had taken a different approach by always supporting evangelism alongside its development activities (Howard 1993: 9).

However, by the early 1990s Tearfund was coming to the realisation that it needed to rethink both its way of working and its fundamental identity. Combining evangelism and development was not as straightforward as it had seemed in the 1970s and if Tearfund wanted to continue to grow and also to ensure that it was doing a distinctively Christian kind of development then it would need to do some serious thinking.

Thus in the early 1990s Tearfund found itself at a critical juncture. It had a new Chief Executive, David Adeney, over 200 members of staff, and an annual income of over £14 million. It predominantly worked as a grant-making and personnel-sending agency supporting several hundred missionary and church organisations in some 70 countries. Its networks were mainly in the evangelical Christian world and it was not well known or well appreciated in the broader secular humanitarian and development sectors. It had become the largest evangelical charity and was firmly part of the Christian establishment. Yet some were feeling that it had become a bit staid and old-fashioned and was not appealing to the younger generation. Many of the staff were increasingly uncomfortable with the dichotomy between the spiritual and the material that was running throughout the organisation. Tearfund's leadership decided that it was time for a fundamental rethink about the purpose of the organisation, its way of working, and the role of faith in all of that.

Notes

1 Interview with Jack Arthey, Senior Organisational Development Consultant, Christian Aid, 11 February 2016.
2 Despite the shift in emphasis, Tearfund never completely stopped working with missionary agencies. During the 1980s Ernest Oliver facilitated the formation of new links with evangelical mission organisations such as the United Mission to Nepal, the International Assistance Mission in Afghanistan, and the Association for Cooperation in Tunisia (Tiplady 2005: 41), and even today Tearfund still supports a number of evangelical mission agencies in their overseas work.
3 The Catholic Fund for Overseas Development.

Part II
Emerging as a development NGO

4 Tearfund joins the mainstream, 1990–2005

By the 1990s much had changed in both the mainstream development sector and in the evangelical missionary world. The mainstream development field had largely secularised. NGOs such as Oxfam and Save the Children had stopped making grants to mainline missionaries – who had since gone into a major decline – and had started instead to work with newly emerging local (secular) development NGOs in Africa, Asia, and Latin America. During the 1980s the new 'NGO sector' had begun to trumpet its 'comparative advantage' in international development, arguing that its small-scale, grassroots, non-technocratic approach was more effective than the large-scale, top-down activities of states. Many donor governments had become more interested in working with them and the 1980s have been described by many as the 'decade of the NGOs' (Hilton 2012: 453). Between 1980 and 1993 the number of NGOs registered in the OECD countries almost doubled from 1,600 to 2,970, with a concomitant doubling of spending (Edwards and Hulme 1996). This trend continued during the 1990s, as neoliberal ideas became increasingly prominent and structural adjustment and privatisation policies in the developing world were leading to a 'rolling back' of the state and a reduction in state provision of social and welfare services. At this time policy makers in many donor countries shifted to a 'new policy agenda' in which significant amounts of development funding were channelled to NGOs to provide these services instead of the state, thus leading to a further rapid expansion of development NGOs in both size and number (Edwards and Hulme 1996).

The evangelical missionary sector was also expanding at this time with new missionary agencies and evangelical FBDOs forming in both the US and the UK (Barnett and Stein 2012: 5). However, by the late 1980s and early 1990s the evangelical world was becoming increasingly divided. The Christian Right had emerged in the US and had become a significant social and political force (Williams 2010), and many of the new evangelical mission agencies were increasingly fundamentalist and resolutely focussed on verbal evangelism and saving souls. Meeting at the Second Lausanne Congress on World Evangelization in 1989, this group had reconfirmed its commitment to bring the gospel to the remaining 'unreached peoples' of the world and had developed the concept of the '10/40 Window' – the area of Africa and Asia located between 10 and 40 degrees north of the equator in which most non-Christians live – as a 'window of opportunity' for a more targeted approach to mission (Gailey and Culbertson 2007: 159–60). More moderate evangelicals, including most of those in the UK, felt rather uncomfortable with this approach and theology and instead were increasingly taking on the idea of 'integral mission', developed by Padilla and Escobar and brought back to the UK by John Stott, which sought to combine evangelism with social action to form a more holistic type of change. Tearfund, of course, sat within this second grouping, and over the previous decade had begun to develop a close relationship with René Padilla, engaging with him in theological discussion and making grants to his organisation in Argentina.

Positioned between these two changing worlds, and unhappy with its current *modus operandi*, Tearfund's Board began to think about what type of organisation Tearfund could be going forward. Could it emerge into the mainstream development world, which seemed so full of possibilities and resources, and still maintain its Christian identity? Should it remain in the evangelical world and try to develop a more holistic approach to its work? How, exactly, should evangelism and development be combined? What type of organisation was Tearfund, and what type of organisation should it be from this point on – a mission agency? an evangelical charity? a development NGO? These and many other questions were high on the minds of Tearfund's leadership in the early 1990s. In 1995 they appointed a new CEO, Doug Balfour, to take the lead on answering these questions and to transform Tearfund into a modern organisation fit for the twenty-first century.

While the previous two leaders of Tearfund had been church men, Balfour came from a business background. Young and dynamic, and part of a new generation of charismatic evangelicals, he saw the task before him in religious terms. He recalls:

> I had that overriding sense that Tearfund could be much, much more than it currently was.... I went along to Stoneleigh [Bible Week] that year and Terry Virgo spoke on Joshua and it was like – you know that experience when somebody is saying something and you can hear it in neon lights blazing as if these words are specifically for you at this time. It was like a hotline to heaven. He was talking about Joshua and he was talking about taking the people across the Jordan River and what did that mean for Joshua and the inheritance that was there in the Promised Land? The inheritance depended partly upon the sort of courage, faith and perspective of Joshua working alongside God and being led by God. It just felt like God was saying to me, 'This is the situation you find yourself in. There is an inheritance in Tearfund that is much, much greater than anything it has seen. You have been given this leadership task for a time and I want you to go and be very courageous and be bold because it needs significant change.'*

Thus in 1996 Balfour launched a major international review process, which, inspired by this experience, he called the Jordan Project. This initiated a period of intense change within the organisation. In 2002 he started a second

International Review Project, known as the Caleb process, which further continued strategic discussions and the change process. Following on from 'Jordan', 'Caleb' was named after the biblical character who went as a spy to see the promised land and who reported that it would be possible to enter it.

This period of strategic review and change was not an easy time within Tearfund. Balfour and much of the senior leadership wanted to see Tearfund grow and enter more fully into the rapidly expanding development NGO sector. They wanted the organisation to professionalise and to become fluent in secular development thinking and best practice. However, not all the staff agreed. They had different opinions about what type of organisation Tearfund should be and how it should go about its work. Thus during these years, as the leadership pushed ahead with the process of restructuring and professionalising, tensions began to increase within the organisation and discussions and debates ensued as some staff pushed back against the leadership and tried to promote alternative strategies and ways of working.

At the centre of all these debates were critical questions about what role faith should play in the organisation and its work. While all Tearfund staff shared the same core evangelical faith, staff held differing views about how this faith should be embedded and operationalised within the organisation. Some staff had come to Tearfund after working in DFID or in secular development NGOs; others had come from evangelical mission agencies. Some had grown up in Christian families, while others had come to faith only recently. Most were from the global North, but significant numbers were from the global South. All of these different life experiences, along with personal character and preferences, influenced the views and approaches of different staff members, both senior and junior, and led to the emergence of various different ideas about what type of organisation Tearfund should be and how faith and development should be brought together. These different ideas and the debates between the different camps will be the focus of the next three chapters. This chapter focusses on the leadership's attempts to professionalise and turn Tearfund into a serious relief and development NGO that could sit at the table with the likes of Oxfam, Save the Children, and Christian Aid. Chapter 5 discusses an alternative vision for Tearfund's future promoted by some of Tearfund's more junior staff, particularly those from the global South. Chapter 6 looks at a different, but related, set of debates that also took place during this same period, as Tearfund considered whether or not to start carrying out campaigning and advocacy work.

Turning Tearfund into a development NGO

Early in his leadership Balfour decided that Tearfund's priority should be to carry out technically excellent work to alleviate the poverty of the most needy, as efficiently and effectively as possible. He wanted to turn Tearfund into a professional development NGO that could emerge from the Christian world and enter the mainstream development sector. He argued that Tearfund's work should be characterised as combining 'spiritual passion and professional excellence'. This was a response to a widespread belief in the evangelical world that spiritual passion and professional excellence pulled in opposite directions – you could have one or the other, but not both. Balfour wanted to challenge that idea and make Tearfund into a highly professional organisation that still retained its spiritual passion. He recalls:

> I came across lots of organizations that were once spiritually hot, that is how they started, and then they became professional organizations that did things very well and had great management techniques and all that sort of stuff, but basically you felt like they were spiritually dead.... I just had that abiding belief that it was possible to do both.*

What combining 'spiritual passion with professional excellence' meant in practice was left somewhat open to interpretation, but for much of this period Balfour put considerable emphasis on the 'professional excellence' part of the equation. One of the first steps in the professionalisation process was a major structural re-organisation. Up until the early 1990s Tearfund's development work was organised in four separate departments – the Overseas Relief and Development Department made grants to overseas missionary and church organisations, the Overseas Personnel Department sent out technical experts to work with these organisations, the Overseas Childcare Department administered the child sponsorship programme, and Tearcraft ran as a separate trading business. A major part of Balfour's institutional change process involved moving beyond this siloed approach and creating a more coherent and focussed approach to development work. The four separate departments were disbanded and a team-based regional structure was instituted. Regional teams with Desk Officers for each country would oversee all the work that Tearfund supported in that country. The sending of expatriate OPs, which in the early 1990s was a larger part of Tearfund's work than its grant making, would be slowly phased out and the focus would shift to making grants for high-quality relief and development work.

As another part of the professionalisation process a number of activity areas were ended and a number of new areas were commenced or given more emphasis. Child sponsorship was ended in 1999 and instead Tearfund set up a new Children at Risk programme so that donors could still support work focussed on children. The Evangelism and Christian Education Department was also closed, but its work was continued by the regional teams, who now included aspects of its work within their remit and continued to give out scholarships, mainly for training in theology or development studies.

During this period Tearfund started to use professional accounting techniques, professional marketing techniques, and the standardised frameworks and logframes used in the mainstream development sector. Rather than simply making grants to 'good Christians' who were 'doing the Lord's work', they began to request more detailed project proposals and to demand more stringent accountability regarding funds and activities. This was resisted by many, who felt that this was not a Christian way of working and that relationships should be based on personal contact and trust.

Balfour also sought to expand Tearfund's engagement and influence beyond the Christian world and to engage more with the secular relief and development sectors. As Graham Fairbairn, then Tearfund's Home Director, recalls:

> In the early days we were ghettoised. We sat in our little sphere of safety and we related to missionary societies and other evangelical agencies. We looked out at the Oxfams and Save the Children and all the others and thought that we were different. They looked in at us and said that we were not really doing development because of the religious thing and it was probably only in the mid-1990s that we stepped outside of that ghetto.*

During this period Tearfund started to participate more in the networks of mainstream development NGOs. It joined the network of British Overseas NGOs for Development (BOND) and began to engage in the discussions and debates that were taking place in the wider sector.

Tearfund also began to think about its fundamental mode of operation. As mentioned in Chapter 3, while most development NGOs, secular or Christian, had started out by making grants to overseas missionaries, by the 1980s most of them had changed this mode of operation. Some had set up Country Offices where expatriate staff managed local teams to carry out development projects directly. Others had started to fund local indigenous development NGOs that had emerged and quickly proliferated in Africa, Asia, and Latin America from the 1980s onwards. Even Christian Aid, which had originally made grants to missionaries and to churches, was now shifting to work more with local secular NGOs. Daleep Mukarji, Director of Christian Aid from 1998 to 2010, emphasised that Christian Aid's mission was to reduce poverty and that it would therefore work with the most effective local partners to do that, whether they were churches or secular organisations. 'Our mission is not to support churches,' he would say, 'but to address poverty' (cited in Ferris 2011: 615). Thus during the 1990s, as Tearfund sought to professionalise and increase its effectiveness, there was a major debate about how Tearfund should work. Should Tearfund go operational and start to carry out development projects itself? Should it work with secular partners if they were more effective? Or should it continue to support only evangelical missionary and church organisations?

Most people in Tearfund were strongly against the idea of working with local secular NGOs. How would it be possible to be distinctively Christian working like that? There would be no way to combine development work with evangelism and no evangelical component to the work. But the question of going operational and working directly themselves was more contentious. Some thought that Tearfund should indeed go operational if this was the most effective way to carry out development. There were several examples of evangelical development NGOs that worked this way, such as World Vision International and Compassion International, and to some this seemed like an appealing model. However, others argued that an important part of Tearfund's purpose was to support local churches to grow and to serve their communities. Therefore it would make no sense for Tearfund to start implementing development projects itself as this would simply undermine the local church and local Christian organisations.

Eventually the decision was taken that Tearfund would not go operational in its development activities but would continue to work with overseas Christian partners. But this then opened up another set of questions: How many partners should Tearfund be working with? Should Tearfund set up Country Offices to be closer to the partners? And how could Tearfund make this work more effective?

In the mid-1990s Tearfund was working with a huge number of church and missionary organisations in many different countries and the average grant size was very small. This was not resulting in any visible impact. In order to become more focussed and effective it was decided to massively reduce the number of organisations that Tearfund supported and to focus its activities on a smaller number of countries. Thus during this period Tearfund reduced both the number of organisations that it supported and the number of countries in which it worked by approximately 33 per cent – from over 450 organisations to just under 300, and from over 90 countries to around 60. This was not an easy process and it was the Desk Officers who had the painful job of informing overseas partner organisations that Tearfund would no longer be supporting their work. Many resisted and tried to make the case that particular countries or particular organisations should continue to be supported. There were heated arguments about whether Tearfund should work in this country or that, and whether this partner or this project was more worthy than that one. For an organisation that prided itself in working in a people-centred, relational way, breaking many long-standing relationships in the name of 'professionalisation' and 'rationalisation' was extremely difficult. Many in the organisation began to wonder why professionalisation was so important and whether it was worth it.

Nonetheless, since Tearfund's leadership had decided to continue to work with partners *and* to professionalise then it followed that Tearfund would need to help its remaining partners to professionalise as well. At the beginning of this period many of Tearfund's partners were the relatively recently established development wings of indigenous church denominations or small Christian NGOs. They were strong on 'spiritual passion' but rather weaker on 'technical excellence'. In the 1990s Tearfund decided that it should expand beyond just grant making and start to develop a closer relationship with its partners and work to develop their organisational capacity and technical ability.[1]

In the mid-1990s Tearfund set up a Partner Support Unit through which it would provide technical consultancy, training, and capacity building to its partners. As well as technical support Tearfund began to help its partners become sustainable organisations, helping them to define their vision, build organisational structures, and use project 'logframes' and professional accounting systems. Jennie Collins, International Director from 1992 to 2000, recalls:

> We moved to saying actually if organisations want to be really able to use this money to do the things they want to do then there needs to be some attention given to not just technical input – you know, how do you dig a well better – but how does this organisation run, what's its focus, what are its financial and personnel systems like.... I think that was a big change at this time.*

In this way Tearfund thus spread Western norms and forms of working to small and previously rather informal church and Christian groups across the global South. Some organisations were not willing or able to adapt to these new working methods and Tearfund thus stopped working with them. Others decided that making the changes was worthwhile in order to continue getting support from Tearfund. And others still considered it as a hugely positive process and saw the support in capacity building as fundamental to their getting established and being able to work effectively. To take just one example, Warmis, meaning 'women' in the Quechua language, is a small Christian NGO in Peru that works with indigenous communities in the Andean region on women's rights, livelihoods, literacy, child development, agriculture, and church mobilisation. Warmis was founded in 2001 by four women who had a lot of enthusiasm but little practical experience. Tearfund came across Warmis in 2002 and decided to partner with them. But rather than giving the team a grant straight off Tearfund instead sent a consultant to work with them for two years to train them to develop the skills needed for project design, project management, accounting, monitoring, and evaluation. During this period Tearfund also invited them to attend national and international trainings, which presented the opportunity to connect with other Tearfund partners doing similar work. This support was pivotal in helping Warmis become a professional organisation that has since grown and diversified.

> We had a dream and a passion but Tearfund helped us to become more professional, to improve participation and project cycle management. They helped us to look forward and have a vision, and to plan strategically.
> (Miriam Moreno, Warmis)

There were many voices that thought that, even if Tearfund was not going to become operational, it would be good for the organisation to decentralise and open up Country Offices in order to have a better and more contextualised understanding of the situation on the ground in different countries and to build closer relations with the partners. Doug Balfour was a strong proponent of decentralisation. He recalls:

> [I thought that the] possibility of actually having somebody in region would add an awful lot of understanding and credibility to our work with partners.... I think there is something basically impossible about making decisions 3,500 miles away with people that are often not of the same cultural

origin.... I thought that what we should do is take the desk officers and put them all overseas and have indigenous research and origination teams.*

However, many were against this idea. They feared that, if Tearfund established an in-country presence, it might end up dominating and undermining the partner. At the most extreme there was concern that this would be the first step of the slippery slope of Tearfund going operational itself and thus stopping work with partners altogether. Voices on this side of the debate stressed that, because the fundamental objective of Tearfund was to build up partner organisations – and in particular the indigenous churches – to develop their ministry to the poor, Tearfund staff should themselves remain in the UK. It would be fair to say that many also feared losing their jobs if their positions were moved overseas. Taken all together, the opposition was extremely strong and during the Jordan process it was decided not to open Country Offices. However, the issue resurfaced a few years later in the Caleb process and in this case the leadership decided that Tearfund should indeed open Country Offices. But there was such resistance from both senior and junior staff that in the end the plans were again shelved and instead a small number of Regional Advisors were hired overseas to provide some local oversight and expert input into partner project work.[2] While many secular NGOs went through processes of decentralisation in the 1990s much faster and in a much deeper way – sometimes re-organising into a federation or confederation of linked and equal organisations distributed around the world – Tearfund's religious nature and its explicit mission of seeking to support local churches led to its taking much longer to implement even a basic process of decentralisation.

Being an organisation that works with partners also brought up other issues for Tearfund as it tried to focus and professionalise. One of those related to strategy. In short, should Tearfund define a centralised strategy or should it support its partners in implementing their strategies? Up to this point Tearfund had let the partners take the lead and had mainly taken a responsive mode, agreeing or declining funding proposals. During this period it started to help partners to clarify their own visions and strategies. Thus there was a strong view within some parts of Tearfund that the most appropriate way forward was to support partners in implementing their own strategies. On the other hand members of the leadership were driving Tearfund to professionalise and become more coherent as an organisation itself, and there was a view that a professional organisation ought to have an overall strategy, purpose, and approach to which all of its constituent parts should contribute. In 1992 Tearfund had started to produce regional strategies to guide the work in each of the regions, and the international review some years later suggested that Tearfund should move towards developing one overarching international strategy in order to bring more focus and coherence in the work that it supported. Thus during this period there was a growing tension between the two views – one that favoured a central and thus Northern setting of the agenda, and one that preferred a more decentralised approach that would enable Southern partners to develop their own, more locally contextualised strategies.

When René Padilla came in as Tearfund's International President in 1998 he brought in a more South-focussed perspective and further raised the issue of having partner organisations involved in strategy and decision making alongside Tearfund. There was a lively debate about what 'partnership' actually meant – didn't it imply some sort of joint decision making? Or was it just a nice word that hid the reality that Northern organisations with money told their poorer Southern 'partners' what to do? This, of course, was an issue throughout much of the broader development sector at the time and was not unique to Tearfund (Lewis 1998).

One idea to resolve this issue was to involve partners more directly in Tearfund's central strategy making. To this end a 'Partner Panel' was set up in the early 2000s, in which key individuals from several of Tearfund's major partners came together to provide input into Tearfund's strategy. This panel only continued for a few years, but it established the principle that while Tearfund would develop its own strategy it would do so in consultation with its partners. Jennie Evans, who was head of the Eurasia Department at the time, reflects on the new, more equal, form of partnership that developed:

> I think there is much more consultation now and there is a greater freedom on the part of partners to dialogue.... There is a depth of relationship with many of the partners that gives them the freedom to tell us when they disagree, and to have that lively debate. There is an increased confidence on their part.... There is a recognition that we are all players in the same field and we have different skills and abilities and gifts to bring and we complement one another.*

Thus throughout the 1990s and early 2000s Tearfund completely re-organised itself, professionalised, and formalised and streamlined its relationship with its partners. It changed from being an organisation that simply gave grants and sent expatriate staff to overseas church and mission agencies, to become a professional, coherent development organisation that worked with a network of increasingly professional partners to carry out high-quality work overseas. And as a result of all these changes, Tearfund's development work grew substantially during this period. It raised more money and gave larger grants to fewer partners to carry out more impactful development projects. It funded partners to carry out development work in a wide range of sectors, with a particular focus on water and sanitation, health and nutrition, HIV and AIDS, education and literacy, and children at risk. Alongside these focal areas a significant amount of work was also carried out regarding land rights, good governance, micro-finance and livelihoods, food security, conflict, psychosocial work, and environment. In many respects Tearfund now operated in much the same way as most of the mainstream development NGOs.

Humanitarian work

The desire to professionalise and enter the mainstream brought up more complicated issues on the humanitarian side of the organisation. In 1988 Tearfund had brought in a dedicated manager to oversee its humanitarian work and in the early 1990s this work initially started to change in much the same way as its development work. There was a shift from working reactively whereby Tearfund responded to grant requests from partner organisations, to setting a more centralised strategy to guide Tearfund's priorities and approach in this area, and there was a big emphasis placed on building the capacity of partners and helping them to professionalise. From the 1990s onwards humanitarian work began to expand enormously. While in 1990 it had accounted for around 15 per cent of international expenditure, by 2001 this had risen to 29 per cent and by 2006 to 51 per cent. Thus changes in this part of Tearfund's work had a very significant effect on the whole organisation.

As discussed above, Tearfund favoured working with local partners as its main mode of operation and it felt that it was important for partner organisations to be responding to disasters. It therefore began to place considerable emphasis on capacity building and in the early 1990s it started a major training programme for its partners. As part of this it produced a manual, *Christian Perspectives on Disaster Management*, which combined practical training with biblical examples such as Noah and his ark as an example of disaster preparedness, and Paul's supervision of famine relief in Judea as an example of Christian response. Tearfund also helped several partners to professionalise, and indeed to get involved in disaster response in the first place, by placing OPs with them. In many cases these expatriate staff would set up and initially run the partner's disaster response team while also training up local staff in sector best practice.

These initiatives led to more partner organisations, mainly Christian NGOs and the relief and development wings of large denominations, getting involved in disaster response and doing it more professionally. Nonetheless, despite the excellent work being done by many partners, there were some cases where working with partners in disaster response proved to be rather problematic. If the partner was located right in the disaster area then they would often also be affected by the disaster and thus not able to adequately respond. On the other hand, if they were located very far from the disaster area they had to spend a lot of time and resources in travelling to the disaster area and setting up camp there before they could respond. In some cases partner organisations simply were not interested in carrying out disaster response work and when the OP had gone home they reverted to doing small-scale community development. And in many cases small Christian NGOs simply did not have the necessary capacity to respond effectively to major large-scale disasters. Furthermore, in countries where there were tensions between Christians and people of other faiths, or where Christians were a persecuted minority, some partner organisations had a desire to help Christians first, rather than to respond to everyone equally, as Tearfund increasingly began to demand.

As major disasters such as earthquakes and floods, and also more chronic political disasters, increased throughout the 1990s, these challenges began to pose some serious moral dilemmas to Tearfund. What should it do when its partners were not able to deliver a response that was efficient, appropriate, and to scale? What if Tearfund's chosen working modality meant that more lives were being lost than necessary? What was an appropriate Christian response to such situations?

In 1993 Tearfund decided to carry out its first operational relief work, sending out a disaster response team from the UK to Armenia. The following year it sent out a much bigger operational relief team to Rwanda during the genocide. Based on these experiences Tearfund's leadership began to seriously consider the possibility that Tearfund should set up its own operational teams.

This was incredibly controversial within Tearfund at the time since some years earlier it had clarified that it would not go operational itself but would support local Christian organisations in their on-the-ground work. However, many staff felt that in these life-or-death situations the most appropriate Christian response was to save lives in the most effective way possible, and if that meant responding directly with operational teams then so be it. Others, however, argued that Tearfund's whole *raison d'être* was to support local Christian partners to respond and that setting up operational teams would just undermine them. Furthermore, they considered that responding directly would make Tearfund just like everyone else in the sector, and that Tearfund would lose its Christian distinctiveness. As Jennie Collins recalls:

> We were seeing more and more large-scale disaster situations, particularly conflict, and we were sort of caught between – if the local partner does it, it will be slow, quite low impact, and small but possibly sustainable – whereas what was actually needed was broad coverage, high impact and speed.*

Going operational

In the end a kind of compromise was reached. Tearfund's leadership decided that Tearfund would work with partners wherever possible, but when there was no adequate local capacity it would respond directly through its own operational teams. Thus in 1997 Tearfund set up a Disaster Response Team (DRT) and began to build up its operational capacity.

This was a significant step-change for the organisation. When a major disaster occurred and there was no partner able to respond Tearfund would set up an office in the country, organise vehicles and logistical support, and recruit hundreds of local staff to deliver humanitarian response. The teams would carry out activities such as food distribution, reconstruction projects after war, building of water supplies and sanitation facilities, and distribution of agricultural inputs. Operational humanitarian relief work grew very rapidly throughout the late 1990s and early 2000s, and by 2002 disaster work made up the highest proportion of the International Group's activity in terms of expenditure. Tearfund would usually have operational teams working in four to six countries at any one time, working in countries such as Afghanistan, Burundi, Indonesia, Pakistan, Sierra Leone, and Sudan, among others. Often this work took place in the context of complex emergencies and several interventions lasted for many years. This work was very different from the small-scale relief and development work with which Tearfund was more familiar and it brought up many new challenges and dilemmas for the organisation.

Operational disaster response was much more expensive than the small-scale work that Tearfund had supported previously. And although most people agreed that the extra cost was more than justified by the number of lives that it saved, this new type of work put new financial demands on the organisation and influenced it to search out new kinds of large-scale funding from different kinds of donors. Furthermore, the mainstream humanitarian sector was going through a number of changes at this time and, as a response to concerns about quality and accountability, was beginning to institute a number of international standards and codes of conduct to guide the behaviour of humanitarian NGOs. If Tearfund wanted to join the mainstream then it would have to sign up to these standards. But how could it retain its evangelical mission and identity in such a context? This became an increasingly serious question for many in Tearfund as work in this area grew. Tearfund aimed for 'professional excellence' in this work, but at least initially it was not clear how 'spiritual passion' would play a role.

Institutional funding and joining the DEC

During the 1980s the British government had started to channel large amounts of funding to relief and development NGOs (Manji 2002: 578). A specialist Disaster Unit had been created within the Ministry of Overseas Development to provide a 'focal point' for all issues connected to humanitarian aid. The Disaster Unit pioneered a more professionalised and technocratic approach to emergency relief and also sought closer integration of its work with the NGO sector (Jones 2014: 15). By the 1990s other relief and development NGOs, such as Oxfam and Christian Aid, were receiving significant proportions of their income from government grants and this had enabled them to expand considerably (Whitaker 1983: 57). Tearfund had been more cautious. From the mid-1980s it had started to receive very small amounts of institutional funding from governments, but by 1993 this only accounted for around £400,000, just 1.5 per cent of Tearfund's total income, with the vast majority of Tearfund's funding coming from evangelical supporters and churches in the UK. However, operational disaster response teams were very expensive to run, and thus as this work expanded there were a growing number of voices within the organisation who thought that Tearfund should start to accept more money from governments and other institutional donors.

The question of seeking and receiving institutional funding had been under discussion for many years. In 1989 David Adeney had considered seeking more institutional funding and in an internal memo he noted that there were three potential risks – that Tearfund might have to comply with external secular evaluation and reporting criteria, that Tearfund might become dependent on this type of funding, and that such a dependence might lead to a distortion, or secularisation, of the organisation's purpose and work. In another internal policy paper written in 1993 Jennie Collins had expressed concern that if projects were supported by government funds then projects documents would need to be 're-phrased' and the Christian content removed before they were to be sent to the UK government. In short, many in Tearfund perceived a tension between the organisation's faith-based nature and receiving funds from secular sources, and they were concerned whether accepting money from secular funders would influence the nature of Tearfund's work and cause it to 'secularise'.[3] Doug Balfour had no such qualms. He believed that accepting institutional funding would enable Tearfund to expand its work, help more people, and become part of the mainstream development sector.

Malcolm McNeil, Tearfund's International Director from 2001 to 2004, agreed with Balfour. He had come to Tearfund after working for DFID and was a strong supporter of the drive to professionalise, join the mainstream, and accept government funding. However, many others in the organisation were not so sure. He recalls:

> When I came in, about 3–4% of the total funding was institutional funding and quite a number of staff felt that this was dirty money, that it was sinful, and that we should not be in the market for that kind of funding. Coming from DFID I put it to them that they were all tax payers ... why should we deny partners the opportunity to get this funding?

The main reason that other staff were not convinced was that they continued to fear that receiving this type of funding would limit their ability to act freely in a Christian manner. However, the leadership pushed ahead and by 2006 institutional funding had risen ten-fold to over £4 million, and the vast majority of this money was funding the new operational teams.

However, institutional donors did have a set of requirements for their NGO grantees. In order to access these large-scale government grants, NGOs had to have in place a raft of planning, accounting, and reporting systems, and it was indeed the quest to access this type of funding that drove much of Tearfund's efforts to introduce all of these things during this period. Moreover, institutional donors also required their grantees to sign up to the new international standards that were being developed at the time.

International standards

After the response to the Rwanda genocide there had been widespread discontent in the humanitarian sector and a feeling that the response had not been good enough. This had led to many discussions between the humanitarian agencies and moves to improve and professionalise their work. New networks were formed, such as the Active Learning Network for Accountability and Performance (ALNAP), and new international standards and procedures were introduced (Walker 2005). In 1995 the Red Cross Code of Conduct was launched and a few years later in 1997 a large group of humanitarian organisations came together to create the SPHERE guidelines – a set of minimum standards in core areas of humanitarian assistance in order to improve the quality of assistance provided to people affected by disasters and to enhance the accountability of the humanitarian system. In 1997 Tearfund was still in the process of setting up its Disaster Response Team and it was not involved in these initiatives.

Nonetheless, as Tearfund's operational teams got going, there was a major internal discussion about whether or not Tearfund should sign up to these guidelines. Malcolm McNeil, International Director in the early 2000s, explains:

> The SPHERE guidelines are basically the bible, the secular bible, of disaster work. And there were those who said, 'No, no, we have our own Bible, the Christian Bible, that's the one we follow'. I said what was wrong with us having both the Christian Bible and the SPHERE guidelines and making sure that the two go together, because on many occasions the SPHERE guidelines were perfectly acceptable and there were only rare cases when our Christian principles would be different.

The main sticking point was regarding the role of religion in humanitarian response. The SPHERE standards, and other standards such as the Red Cross Code of Conduct, all insisted that humanitarian agents should not use the disaster situation to impose their faith onto the recipients of aid and relief. They called for a clear distinction between religious activities and humanitarian activities. This rubbed up against Tearfund's evangelical identity and stated purpose, which included proclaiming the gospel.

It is worth noting that several Christian organisations had been involved in the formulation of the SPHERE guidelines. These organisations, including the World Council of Churches, the Lutheran World Federation, and members of the Caritas family, came mainly from mainline Protestant or Catholic backgrounds, and they saw no problem with the separation of religious and humanitarian activities. Monika Krause reports that, when she asked a senior member of the Lutheran World Federation and a leading early proponent of the SPHERE standards about this issue, she replied by quoting Martin Luther: 'The Christian shoemaker does his Christian duty not by putting little crosses on the shoes, but by making good shoes, because God is interested in good craftsmanship' (Krause 2009: 128–9).

However, for Tearfund, as an evangelical organisation, this was a much more contentious issue. A period of intense discussion and debate ensued about whether signing up to these codes of conduct was compatible with Tearfund's mission and purpose. David Bainbridge, who at the time was Operations Manager in the Disaster Response Team, recalls:

We used to have this debate: if the Red Cross Code of Conduct didn't exist what would Tearfund's approach be? One extreme was that everyone who receives food distribution needs to know that Tearfund is a Christian organisation and here are some key messages about the Christian faith. The other extreme was that our faith should be completely invisible. You're receiving food from an NGO because their mandate is emergency relief and you will never know that they were Christians. I would argue we would do the same as we do now – we would quote the parable of the Good Samaritan and we would distribute without pursuing a particular religious belief. We never wanted to hide the fact that Tearfund was a Christian organisation and our motivation was faith-based ... but there were no strings attached.

Eventually Tearfund decided that, in order to be a significant player in the humanitarian sector, it was necessary to sign up to these codes, and a few years later it signed up to the SPHERE guidelines and to the Red Cross Code of Conduct, whose Article 3 states that 'Aid will not be used to further a particular political or religious standpoint' and insists that its signatories 'will not tie the promise, delivery or distribution of assistance to the embracing or acceptance of a particular political or religious creed' (ICRC 1994). Tearfund also took the further step of asking its overseas partners to sign up to the codes. Then in 1998, after it had signed up to these codes and standards, Tearfund joined the Disasters Emergency Committee (DEC), the umbrella group of UK charities formed in 1963, which by this time had expanded to many more than its five original members to become the major body that coordinates and launches collective appeals to raise funds for emergency aid. This led to very high flows of funding coming in to support Tearfund's humanitarian work.

By joining DEC Tearfund could show that it was now clearly positioned in the mainstream humanitarian sector. It had left the 'Christian ghetto' and was now sitting round the table with the likes of Oxfam, Save the Children, and Christian Aid. To consolidate its new position in the mainstream, Tearfund also joined a number of other networks of humanitarian NGOs, such as ALNAP and the Start Network, through which it sought to take part in discussions regarding humanitarian thinking and to improve best practice, and the Global Network for Disaster Reduction (GNDR) and Voluntary Organisations in Cooperation in Emergencies (VOICE), which advocated around humanitarian issues. At the same time it was instrumental in setting up Integral Alliance, a consortium of evangelical humanitarian agencies that could fundraise together and collaborate when working in the same country, sharing offices, logistics, and information.

Whither evangelism?

However, joining the mainstream brought with it many challenges and dilemmas. Signing up to the international standards and codes started a long discussion within Tearfund about how, and in what ways and in what situations, it was possible and appropriate to evangelise. This, after all, was of fundamental importance to Tearfund as an evangelical organisation, and yet it appeared to have just signed up to standards that ruled out evangelism. How could Tearfund hold these things together? As Malcolm McNeil explains:

> The key issue was regarding proselytization. The SPHERE guidelines would say you mustn't make your help for people contingent on them signing up to your church or something like that. And, of course, we would agree with that. We would give help to all religions and none. But we would like to say that we were doing it in the name of Jesus Christ. Not heavy evangelising but making it clear that this is the motivation for our work.

These issues became even more heated when in 2001 aid workers from a Christian organisation called Shelter Now were arrested in Afghanistan for 'proselytising'. This led to intense media interest in the activities of Christian relief and development organisations, particularly in countries where there was no religious freedom. Tearfund thus had to think hard about its approach to evangelism and how it fit in with its humanitarian and development work. In 2003 it produced a Proselytism policy statement. In this document it differentiated between 'evangelism' and 'proselytism', stating that proselytism involved the 'unjustified manipulation or use of coercive techniques or force to achieve conversion' whereas evangelism was 'telling the good news of God's love in Jesus Christ' (Hughes 2003: 1). The document clarified that, while Tearfund longed to see people come to faith, its staff would not use manipulate or coercive approaches. Nonetheless, Tearfund did wish to see people come to the Christian faith, and thus the document continues:

> There is a crucial difference between using aid in order to put pressure on needy people to convert and dispensing aid while hoping and praying that those who receive it come to believe in Jesus Christ.
>
> (Hughes 2003: 2)

A similar differentiation between 'evangelism' and 'proselytism' was taken up by most evangelical NGOs in subsequent years (cf. Fountain 2015, Lynch and Schwarz 2016). However, making this distinction clear in practice was not always so simple and the issue of how to integrate 'evangelism' into relief and development work, and yet not to 'proselytise', became an ongoing issue in Tearfund's work in the coming years. What activities were appropriate and what were not? Were some activities very subtly manipulative in ways in which Tearfund had not thought through before? Where should Tearfund draw the line in these grey areas?

These questions were often rather more complex for Tearfund's partners, many of whom were the development wings of church denominations. Several of these considered that part of the reason for doing humanitarian work was indeed in order to get a captive audience to whom to give Christian teachings. Others found the impartiality clauses more difficult and argued that the Bible said that they should help Christians before others, quoting Galatians' saying that you should help your own household first. Tearfund, however, developed a zero-tolerance policy on this and made it clear that it would only work with partners that agreed to sign up to the international standards. This process led to the imposition of the Northern conceptual separation between religion and society, church and state, onto the network of churches in the global South that were linked to Tearfund, and as a result several of them had to make changes in the way that they worked, such as stopping distributing Bibles during development work or preaching at disaster sites. In this way these local, Southern religious organisations became subjectivised to global norms.

Thus as Tearfund emerged into the broader humanitarian field, seeking institutional funding, signing up to international codes of conduct, and taking part in broader coalitions, it was indeed faced with 'secularising' demands as many had feared. What, then, would it mean to be an evangelical humanitarian relief organisation in the 2000s?

How to work operationally in Muslim countries?

A further question that arose during this period with regard to the new operational humanitarian work was, how to work in Muslim countries? During these years Tearfund responded to humanitarian crises in several Muslim-majority countries, such as Afghanistan, Pakistan, and Sudan. Working in countries such as these, with very few local Christians, raised lots of new issues for Tearfund. One issue that quickly arose concerned the employment of local staff. Tearfund had a policy of only recruiting evangelical Christians. But in Muslim-majority countries this was simply not possible. So during these years Tearfund took the decision that in these contexts it would employ local staff from other faiths, who would work in Tearfund's operational teams under the leadership of Christian expatriate international staff. Thus in countries such as Sudan and Afghanistan, Tearfund's on-the-ground operational teams consisted almost entirely of Muslims. Many within Tearfund wondered how they could make their work distinctively Christian in such situations.

In the early 2000s Tearfund's humanitarian team put a lot of effort into trying to work this out. They focussed on three areas. First, they put a lot of effort into developing theological resources for the organisation's expatriate international staff and framing their work in a biblical way. In the early 2000s the team developed its own internal training programme – the Disaster Management Development Programme (DMDP) – which stressed that international staff should model Jesus in their actions and relationships and should pray before making major programming decision. Second, they put particular emphasis on acting respectfully towards local cultures and other faiths. Tearfund's Code of Conduct for the behaviour of staff in the field was significantly different from the codes used by other secular organisations in that it called for 'whole life discipleship', meaning that Tearfund staff should be modelling good behaviour and values all the time, even outside work hours. And third, the team developed spiritual resources to align Christian and Muslim staff so that they could all work according to Tearfund's Christian values. For example, Oenone Chadburn, who has worked in Tearfund's humanitarian team since 2004, explains how they worked with Muslim staff in Afghanistan:

> When we introduced the core values of Christ-centred, compassionate, courageous – the Afghanistan Country Director held a training program going through each of these values and what they meant and going through the synergies between the Muslim faith and the Christian faith, and how the national staff could demonstrate these values just as much.

Nonetheless, despite these efforts to make their operational humanitarian work distinctively Christian, an outside observer would have been hard pushed to differentiate between Tearfund and any other humanitarian NGO working on the ground. While for many in Tearfund this was good and appropriate, for others it was a troubling loss of evangelical mission and identity.

Managing the risk of secularisation

During this period, it is clear that there were many 'secularising' forces influencing Tearfund's work. An increasing number of voices began to question the direction of travel and to talk about the seemingly very real risk that Tearfund might secularise and become just like any other relief and development NGO. The risk that an evangelical development NGO might secularise is widely recognised in the evangelical world. There is an awareness of the historical trend for Christian social action organisations to become progressively more secular and a recognition that many contemporary secular development NGOs were formed by Christian leaders and started off explicitly imbued with Christian values. Leaders of many evangelical organisations share a concern that the same might happen to them. Thus, when the Charity Commission started to require that all UK charities keep a risk register in order to monitor and assess the risks that the organisation faced, Tearfund's board identified the risk of secularisation as the number one risk.[4]

So from the early 2000s onwards Tearfund's Board meetings always started with a review of the risk register and a discussion about the risk of Tearfund's secularising and what needed to be done to mitigate against this. As part of this exercise the Board would review the activities of the organisation, its visions and values, and its statement of faith. They would ensure that all staff and public figures who represented Tearfund agreed with this statement of faith, and they would keep an eye on the choice of organisations with which Tearfund partnered. They also ensured that prayer and devotional time continued to be embedded into the day-to-day workings of the organisation. A few years later a Theological Committee was also established to advise the Board on these matters. Thus the risk of secularising was discussed at the highest level.[5] Would this risk management exercise influence Tearfund's way of working?

Conclusion

In the 1990s and early 2000s there was a major growth and professionalisation of Tearfund's development and humanitarian relief work. On the development side of the organisation Tearfund implemented new accounting and managerial systems and put considerable effort into building the capacity of its partners so that they could professionalise and meet best practice standards. Tearfund emerged out of the 'Christian ghetto', joined mainstream networks, and was accepted and recognised as a major development NGO.

On the humanitarian side of the organisation Tearfund set up new operational teams, developed impressive technical excellence, and joined the DEC. But in many ways the demands and operating modality of this sector created 'secularising' pressures within the organisation – starting to work in a direct operational manner threatened to undermine Tearfund's role in supporting the local church and its broader evangelistic and spiritual mission, hiring local Muslim staff made it very difficult for operational teams to act in a distinctly Christian way, receiving institutional funding and money from DEC pushed Tearfund to do only secular programming and to remove mention of any spiritual work from its proposals and reports, and signing up to international standards threatened to straitjacket Tearfund into a secular way of working that separated religion and humanitarianism and left little space for spiritual interventions.

While the 'mainstreamers' saw all this as good change that had turned Tearfund from a small, quasi-missionary organisation into a major relief and development NGO, others in the organisation were not convinced. They feared that Tearfund was losing its fundamental mission and purpose and was at risk of becoming just like any secular NGO. They resisted the changes and argued that Tearfund should develop a different, more 'transformational' approach to its work. Their ideas will be discussed in more detail in the next chapter.

Notes

1 This was a common realisation also among secular NGOs that had started to partner with indigenous locals NGOs during this time. The 1990s is widely considered to mark the beginning of the era of 'capacity building' in the broader development world.
2 It was only in 2008, under the leadership of Matthew Frost, that Tearfund finally set up Country Offices and only in 2018, under the leadership of Nigel Harris, that significant work functions and decision-making powers were transferred to them.
3 Many people in the wider NGO sector have also drawn attention to potential problems in accepting government money, particularly that NGOs may lose their independence and become susceptible to the political whims of governments (e.g. Hilton 2012: 462, Edwards and Hulme 1996).
4 Other risks were more similar to those faced by other NGOs, such as operational risks, security risks, and reputational risks.
5 Tearfund is not alone in monitoring the risk of secularisation and in implementing measures to mitigate against it. World Vision, for example, carried out a 'Christian Witness Commission' in the mid-1990s in which a team spent two years carrying out surveys and in-depth interviews, and reviewing country strategies, policies, plans, and evaluation reports relating to Christian witness in order to 'determine if there was any evidence that World Vision was sliding toward secularism' (Myers 2015: 119).

5 The religious revitalists and the quest for transformation

As Tearfund grew, professionalised, and entered into the mainstream, many staff members were not happy with the way in which the organisation was changing. They felt that, in the attempt to professionalise, it was losing its Christian character and its evangelical emphasis on sharing the gospel. It was becoming just like any other relief and development NGO instead of being a distinctive evangelical agency. While these sentiments were shared quite widely in the organisation, some of the most vocal and active voices calling for another way of doing things were coming from staff in or from the global South, junior staff that worked closer to the field level, and the theologians that had joined Tearfund in the early and mid-1990s. These were the voices that were complaining and resisting in Chapter 4. This chapter sets out the alternative, more transformational, approach that emerged from their discussions and experimentations during this period, even as the drive to professionalise and mainstream was pushing full steam ahead.

Developing Tearfund's theology of development

In 1993 Tearfund had closed the Evangelism and Christian Education Department, merged its work into that of the Overseas Relief and Development Department, and recruited Dewi Hughes as its first Theological Advisor to help the organisation develop a coherent theological underpinning for its overseas work and to clarify what made its work 'Christian'. This proved to be a much more complex task than anyone in the organisation had foreseen. The process of developing Tearfund's theology of development and then trying to work out how to implement it in its practical work will be discussed here in some detail.

In the mid-1990s Hughes had put together a group to work on articulating Tearfund's theology of development.[1] This group had consisted of both theologians and development practitioners, and the aim was to produce something that genuinely brought together Christian thinking and development thinking into one seamless whole. After much discussion and debate, with input from staff, overseas partners, external experts, Board members, and international sister organisations, in 1996 the team produced a document called *Tearfund: Mission, Beliefs, Values*, which sought to clarify the Christian nature of Tearfund's work.

This document had four parts. The first set out Tearfund's mission and purpose as it was understood at the time:

> The purpose of Tearfund is to serve Jesus Christ by enabling those who share evangelical Christian beliefs to bring good news to the poor.
> (Tearfund 1996: 1)

The second was a statement of faith, outlining the evangelical beliefs that were central to Tearfund's worldview. The third was a list of nine core values that should underpin all of Tearfund's work. And the fourth part was a statement of Tearfund's Operating Principles. This document set out Tearfund's theology of development and sought to define 'Christian development' in a way that 'tried to be faithful to the Bible and to honour both Christian tradition and development practice' (Tearfund 1996: 4).

The Operating Principles sought to create a framework for a specifically Christian type of development. Drawing on the approach developed in Wheaton, which re-framed development as 'transformation', it based its thinking on the biblical doctrine of creation, Fall, and redemption, in which the Fall is understood as the ultimate cause of poverty and injustice and redemption as the ultimate solution. Looking at how humans, and Tearfund, could help to improve things in the meantime before God's final redemption, the Operating Principles suggested that the underlying cause of poverty was broken relationships – between people and God, between people and people, and between people and the environment. This formulation derived from the work of Croatian theologian Miroslav Volf, whose books had been influential in the thinking of Tearfund's theologians. Bringing this into the development context led to the conclusion that the fundamental aim of 'Christian development' should be to restore these broken relationships. This was stated clearly in the Operating Principles:

> The causes of poverty and marginalisation are complex, but we believe they stem from broken relationships. The goal of Christian development is restored relationships with the Creator, with others in community and with the environment.
> (Tearfund 1996: 5)

To this aim the Operating Principles set out two priorities for Christian development – a focus on social relationships and reconciliation, and a commitment to proclaim the gospel in order to bring about 'reconciliation with God through submission to Jesus Christ' (Tearfund 1996: 5). According to Tim Chester, one of the theologians on the team, development approached from this perspective should always ask, 'how does what we are doing affect relationships?' (Chester 2002: 8). This approach, at least in theory, shifted the focus of development away from products – wells, immunisation, homes, loan schemes, and so on – to people. And reconciliation with God implies the need for evangelism as a fundamental part of Christian development.

The Operating Principles then set out 11 characteristics of 'Christian development' – compassion, justice, character, cultural sensitivity, cultural transformation, accountability, leadership, empowerment, participation, sustainability, and integration. However, they acknowledged that these could not define 'Christian development' because many secular organisations held similar values. But it was rather a case that if these values were not upheld then the development was definitely not Christian.

The document ended by stating that Christian development needed to take place in the context of prayer because 'there is a spiritual reality to development which a secular worldview often ignores. We are engaged in a spiritual conflict. Therefore prayer is essential for Christian development' (Tearfund 1996: 8).

Finally it suggested that the local church was the best vehicle through which to bring about reconciliation in communities, and therefore committed Tearfund to working with the local church to enable it to fulfil its ministry to the poor.

The idea that Christian development should be carried out by the local church was rather novel at the time and very much came from the theological convictions of the theologians, rather than from ideas about good development practice. Their thinking was particularly influenced by the work of René Padilla and other Latin American theologians who had developed the concept of 'misión integral' decades earlier, and by British theologians such as John Stott and Chris Wright, who had been instrumental in importing this theology into the UK. What was unusual in this theology was the insistence that mission should be both spiritual and material and that the church should play a central role in both areas.

Furthermore, when the theologians talked about the 'local church' they were referring to a local congregation, or what we might call a local village church (although of course it may also be in a town or elsewhere). At this time Tearfund used the phrase 'local church' to mean a number of different things – the local church in another country (i.e. a large denomination), Christian NGOs in another country, and indeed also local congregations. Using this broader formulation Tearfund has always said that it works 'with the local church' – meaning in most cases mission organisations, the development wings of large church denominations, and Christian NGOs. But what the theologians were talking about was working with *local congregations*, the community church in the village or neighbourhood. This was actually a radically new idea, but because of the confusion over terminology, it went largely unnoticed at this early stage.

Putting all this together, the theologians argued that what made 'Christian development' Christian was that it focussed on relationships, that it was committed to evangelising the poor, that it included prayer, and that it was carried out by the local church. This sounded vague and general enough that it was accepted by Tearfund's leadership without too much question.

This formulation was the first time that the idea that the local church should be involved in community development began to emerge. The theologians felt that there were strong theological reasons to have the local village church as the lead development actor, since the local church is 'the community in which God lives by his Spirit' (Tearfund 1996: 8). They began to see working through the church as the way to overcome the dichotomy of development and evangelism that had pervaded so much of Tearfund's work in the 1980s and early 1990s. As the final paragraph in the Operating Principles put it:

> The New Testament gives little explicit teaching on either evangelistic or developmental methods. Instead it calls upon the church to be a caring, inclusive and distinctive community of reconciliation reaching out in love to the world. When we see the church in this way there is no opposition between evangelism and social action.
> (Tearfund 1996: 8)

However, while this text made its way into the Operating Principles there was at this time no clear model of what a church-centred development programme might look like. Nonetheless the theologians continued to push the idea of working more with the local village church in their other theological writings for Tearfund. Jennie Collins, who was International Director from 1992 to 2000, recalls the type of discussions that were taking place at this time:

> We knew what we meant by holistic development but we weren't sure quite how to do it. I think the theologians started to do more reading, more writing. They started to help us to look at it differently, even if we weren't practically doing things differently. The question was also about church and what was church and who was church? ... We started to think more about this at that time.*

The idea of the local village church itself carrying out development work was extremely radical at the time and was not something that Tearfund's leadership and departmental heads had thought much about. They were busy professionalising and planning projects according to logframes and using new kinds of project cycle management tools and accounting software, and all this seemed a million miles away from a local village church, often with a thatched roof and no electricity, out in an African village. How could these two worlds possibly be brought together?

Finding a name for Christian development

At this time there was a lot of discussion about what language should be used to refer to the new hybrid change process that Tearfund's staff were seeking to conceptualise. They wanted something that would effectively signal the bringing together of the Christian and the development worlds. The language of 'faith-based' development had yet to emerge, but there were several terms in use in evangelical circles that might be appropriate, and the group mulled them all over. Should they call what they sought to do 'holistic development'? or 'transformation'? 'integral mission'? or simply 'Christian development'? Tim Chester recalls:

Should we talk about 'holistic development'? That was what Tearfund initially talked about – meeting the whole person, spiritual and physical. The problem with that was it didn't really describe the nature of the interaction between the two.... A lot of people favoured 'transformation' and that was a term that had been coined by an evangelical fellowship at its conference in Wheaton in 1983 as a term that could describe both physical and spiritual change. My complaint with that was that it was just too vague. It could really describe anything. Also my contention is that evangelism and social action are not the same thing, and the danger with using a sort of cover-all term like transformation is that it allows you to just do one without the other. It doesn't actually integrate them in the way that a term like 'integral mission' does. I don't think 'integral mission' had kind of gained the status that it later did through Micah so in the end we went for 'Christian development.'*

However, a few years later in 1998 René Padilla became Tearfund's International President, and the decision was taken to stop talking about 'Christian development' and to link more closely with the Latin American theology by talking instead about 'integral mission'. As a later Tearfund document explains, this phraseology sought to emphasise more clearly the interconnectedness of evangelism and social action – not that they were two separate forms of action that could be brought together, but rather that they were fundamentally one type of action that should not be mistakenly broken apart:

> 'Integral' in the Spanish is also the word used for 'whole wheat' or 'wholemeal' bread: if something is not integral, therefore, it has lost something of its essential self. If something is not integral, it is because something has been removed as the husk is removed from the wheat when whole wheat is milled to make non-whole wheat flour. In English, by comparison we understand integral and integrated as meaning essentially a whole, but we bring to this the understanding that something that is integrated has component parts that are brought or held together. This means that in the English understanding of integral mission, integral is effectively understood as the sum of a number of parts, while in the Spanish understanding it is effectively understood as something that has never been separated. This is why English explanations and definitions of integral mission have often employed the language of verbal evangelism and social action – but this means that we have never fully escaped the dualism that comes from talking about different types of mission being brought together and that we have never escaped the question of which is more important.
>
> (Tearfund 2016a: 17–18)

While this thinking about development had much in common with ideas discussed within the ecumenical missions in the 1940s and 1950s, it was very different from the ideas being discussed in most of the secular development

NGOs at this time. During the 1990s and 2000s many of these organisations had begun to frame their work in terms of human rights and were talking about 'rights-based development'. In 1995 Oxfam issued its Global Charter for Basic Rights, and Christian Aid, ActionAid, and War on Want followed in the next few years with similar rights-based approaches (Hilton 2012: 468). Conceptualising development as a 'right', accorded to all humans, portrayed a fundamentally secular and universalistic conceptualisation of the world, and zoomed out to a level of focus in which governments and international organisations were important agents in manifesting everyone's right to develop. Tearfund's concept of 'integral mission', however, remained focussed at the community level, where beliefs, relationships, and church could play a significant role.

Micah Network and Global Connections

Many Tearfund staff were keen to spread their new approach in the evangelical relief and development sector. Thus in 2001 the organisation was instrumental in establishing an international network of evangelical relief and development NGOs with the express aim of promoting the vision and practice of integral mission. This network was named the Micah Network, taking its inspiration from the biblical passage Micah 6:8, which says, 'And what does the Lord require of you? To act justly, to love mercy and to walk humbly with your God.' Members further discussed just what was meant by integral mission and then Tearfund's Tim Chester drafted the Micah Declaration on Integral Mission, which was agreed by a global conference of 140 Christian leaders and which summed up their thinking succinctly. The Micah Declaration presents a holistic or integrated vision of mission in which evangelism and social action are not seen as two separate things that must be combined, but rather as one integrated and inseparable whole. Thus the Declaration states that:

> Integral mission or holistic transformation is the proclamation and demonstration of the gospel. It is not simply that evangelism and social involvement are to be done alongside each other. Rather, in integral mission our proclamation has social consequences as we call people to love and repentance in all areas of life. And our social involvement has evangelistic consequences as we bear witness to the transforming grace of Jesus Christ.
> (Micah Network 2001)

The Micah Network has grown considerably over the years and now has well over 500 member organisations and national networks in over 80 countries, all working to spread the idea of integral mission and to make it more mainstream. Many of these are Tearfund partners. This has led to the concept of integral mission becoming widely accepted among evangelical development NGOs, and for the most part it now guides their approach to engaging in relief and development work.

86 *Emerging as a development NGO*

During this period Tearfund also remained connected with the evangelical missionary sector and continued to be a member of the Evangelical Missionary Alliance. During the 1990s the number of UK evangelical mission agencies continued to expand and many of the older agencies changed their names to something with a more contemporary sound. Thus the Bible and Medical Missionary Fellowship became 'Interserve' in 1987 and the Bible Churchmen's Missionary Society became 'Crosslinks' in 1990. In 2000 the Evangelical Missionary Alliance rebranded itself as 'Global Connections' and counted well over 100 member organisations. A few years later it set up a Relief and Development Forum in which evangelical relief and development NGOs could discuss the missional aspects of their work. Tearfund was active in this forum and sought to share its new integral mission approach through seminar presentations and papers.

Putting this new theology into practice

Nonetheless, despite these theological developments, it was still far from clear for the rest of the organisation how this transformationalist theology of development could be put into practice. In the early 2000s another team was put together to try to answer this question. This team consisted only of practitioners – senior people in Tearfund's main relief, development, and advocacy teams. In 2002 it produced the first version of what was to become another foundational document for Tearfund's work going forward – *Paths out of Poverty*.

This document aimed 'to link the concepts of Integral Mission and God's concern for the poor discussed in Tearfund's Operating Principles with secular development thinking' (Tearfund 2002: 2). In doing so it sought to provide a Christian framework that could underlie and guide Tearfund's practical work as the organisation grew and professionalised. In practice the document sought to bring together the Christian understanding of sin, broken relationships, and poverty with a secular model of poverty alleviation developed by the World Bank that focussed on providing the poor with opportunities, empowerment and security.

While there was a clear desire to try to unite Christian and secular thinking into one model, this proved extremely difficult. There were fundamental differences in the Christian and secular approaches, particularly with regard to the causality of poverty and the steps necessary to alleviate it. The Christian model developed by the theologians implied that the first step to alleviating poverty was forgiveness of sin and reconciliation with God. This would then lead to a change in behaviour from sinful to righteous, which would in turn lead to the restoration of relationships within families and communities and with the environment, in which oppression and injustice would be removed. This would result in transformed communities in which the rich would help the poor and people would have sustainable livelihoods. The approach is summarised in the following diagram, taken from the *Paths out of Poverty* discussion paper (Tearfund 2002: 8):

> **Restored relationships as the ultimate solution to poverty**
>
> Forgiveness of sin
> ↓
> Restored relationship with God
> ↓
> Recognition of accountability to God and hence a responsibility towards others
> ↓
> Righteous, selfless attitudes, actions, and values (love, humility, compassion, justice ...)
> ↓
> Striving for restoration of relationships with others and environment
> ↓
> Equity, justice, equality, hope, rejection of oppression and prejudice, honesty & fair governance, richer helping the poorer ...
> ↓
> Sustainable livelihoods
> Transformed communities

The secular model from the World Bank, however, focussed on promoting opportunity, facilitating empowerment, and enhancing security (World Bank 2001). Tearfund sought to adapt and integrate this framework into its Christian approach but also criticised the secular analysis for misunderstanding that many of the causes of poverty were actually, in their view, consequences of sin. Thus lack of assets or access to services, lack of income, and lack of empowerment should be understood as consequences of sin. For example, the paper states:

> We can see the limitations of a secular viewpoint, because where there is no acknowledgement of sin and accountability to God, what a Christian can see as *consequences* of sin are here listed as *causes* of poverty.... Tearfund's understanding suggests such secular models will always remain incomplete.... Selfish attitudes and actions of a sinful heart lead to lives lived with a lack of recognition of responsibility to others. This is the link between the spiritual causes of poverty and the practical outworking noted above in the secular viewpoint.
>
> (Tearfund 2002: 7)

The paper suggested that evangelism was necessary to reconcile people with God and bring about 'Christian development', and even suggested that evangelism could be an important tool to bring about development:

> Tearfund works exclusively with those who share the gospel of Jesus Christ in both word and deed precisely because this gospel has the power to transform individuals and communities and have a profound and lasting impact on material as well as spiritual realities. Effective evangelism, delivered

sensitively and appropriately in the context of integral mission, is in itself part of a meaningful strategy for helping people escape poverty.

(Tearfund 2002: 10)

But despite references here and there to doing these things 'in the name of Christ', the activities that the paper suggested Tearfund should focus on – under the broad headings of community development, trading, advocacy, and disaster management, seemed decidedly mainstream and secular. It insisted that Tearfund itself would not support evangelism, but would work with partners who in other areas of their work carry out evangelism. So despite the desire to unite the spiritual and the material and to define a distinctive form of 'Christian development' the paper still ultimately fell back into the dichotomy of 'development' and 'evangelism'. Tearfund would support development activities that were essentially the same as those carried out by secular organisations, but they would be carried out by Christian organisations who would also evangelise and preach the gospel.

When the discussion paper was sent out to partners it received a great deal of criticism from many different angles. Almost all the partners refused to accept the implication in the theological model that individuals had brought about their own poverty because of their sinful behaviour. Asian partners further criticised the idea that there were linear paths from sin to poverty and from forgiveness of sin to transformed communities. African partners thought that Tearfund should also support evangelism and wanted to see evangelism and Christian education foregrounded as a fifth core area of intervention, arguing that this is what made Tearfund different to other development agencies. Partners in Latin America wanted to have more of a focus on justice and also to change the language from the rather neutral 'paths out of poverty' to something that emphasised structural inequalities, such as 'confronting the abuses of poverty' or 'the fight against poverty'. In almost diametric contrast partners from the Middle East preferred an approach that focussed on the provision of welfare, arguing that even though this was not considered good development practice it was deeply compassionate and deeply biblical. Many also wondered where exactly the 'paths out of poverty' would lead to, and what precisely a transformed community looked like (Adeney 2003: 2–3).

A revised version published in 2003 sought to address some of these issues. It emphasised that poverty, and the lack of opportunity, empowerment, and security that characterised it, were not caused by the sinful behaviour of the individuals themselves but by 'a profound spiritual and moral disorder that affects the whole of humanity' (Tearfund 2003: 6).

It also sought to place more emphasis on the importance of evangelism and the limitations of purely material development interventions. It suggested that converting to Christianity could empower people who had been disempowered by other religious systems, such as through the caste system in India, which claimed that the lower castes emerged from the feet of the gods and were thus worth less than the upper castes. Bringing these people to Christianity, with its emphasis on equality before God, it argued, could help to empower them far more than any material intervention.

> We are able to see that practical interventions can assist people escape, or at least be relieved from poverty, although ultimately only the spiritual dimension can address the problem of sin and our broken relationship with God. This is why Tearfund has objectives that demand that any responses are based on the integral mission of the Church being both practical and spiritual, challenging underlying value systems.
>
> (Tearfund 2003: 8)

Many of Tearfund's staff and partners still found this formulation unsatisfactory, so a small team consisting of a theologian and a policy and advocacy specialist sat down to try again (see Chapter 6 for a discussion of the emergence of the advocacy team). Their new version was completed in 2004 and took the new title, *Overcoming Poverty*. This paper made two key innovations. First, it reformulated its understanding of the link between sin and poverty, by widening out its understanding of sin from a notion of individual sin to a notion of a more collective and structural type of sin:

> This wilful alienation from God that infects the whole of human life is what we call sin. This is the ultimate cause of poverty. However, by saying that the ultimate cause of poverty is sin we do not imply that the poor are poor because of their own sins. In fact the Bible is very clear that the vast majority of the poor are poor because of factors that are beyond their control. They are held captive by the accumulated legacy of sin that is embedded in oppressive political, economic and religious structures.
>
> (Tearfund 2004: 4)

Second, the paper placed much more emphasis on structural issues in the global political economy, such as unfair trade rules, crippling developing-world debt, and the lack of pro-poor investment. This led it to give much greater emphasis to the role of the rich and powerful in causing, and then alleviating, poverty, and on the importance of advocacy for bringing about change at the global level. There were new sections arguing for the importance of advocacy work in rich countries and in international institutions such as the United Nations and the World Bank, and a new section that emphasised the importance of Christians in the UK sharing their wealth with poor communities overseas:

> Coming to know God in Jesus Christ enables the rich to re-evaluate their wealth and to begin to use it not to satisfy their own lusts but to serve God and the needy.... Tearfund has always believed that an important part of its calling has been to educate the church in the UK about world poverty and the role of the church and Christian organisations in serving the poor. Underlying this belief is the conviction that when Christians and churches

know that there is a need their knowledge of God will stir them to respond with their diverse resources.

(Tearfund 2004: 8)

Nonetheless a number of problems still remained. First, while there was growing acknowledgement of the importance of thinking globally and addressing global issues, much of the paper still focussed at the level of the community and indeed on the individual. The very question that initiated this work – how could *people* overcome poverty? – implied this level of analysis from the very beginning. This was most likely because the majority of Tearfund's international work at this time was indeed small-scale community development, and also because Tearfund's evangelical worldview led it rather naturally to place a great emphasis on the individual and on individual transformation. At this time Tearfund struggled to bring together the different scales of analysis into a coherent whole. This would come in later years. The 2004 document ultimately fell back to a focus on the individual. Thus the document concluded:

Our conceptual framework for how people overcome poverty can be summed up as service of God and neighbour in the name of Jesus, in the power of the Holy Spirit and in the context of the church.

(Tearfund 2004: 8)

Second, there was still no discussion of what a transformed community would actually look like and therefore what the end goal of Christian development was. This too would come only in later years. For now the document simply suggested the types of activities that could be taken to practically help the poor to overcome poverty. These were largely the types of activities that Tearfund, and indeed many secular NGOs, were already supporting – community development projects, disaster mitigation, and advocacy.

From all these documents the main thing that emerged that would make Christian development truly distinctive was the vision, again, that the church, at all levels, should be carrying out this work. But at this point in time Tearfund was not yet clear how to actually work with the local village church in practice.

However, while all these long and involved theoretical discussions had been taking place, a number of staff closer to the ground had already begun to experiment with practical ways to work with the local church and to make Tearfund's work more Christian.

Church and community mobilisation (CCM)

While all this theological reflection was taking place, Tearfund's Desk Officer for East Africa, Gladys Wathanga, was also wondering how to make Christian development really Christian. She would go out and visit projects that Tearfund supported and which were typically delivered by the development departments of large denominations, and she would wonder what was distinctively Christian about it. She recalls:

> I was getting rather dissatisfied because I still had a question of how different is Christian development? ... There were mission statements that talked about 'Christian development' and I wondered what is the difference in what we are doing and what others are doing? If I visited this community where we had carried out this project and I wasn't told that it had been done by a Christian organisation, how would I know?

Gladys had previously worked at World Vision, where she had come across a development tool called the Participatory Evaluation Process (PEP). This had been developed by Judy Hutchinson in the early 1980s and had been used by World Vision to enable communities to reflect on their situation and decide what they could do to improve it using their own resources and initiative. Gladys had used the tool when she was working at World Vision and found it to be effective and positive. In 1998, when she was with Tearfund, she suggested that one of Tearfund's partners, the Africa Inland Church of Tanzania, consider using PEP in the community development work that its development departments were carrying out in the diocese of Mara and Ukurewe. Using this participatory tool, staff from the development department of the diocese went to local communities and facilitated them to discuss their situation and find activities that they could do to improve their lives. While these projects produced significant outcomes, with communities creating their own projects and activities, Gladys was concerned at the lack of Christian content.

At around the same time, Tearfund was supporting another partner, an Anglican diocese in Uganda. The project was helping children with disabilities caused by cerebral malaria. The development department of the diocese was working with affected children to help them strengthen their limbs. It taught people how to make a simple frame out of materials collected from the forest that could help support the child while he or she exercised. Gladys went to visit the project and came across a disabled boy living alone with his grandmother, who did not have a frame. The grandmother explained that, because she was alone looking after the boy, and she could not leave him unattended, she did not have time to go to the forest to collect the materials needed to make the frame. Gladys recalls:

> I asked the social worker, 'Have you talked to the local church about helping this lady have the materials that she needs to make a frame?' Because the church was just close by. And the social worker looked at me and said, 'What's the church got to do with it?' I was sure that if the church knew about this woman then they would help her, but the social worker did not see the connection. That is what made me really unhappy with what we were calling 'Christian development'. I knew from that day that it had to involve the local congregations, the local Christians. It had to be about Christians loving their communities, and the local church was the best institution for that.

An evaluation of the project came to the same conclusion – the local village church was being left out of the process. So Gladys and her colleagues in Nairobi, Francis Njeroge and Peter Gitau, started to think about different ways of doing 'Christian development'.

Tearfund's Operating Principles focussed on relationships and stated that the key to Christian development was its emphasis on improving relationships, and yet Gladys was not seeing this in the work on the ground. The team liked the PEP tool as a way of mobilising and empowering the community to improve their own situation, and they started to wonder if there was a way to get the local village church involved in the process. When they heard about a new methodology that was being used in some of Tearfund's work with UK churches they realised that they had found the final part of the puzzle.

In 1996 Tearfund had started to work with partners in poor communities in the UK in its UK Action Programme, which was to run from 1996 to 2015. The idea of this programme was that local churches in poor areas would work to improve the situation of their surrounding communities. David Evans, who was head of the UK and Ireland team at the time and who set up the programme, recalls:

> Its vision was to get local churches to a position where they could do something constructive. They could help the poor. They were the ones that were there 24/7.... It was addressing the crucial role that the local church can have in our poorest communities.*

This was a novel approach at the time because most welfare work was being done by Christian NGOs or para-church organisations. Tearfund had begun to work with local churches on three-year cycles and supported them to set up and run projects in their local community. Tearfund gave them grants, training, and one-to-one organisational development support, and networked them up with similar churches for peer-to-peer learning. One of the first projects supported by UK Action was the Toxteth Tabernacle. David Evans recalls:

> They converted the basement of their church – a massive great preaching barn ... into a skills school which was specifically for children who had been permanently excluded from school because of disruptive behaviour.... They offered things like literacy, computers, numeracy, woodwork and IT.... I remember visiting and the project leader said to me, 'You know we've got a bit of a problem. The kids have asked for more maths....' I paused and thought, 'Well that is a miracle because six months ago they were assaulting their maths teacher or throwing desks through windows. What on earth had happened and ... how does that chime in with their understanding of the fact that there is somebody who cares for them and has helped them change?' I was amazed at the profound evangelistic potential of that sort of situation.*

In other projects partners were working with homeless people, drug abusers, sex workers, vulnerable children, and youth. The approach of working with the local church had struck a chord with a number of UK churches, and they had started to contact Tearfund to ask for practical training resources to help them do community development work. This had led to Tearfund's developing a toolkit called *Church Community Change*, which set out a participatory process whereby churches would be envisioned through Bible study to think about how they were called to serve their local communities.

When Gladys and her team heard about this work and the *Church Community Change* approach they realised how they would develop their approach to Christian development. They took the first part of the *Church Community Change* methodology, where churches are envisioned through Bible studies to work with their communities, and added it to the PEP methodology, so that the envisioned church would then lead their community through the PEP process. They tentatively called this new approach 'Church and Community Mobilisation' (CCM).

Gladys and her team returned to the diocese of Mara and Ukurewe in Tanzania to pilot the new approach. This time they asked the development department of the diocese to work directly with the local village church and to use the UK tool and its Bible studies to help the village church think about its role in the community. Then they asked the development department to train the church leaders in how to use the PEP tool with the community. The results were very encouraging. The local community started to get organised and carry out small-scale development activities, like building a small nursery and primary school, and the local village church was right at the centre.

As Tearfund gets most of its funding directly from supporters, Gladys and her team were able to experiment with this innovative new approach without having to write extensive project proposals and convince donors (see Appendix). Gladys reflects:

> It was the unrestricted funding that we got from churches and supporters in the UK that made this possible. It gave us the flexibility to try out new things. If we had had to write a proposal to be funded by an outsider it would not work because they want to see planned and quantifiable outcomes. They are not interested in processes where the outcome is not known.

Gladys and her team decided to try this approach in other places. The Pentecostal Assemblies of God (PAG) in Uganda and several Anglican dioceses in Kenya began to use the process to envision local churches. The churches then mobilised their communities and started to carry out projects, such as digging shallow wells for clean water, setting up gravity irrigation systems, and starting a community dairy. But what really inspired Gladys was that in this approach the church was at the centre of all the good work. And, as she explains, in this way the church had new opportunities to evangelise, thus bringing development work and evangelism much closer:

The beauty about the church being involved is that Christians serve and interact with the community. The results might be the same, the same schools and clinics, but as Christians interact with the community people start attending church, and that gives the church the opportunity to evangelise and the church membership grows and more people get to know God. And that is transformation.

By the early 2000s there were CCM projects in Kenya, Uganda, Tanzania, and Southern Sudan, and a small, committed group of Tearfund staff who believed in this methodology. For the time being they were just a small minority, but they invited other Tearfund staff to visit the projects and see what was happening on the ground and worked hard to encourage it to spread within the organisation.

Meanwhile, another group of Tearfund staff was experimenting with a different way of working with the local church. This area of work focussed on HIV and AIDS.

Working with churches in response to HIV and AIDS

In the late 1980s the issue of HIV/AIDS had emerged and staff in Tearfund had begun to wonder what a Christian response to the pandemic would look like. In 1991 the organisation started to encourage many of its African partners to start working on raising awareness and provide voluntary HIV testing and counselling. However, Tearfund's Africa Desk Officers had found it very difficult to convince its Christian partners to take on this work because the predominant view of the evangelical churches in Africa at that time was that HIV and AIDS was a problem that was 'out there' and not part of the church. They held conservative attitudes towards sex and towards gender and believed that HIV was associated with promiscuity and immorality; thus they refused to acknowledge it could be a problem within the Christian community. In many cases religious leaders were central in stigmatising and ignoring people living with HIV, and in some cases even punishing them (Marshall and Taylor 2006). Churches, at this point, were very much part of the problem. While the Catholic and mainline churches in Africa had begun to carry out piecemeal responses to the pandemic during the 1990s, mostly involving home-based care, counselling work, and caring for orphans, the vast majority of the evangelical and Pentecostal churches had refused to engage with the issue (Prince 2009: vii).

In 2000 Tearfund hired a new staff member from India. Veena O'Sullivan had been working with a coalition of NGOs establishing best practices in HIV and AIDS interventions in Karnataka, India. After moving to the UK she started to lead Tearfund's work on HIV and AIDS and began to push it into a new direction. She was shocked when she saw the attitude and behaviour of the evangelical churches in Africa, and decided that an important intervention would be to try to change the attitudes of these churches – to shift them from being part of the problem to being part of the solution. She recalls:

When we started this work the church was harsh. They were really mean. They were slammed at by everyone in the development world for their inaction and their negative action. So it was a very difficult time and a very difficult space for us as people of faith who were committed to enabling the church to be a compassionate space for those suffering stigma and shame. And I suppose that made us think that we had to stick with this, even if the going was tough. We had to find a way to win the church over and get them involved.

The key issue was to try to convince the evangelical churches that HIV was an issue for everyone, including Christians, and that they should get involved. Veena believed that people living with HIV had to be central to the response and that change would be most powerful if it was championed by the people who were themselves affected. So she slowly and gently sought out African faith leaders who were themselves living with HIV. She then formed a network of these 'HIV Champions' in Kenya, Uganda, Malawi, Nigeria, and South Africa, and worked with them to empower them to speak out about their situation and educate the wider community and leadership about HIV and AIDS. Tearfund and its local partners then organised meetings and discussions with church denominations in these countries to discuss HIV. They would start by talking about technical issues, such as health outcomes, physiology, sociology, and so on. At some point someone in the group would generally ask, 'But what has all this got to do with us?' Then the HIV Champions, who were often senior and respected church leaders, would talk openly about their own personal experience with HIV. Hearing these respected leaders talk like this about HIV was often shocking and humbling for the other participants and was instrumental in changing their views and getting them to understand that anyone could get infected with HIV and that HIV was not the result of sin.

Tearfund's work with HIV and AIDS continued well after 2005 and will be further discussed in Chapter 7. What is important here is to note the very specific and distinctive faith-based and church-based response to HIV that some of Tearfund's staff members were beginning to develop. Veena and her team reasoned that, as a Christian organisation, Tearfund had the potential to play a distinct and particular role working with churches and with faith leaders to change people's attitudes and behaviours in a very deep and meaningful way. And the team experimented with a new kind of methodology to carry out a particularly Christian type of development work that, like the CCM approach, was centred on the local church.

Thus by the mid-2000s two new church-based methodologies had been developed by more junior, Southern, predominantly female staff in different teams within Tearfund's International Department. These methodologies were inspired by the theological discussions and writings that had started in the mid-1990s and many felt that they were a truer reflection of what a distinctively Christian form of development could look like – one that kept evangelism and development close together and sought to work in a more holistic way. These 'religious revitalists' felt strongly that Tearfund was going in the wrong direction with the growing emphasis on professionalisation and moving into the mainstream, and felt compelled to push against the leadership and to develop an alternative vision of a more Christian kind of development.

Dilemmas of faith-based development

The organisation was torn. While some staff members were excited by these new church-based approaches, others agreed with the leadership and thought that the best way forward was to become more effective and more efficient, to work with higher-capacity partners, and to do top-quality development work with a Christian motivation. CCM did not fit into this vision at all. It was small scale, messy, and focussed on process as much as results. Some staff wondered whether CCM was a suitable methodology for large-scale relief and development. Did it have appropriate systems and transparency to be able to fit in with the requirements of the mainstream development world? Would it ever get funding? Others were concerned that it might distract churches from their core, spiritual work. And others still were concerned that it would lead Tearfund back into the little Christian ghetto. All in all, CCM and the other church-based methodologies were incredibly controversial at this time. Tulo Raistrick, who worked in the UK Action team in the late 1990s and then later as Tearfund's Church and Development Advisor, was one of the early supporters of CCM. He recalls the angst and tensions that these different views caused:

> For some people in the organisation there was a feeling that what we needed was much more professional NGOs on the ground. So the key thing was to develop the professional capacity of our local partners, so that there was greater transparency and greater accountability and so on. And I think as Tearfund accessed more and more DFID funding it was understandable that some preferred to go that route. But I think going that route worked against working with local churches, who by their very nature aren't very good at those kinds of things. So there was a body of opinion in the organisation that was wanting to go that way, and then another body of opinion that wanted to go the other way .... And during that period there was quite a lot of debate and angst about what was the right direction to go....

Conclusion

By the mid-2000s there was thus a major debate within Tearfund about what kind of organisation it should be and what kind of work it should be doing. As the leadership pushed Tearfund to professionalise and enter the mainstream, the secularising forces that this gave rise to set in motion a reaction from several passionate, 'spiritually hot' staff members who fought to keep faith and evangelism at the centre of their work. At its core, the debate was about whether Tearfund should be 'Christians who do development', or whether they should 'do Christian development'.

Before we look at how these issues were resolved, however, the next chapter will discuss another set of dilemmas and debates that were taking place in parallel to the issues discussed in this chapter and the previous one. As if all this were not enough, in the mid-1990s Tearfund's leadership was also considering whether or not to start campaigning and advocacy work, something that had been taboo for evangelical organisations for a long time but which was beginning to seem like an important component of work as Tearfund sought to enter the mainstream.

Note

1 World Vision was working on its theology of development at around the same time. The results are extremely similar. World Vision decided to refer to its approach as 'transformational development'. Its ideas are elaborated in *Walking with the Poor: Principles and Practices of Transformational Development* (Myers 1999).

6 The globalists and the localists – the start of campaigning and advocacy

Introduction

As Tearfund sought to professionalise and enter the mainstream, the question arose of whether it should start doing campaigning and advocacy work. Mainstream development NGOs had come to the realisation early on that poverty and inequality could not be alleviated by small-scale interventions alone and that structural changes to the world economy would be needed. Already in the late 1960s and 1970s they had started to lobby the government to change the terms of its trade deals with the newly independent countries of Africa and Asia and to give more money in overseas aid. This work had grown in the interim years and by the 1990s campaigning and advocacy were core elements of the portfolio of work carried out by most mainstream development NGOs. In contrast, however, twentieth-century evangelicalism had historically been characterised by its individualistic approach to social change. As Christian Smith has described it, evangelicals tended to subscribe to a 'personal influence strategy' of social transformation, whereby if enough people were converted to Christ, society would change for the better (Smith 2002). Structural and systemic thinking was not part of the evangelical approach and in the early 1990s, when Tearfund was still more mission agency than development NGO, things such as trade deals and UN policy seemed very far from its core concerns. Should it, then, step into this new area? This chapter looks at the discussions around this issue and the resulting activities that were undertaken.

The pre-history of campaigning and advocacy at Tearfund

The idea of engaging in political advocacy was actually discussed in the very first meetings of the Evangelical Alliance Relief Fund Committee in 1968, but at that time it was decided that such action was 'too political' and too radical for evangelical Christians (Hollow 2008: 167). In 1969 some members of that committee, particularly the young Mary-Jean Duffield, had suggested that part of Tearfund's work should include mobilising UK evangelicals to try to influence government policies to help the overseas poor, but many on the Committee were not convinced. Later that year the Committee had agonised over whether to join a national campaign organised by Oxfam, Christian Aid, and other relief and development NGOs that called on the UK government to give 1 per cent of GNP in overseas aid and to negotiate more favourable trading conditions with the poorer countries. The mainline churches supported this endeavour and launched a 'National Sign-In on World Poverty' in which they invited congregations to sign a declaration to be presented to MPs throughout the country (Black 1992: 158, Endersbee 1973: 90). But in the end Tearfund had decided that the campaign was too political for them and they did not join. Instead they wrote an insert into the Church of England newspaper suggesting that Christians should write to their MPs about international aid (Hollow 2008: 168–9, Endersbee 1973: 90–7).

During these early years Tearfund argued that political advocacy and campaigning were important, but not something that Tearfund itself did.[1] Instead, starting from the early 1970s, Tearfund encouraged those supporters who were interested in such issues to get involved with the World Development Movement (WDM), now called Global Justice Now, a secular, non-charitable pressure group that had been set up by Oxfam and Christian Aid in 1969 when UK Charity Law had made it difficult for charities to engage in campaigning. At that time it was run by John Mitchell, an evangelical, a Tearfund supporter, and a close friend of both Tearfund's founder and its then President. A survey in the late 1980s suggested that over half of WDM's supporters were Tearfund supporters.

However, even when it became easier for charities to engage in campaigning in the 1980s, and when Oxfam, Christian Aid, and others began to develop and build up their advocacy and campaigning teams, Tearfund continued to shy away from this kind of work. In these years it did only some ad hoc political work. In 1985, for example, on the first anniversary of the BBC's reports about the Ethiopian famine, Tearfund collaborated with WDM and other development agencies to organise a mass lobby of Parliament to urge government action to increase its overseas aid budget. Tearfund also put its name to a joint letter from development NGOs in *The Times*, calling for the government to tackle world poverty and hunger (Hollow 2008: 176). In 1989 there was a piece in *Tear Times* about the European elections, which encouraged supporters to challenge candidates on social justice and development issues (Tear Times 1989: 22). But for the most part Tearfund kept away from politics and political issues. Tearfund's leadership thought that, while UK evangelicals at this time had largely come around to the idea that they should be involved in social action for the poor, many were still very wary about political engagement.

Tearfund decides to start campaigning

By the 1990s some people in Tearfund were beginning to feel that this was not enough. There was a growing awareness in the development sector at this time that community development on its own was not working in reducing poverty at scale or in tackling most of the causes of poverty, and that large-scale structural change in global affairs was needed. Thus many relief and development NGOs had stepped up their advocacy and campaigning work in the 1980s and early 1990s. Some of this thinking was seeping into Tearfund, as Jennie Collins recalls:

> I think we were beginning as an organisation to make many more connections between what was happening in the developed world, as it was called, the global North, and to see trade issues, debt issues particularly and saying, 'Gosh our lifestyles ... if something really happened about them it would make more difference than all of the money Tearfund put in to development.' So those issues were becoming much more conscious at that time.*

At the same time, as discussed in Chapter 5, Tearfund's own theological reflections were also beginning to lead in this direction. Some people in Tearfund were beginning to feel that a rigorous analysis of major world problems from a biblical perspective was necessary. At the time no other organisation was doing this and they felt that it was an important space for Tearfund.

Furthermore, during the 1980s the Evangelical Association had been growing and becoming more publicly engaged and committed to social action, and under Clive Calver's leadership a new Public Affairs Department had been formed (Randall and Hilborn 2001). By the mid-1990s this had grown into a strong and effective department and its Director, Martyn Eden, suggested that Tearfund should also get involved in lobbying and advocacy, and even proposed that the EA could carry out parliamentary monitoring and other public affairs services on their behalf. Several meetings took place between staff from the EA and from Tearfund, but ultimately this partnership did not materialise. Instead Tearfund decided to venture into policy and advocacy on its own, starting in a slow and measured way.

In 1992 Tearfund decided to test the water by taking part in a joint campaign with two other evangelical organisations – Spring Harvest and Youth for Christ – to mark the Rio Earth Summit and the first global agreement about climate change. In this campaign, called *Whose Earth?*, they talked to UK supporters and churches about climate change and organised a big rally in Hyde Park. The campaign went down well and there was no major backlash from supporters.

Nonetheless Tearfund decided to progress slowly and in a way very influenced by its Christian approach. It started to educate its supporters more about global issues and encouraged them first of all to pray. In 1992 it launched World Watch Prayer Link, a monthly prayer update enabling supporters to pray in an informed way for topics of international concern. And in 1993 it hired a Public Affairs Officer, theologian Tim Chester, to research about major world problems and campaigning issues and write articles about them in *Tear Times*.

At this time a small number of Tearfund partners were already doing some local-level campaigning and advocacy, mainly in Central and Latin America. Mopawi in Honduras were advocating for land rights for the indigenous Miskito people, and Paz y Esperanza in Peru were doing advocacy on human rights issues. But the majority of partners were not doing advocacy at this time and most were not even sure what it was.

Finally, in 1994, the Board took the decision that Tearfund should begin campaigning work. But it stressed that Tearfund should start this process slowly and make a concerted effort to take its supporters along with them on this journey. Tearfund also began to think about starting policy and advocacy work, directly engaging with politicians in the UK parliament and perhaps also in international forums such as the UN. A further question discussed was whether it was appropriate for Tearfund to join non-evangelical advocacy networks, such as the burgeoning Jubilee 2000. But while the senior leadership mulled over these questions, more junior staff again led the way into action.

Jubilee 2000

In parallel with all these internal discussions, a young, female Tearfund consultant, acting independently, was instrumental in the formation of a large developing world debt cancellation campaign called 'Jubilee 2000'. This campaign was to become the largest campaign organised in the twentieth century. It had a strong faith element in it and in many ways it was pivotal in getting both Tearfund and its UK evangelical constituents over their reticence about engaging in political campaigning and advocacy.

In September 1994 Isabel Carter, the Editor of Tearfund's *Footsteps* magazine,[2] was flying across Africa during a visit as a Tearfund consultant when she had what she describes as a vision. She had been reading Susan George's book, *The Debt Boomerang* (1992), and seeing Africa unfold beneath her it struck her how so many of Africa's problems stemmed from the fact that all the countries were struggling with the huge burden of debt. Then it came to her – the vision that there would be a jubilee in the year 2000 and debt in the developing world would be cleared. And that she somehow had a role in making that happen.

A few months later, in early 1995, she asked senior people in Tearfund if they would take this forward and make it happen. Senior staff in Tearfund were not yet ready for this and so they declined. Isabel then went around many of the other big relief and development agencies and one by one they all said no. However, in the course of these early discussions, she came across some other people who had had the same idea. In particular she met Michael Dent and Bill Peters. Michael Dent, a retired politics professor from Keele University, had had the idea some years earlier of using the Jubilee as a frame for a debt forgiveness campaign.[3] In 1990 he had organised a group of students into a 'Jubilee Campaign' where they signed a petition calling for a one-off dropping of the debt (Reitan 2007: 75). In 1993 he had joined forces with Bill Peters, a retired British diplomat, and together they had started to write to MPs, ambassadors, bishops, and bankers about the idea. Both were committed Christians.

This group of three, and a few others, started to work together developing ideas for a grassroots campaign to write off the unpayable sovereign debt of developing countries. Dent was a member of the Debt Crisis Network (DCN), a network of organisations working on debt that had been established in the UK in 1987 following initial work by War on Want, and soon afterwards members of the DCN, and in particular Ann Pettifor, began to come around to the idea and started to work with them on the details of the Jubilee 2000 campaign to press G8 governments and banks into cancelling unpayable debt owed by the poorest countries by the end of the year 2000.

They set up Jubilee 2000 as an independent organisation, registered with the Charity Commission, and organised a small office within the Christian Aid building. While Tearfund as an organisation would not get involved at this time, a number of Tearfund staff started to attend these early meetings and provided important advice about promoting the campaign's ideas.

While three out of four of the initial team were Christians, they did not intend for Jubilee 2000 to be a Christian campaign. They wanted something much broader than that. But the framing of the campaign was decidedly biblical, rooted in the Book of Leviticus' prescription that at certain points in time economic relations should be reset by freeing slaves, returning or redistributing land and wealth, and cancelling debts. The centrality of the religious frame drew faith-based organisations to the forefront of the campaign, inspiring a fairly establishment group of people to join with more radical activists. And indeed it motivated more and more Tearfund staff, who began to push the leadership for Tearfund to be directly involved. But still the leadership were hesitant.

In late 1996 Tearfund's leaders took a step forward and decided to include a Jubilee 2000 flyer inside *Tear Times*. They sent it out to all its supporters and encouraged them to support the campaign and make a donation. Tearfund was the first major NGO to do this, and the response was massive. Donations started to pour in to the fledgling campaign. Other Christian organisations soon followed suit, followed then by the secular NGOs. A large number of people sent in cheques and this enabled Jubilee 2000 to properly get off the ground. In April 1997 the organisers launched the 1,000-day countdown to the millennium in a public event in London.

As interest in the Jubilee 2000 campaign grew among the public, many relief and development agencies finally decided that they also wanted to be involved. For Tearfund the decision was more difficult because it had never been deeply involved in a campaign before, and certainly not in a large coalition with a variety of non-Christian organisations. David Westlake, Tearfund's Youth Director at the time, recalls:

> There was the big discussion as to whether Tearfund should get involved in the Jubilee 2000 campaign. With hindsight it seems ridiculous but I remember great angst about whether this was too political, would our supporters accept it. There was great wrestling with these kinds of issues.*

After long discussions Tearfund finally decided to take the risk and get actively involved. In October 1997 the Jubilee 2000 Coalition was formed. Tearfund was a founding member and Stephen Rand, then Prayer and Campaigns Director, was elected to the Board.

One of the first things that they did was to set up the Global Action Network, Tearfund's first full-scale programme equipping supporters to campaign on poverty issues from a biblical basis. One of its first actions was to urge supporters to get behind Jubilee 2000. It found that its supporters needed little pushing – they were excited and inspired by the campaign and by its biblical framing. As Stephen Rand explains:

> The Jubilee framing was enormously significant for the Tearfund constituency because they bought into the biblical argument quite strongly. That was the rolling tide that bought the evangelical constituency into that movement.

Tearfund found that it was able to mobilise huge numbers of supporters, often dwarfing the numbers mobilised by secular NGOs. On one day it gathered a record-breaking 232,927 signatures for the petition and mobilised large numbers of supporters to go to the human chain demonstration around the G8 summit. This was partly because it had access to supporters in ready-made church networks, and partly because for many evangelicals campaigning for debt reduction became a deeply meaningful religious experience. Stephen Rand describes a prayer vigil that was held in his Baptist church during the 2000 G8 meeting in Okinawa, Japan:

> The G8 leaders were in Okinawa. A small group of us were in a West London church. As we followed the Summit Watch vigil guide I realized that this was not just a routine ceremony, it was another step of faith.... As the vigil ended we were invited to light a candle and place it at the front of the church. At first no-one moved. Then, in deep silence, one after another solemnly took their candles forward. The silent movement spoke eloquently of commitment, of determination, of faith, of hope. The candle flames flickered, as the highest aspirations of the human spirit were fueled again by God's compassion and justice. The spirituality at the heart of Jubilee 2000 had never felt so powerful.
>
> (Stephen Rand, quoted in Barrett 2000: 19)

This faith-inspired approach, in which political campaigning becomes an intensely religious activity, was to set the course of much of Tearfund's campaigning work in the coming years.

In June 1999 Tearfund uniquely arranged an internet link-up between Gordon Brown, then the UK Chancellor of the Exchequer, and Elinata Kasanga, a poor mother of seven in the village of Balakasau in Zambia (Barrett 2000: 24). In this live webcast Elinata was able to explain directly to the Chancellor how Zambian unpayable debt was having an impact on her life and how she could not afford to buy medicines for her children or to send them to school because debt had stolen money from the Zambian economy. Mike Webb, who organised the webcast, recalls:

> It was a lot of hard work but we managed to do it with God's grace and help. To me it really symbolized something about Tearfund: it was giving a voice to the voiceless.
>
> (Quoted in Hollow 2008: 184)

Innovative activities such as this, plus Tearfund's ability to mobilise really high numbers of supporters to sign petitions and come to demonstrations, established Tearfund as a serious player in the campaigning sphere.

The Jubilee 2000 campaign succeeded in getting debt onto the global agenda and led to world leaders eventually agreeing to write off over $130 billion of the poorest countries' debts. At the same time it also had a profound effect on many quarters of the UK evangelical church, making campaigning and advocacy something that was acceptable, and indeed even religiously important. Stephen Rand explains the sea change that took place:

> From Jubilee 2000, from say 1997 to 2005, and I think because of Jubilee 2000 largely, the evangelical constituency broadly moved into acceptance of political campaigning. That's a whole load of individual journeys, but it's also about the tone and it's about what church leaders are saying. And I think more and more church leaders, the ministers in the pulpit, would be positive about signing petitions and all of those things.... I'd like to think that Tearfund itself, and the involvement in Jubilee 2000, significantly shifted the evangelical constituency towards an understanding of concern for the poor ... including campaigning for change.

The experience of the Jubilee 2000 campaign was extremely significant for Tearfund. It showed that it could do this work well and that it could do it in a distinctive, faith-based way even while it entered into large coalitions with those from other faiths or with no faith at all. In many ways it set the course for Tearfund's campaigning and advocacy work in the coming years.

Integrating advocacy and campaigning in the 2000s

By 1997 a major shift had taken place within Tearfund. It had joined the Jubilee 2000 Coalition and had also employed its first Public Policy Advisor, Andy Atkins, to set up policy and advocacy work within the organisation. At this time Tearfund was still quite isolated from other NGOs and had little research and policy capacity. So as a first step it decided to build up its capacity to lobby on macro issues, such as debt, trade, and food security, and on regional issues, such as disasters, governance, or human rights in particular countries, and to begin to see how it could build the capacity of its partner organisations to start engaging in advocacy and campaigning. The new Advocacy Strategy suggested that

Tearfund should focus on three macro issues at a time, and the first three should be debt, trade, and the environment. Furthermore, it also suggested that Tearfund should join advocacy networks and develop a reputation in this field.

In 2000 a new Advocacy Department was created, bringing together the Campaigns and Public Policy teams that had largely run in parallel up to this point. Now they began to work together towards shared objectives – the Public Policy team would do research and engage with politicians, while the Campaigns team would mobilise the church and get supporters to attend marches and demonstrations on the same issue. More resources were given to the team and new staff were employed. The overall aim was that Tearfund would become 'the primary channel by which UK evangelicals campaign on development issues' (Atkins 2002: 2).

The first big integrated campaign that Tearfund initiated and led was the *Water Matters* campaign, which it ran in collaboration with Water Aid. Together the two organisations worked with the UK government's Department for International Development (DFID) to convince the EU to negotiate at the 2002 World Summit on Sustainable Development for a new international target for providing sanitation to poor people. Tearfund attended the summit with 12 of its partner organisations, enabling them to speak directly about the situations in their communities, and also mobilised its supporters to send postcards to their MPs.

The campaign was a success and a new international sanitation target was set. This led to various governments putting more money into water and sanitation projects. The UK government doubled its aid budget for water and sanitation in Africa. The amount of money raised for water and sanitation work in the South through this intervention was much larger than Tearfund's entire budget. Even the sceptics within Tearfund began to see the effectiveness of advocacy work. Furthermore, the media coverage generated by the campaign was raising Tearfund's profile. And this, in turn, was leading to more donations.

In 2002 Tearfund also ran another campaign called *Whose Earth?*, echoing its first foray into campaigning in 1992. This campaign was significant because it marked the start of Tearfund's advocacy and campaign work about climate change, which would continue to be a major focus of its work up until the present.

In the following years Tearfund ran several other campaigns, on issues such as HIV and AIDS, ethical tourism, and trade and livelihoods. And it continued to educate and mobilise its supporters. By 2006 Tearfund had about 12,000 regular campaigning supporters who carried out around 50,000 actions per year. By 2006 Tearfund had one of the largest advocacy capacities on development issues in the evangelical world. While Tearfund had begun to encourage its overseas partners to start advocacy or campaigning activities, little emphasis had been put on supporting them at this stage and the focus had been on building up its UK advocacy capacity.

The role of faith in advocacy and campaigning

Tearfund's campaigning and advocacy work started soon after the Operating Principles had been launched and in the context of major discussions about what it meant to do 'Christian development'. Therefore, from the beginning Tearfund put considerable thought and effort into making its campaigning and advocacy work distinctively Christian. It did so in three main ways.

First, as discussed above with regard to the Jubilee 2000 campaign, Tearfund sought to make campaigning a fundamental part of the outworking of people's faith. It produced material on 'biblical campaigning' and built reflection, prayer, and ethical living into a 'whole life' approach. Campaign events would generally start with a period of worship and might end with a spiritual workshop in a nearby church.

Second, Tearfund developed theological resources to convince evangelicals – including church leaders, theologians, partners, supporters, and staff – who were still unsure that advocacy and campaigning for justice was biblical and Christian. In 2002 it produced a discussion paper – *The Mission of the Church and the Role of Advocacy* – to address the theological basis of advocacy and to argue in more depth why evangelicals should get involved and why arguments that they should not were biblically false.

Third, Tearfund thought about what faith-based advocacy and lobbying might look like. This was rather more difficult as it was hard to see how evangelism or spirituality could be combined with talking to politicians or going to UN summits. For some this was a reason for Tearfund not to put too much energy into this area of work. Others, however, felt that advocacy and campaigning could indeed be carried out in a distinctively Christian way. Tearfund's advocacy staff decided that faith would shape its work in two main ways: it would influence the choice of issues on which it advocated and it would influence the way that Tearfund staff went about their advocacy. Tearfund would ensure that there was a biblical basis for all the issues on which it advocated and that its messages were biblically sound. It would also ensure that its staff conducted themselves according to Christian values, seeking to act respectfully and to build relationships rather than to confront or publicly shame. Andy Atkins, who was Advocacy Director from 2000 to 2008, explains:

> We wanted our Christian distinctiveness to be evident in *how* we did advocacy. We would treat people like human beings and not be rude to them in public. We didn't want to just criticise or be confrontational, we sought a more relational approach – 'Don't assume you've got an enemy before you check if you have a friend.'

Tearfund also decided not to publicly target individuals or specific companies in its campaigns. One outcome of this intentionally Christian approach was that Tearfund's advocacy perhaps tended to steer clear of some of the more contentious topics that other organisations took on.

Joint campaigns and coalitions

Since policy changes tend to happen when many organisations lobby and campaign together, Tearfund was soon faced with the decision whether to join broad-based campaigns with other organisations. Some staff felt that this was not appropriate as Tearfund would lose its evangelical distinctiveness if it worked side by side with secular organisations and that some of its more conservative supporters might be put off if they saw Tearfund acting jointly with some of the more radical organisations that took part in these coalitions. Other staff, however, felt strongly that this was a necessary way of working if Tearfund was to join the mainstream and become a serious player, and that furthermore the experience of Jubilee 2000 had showed that it was possible for the organisation to work alongside secular NGOs and those of other faiths and not lose its Christian identity. The second view predominated and so Tearfund started to join these large coalitions.

When working with large coalitions each organisation would message its own members using their own language and frame, while the overall goal remained shared. For example, when campaigning about climate change Tearfund would speak to its supporters about 'creation care' and bring biblical examples to support the importance of looking after the environment. The Royal Society for the Protection of Birds might also be a part of the same coalition, but it would most likely speak to its supporters about the importance of environmental protection for birdlife. And in this way each organisation would be able to maintain its different motivations and approaches while all coming together to push for the same policy change.

Tearfund was actually the first large development NGO to work on climate change as a development issue and paved the way for others to follow. It was a founding member of the Stop Climate Chaos Coalition (now called The Climate Coalition) and was also active in the Trade Justice Movement. In 2005 it was a founder member of the Make Poverty History (MPH) campaign, an extensive broad-based UK coalition formed to pressure the UK as G7 hosts that year, calling for changes in policy on trade, debt, and aid in order to help the poor in developing countries. In all these coalitions Tearfund's key strengths remained its faith-inspired ability to mobilise large numbers of campaigners and its ability to mobilise supporters across the political spectrum.

Conclusion

This chapter has described the evolution of Tearfund's campaigning and advocacy work in the late 1990s and early 2000s, and the tensions and dilemmas that surrounded the decision to start this work. This work also set in motion a new set of tensions within the organisation – between working at the global level or at the local level, between focussing on justice or on charity, and between working to change the system or to alleviate immediate suffering. To a large extent this tension is evident in many secular NGOs as well, but in Tearfund it was exacerbated by the evangelical tendency to focus on the individual, which made it somewhat harder to integrate structural and systemic elements into their thinking. And of course, the fact that it was difficult to think of ways in which evangelism could be combined with advocacy work meant that some people in the organisation continued to think that advocacy was not central to an evangelical way of working and should not take up too many resources that could be better spent on small-scale community development work with its greater potential to transform individual lives.

However, despite all the dilemmas and debates, looking across the work of all the departments, it is clear that by 2005 Tearfund had grown enormously and had changed almost beyond recognition from the organisation that it was at the beginning of the 1990s. It had transformed from a small quasi-missionary organisation to a major relief and development NGO. Its annual income had increased from around £15 million to over £50 million, making it one of the larger relief and development agencies in the UK. It had professionalised and gained respect and recognition from secular relief and development actors. It had started its own operational teams in the field of humanitarian relief, increased the amount of institutional funding it received, and signed up to international codes of conduct. And it had developed a significant campaigning and advocacy capacity, and had taken part in several broad-based international campaigns.

However, these changes had brought in some secularising forces and had led to a counter-movement within the organisation as a growing number of staff had started to push back against the leadership. They had started to develop a new theology of poverty and development and had begun experimenting with specifically Christian forms of church-based development. Being a major relief and development NGO and also an evangelical organisation was proving to be rather difficult. Different members of staff had different ideas about what kind of work Tearfund should be doing and how faith should be embedded in its activities. Different parts of the organisation were pulling in quite different directions. There were many different views and a lot of tension and angst, and it was not clear which way to go and how to pull all these strands together to make a more coherent and impactful organisation. By 2005 both the CEO and the International Director had resigned. A new leadership and some major decisions were required.

Notes

1 Tearfund was not unaware of global issues during this time, but it did not feel confident that its constituency would support this type of involvement. During the 1970s progressive evangelicals in the US, such as Ron Sider and Jim Wallis, were developing their thinking about poverty and justice in the world order. They wrote in evangelical publications such as *Sojourners* and *The Other Side*, in which they critiqued capitalism for allowing powerful elites to oppress the poor and spoke out against unfair trade rules, debt, and other such issues (Gasaway 2014: 212). Ron Sider's book, *Rich Christians in an Age of Hunger* (1978), became an iconic book for progressive evangelicals and was read by Tearfund staff and enthusiastically reviewed in *Tear Times*.

2 *Footsteps* is Tearfund's flagship publication and it still runs today. It was started in 1987 as *Footsteps to Health* and then in 1989 it changed its name to *Footsteps* and widened out to focus on a much broader range of topics. It is produced several times per year and sent out to partners and other interested individuals. Editions are produced in English, French, Spanish, and Portuguese, and a reader survey in the early 2000s suggested that *Footsteps* was read by some 45,000 people in 170 countries (Rhodes 2002). It was edited for many years by Isabel Carter, who herself had been a Tearfund OP in a remote part of Western Kenya during the mid-1980s, and thus had first-hand practical experience of how important this kind of publication was for both community development workers in the field and also for farmers themselves.
3 The idea had also independently been suggested by the All African Council of Churches, who in 1990 had issued a call for a jubilee year to cancel Africa's debts (Friesen 2012: 51).

Part III
Becoming an FBO

7 Trying to institutionalise faith-based development, 2005–2015

Introduction – new era, new approach

By 2005 there were major differences of opinion regarding what type of organisation Tearfund should be and what type of work it should be doing. At the centre of the debates was a critical discussion about how it should integrate faith into its development practice. The 'mainstreamers' thought that Tearfund should become a more professional organisation meeting the needs of poor people in the most efficient way possible, while the 'transformationalists' believed that Tearfund should lead with its Christian distinctiveness and work through the local church with the aim of bringing about a deeper, holistic faith-centred type of transformation. The choice of direction had implications for all areas of Tearfund's work – should development projects emphasise highly expert and technical input or should they be community led and based around the church? Should Tearfund be funding theological training of church leaders? Should humanitarian work be carried out by operational teams or only through local Christian partners? Should Tearfund prioritise global advocacy campaigns in partnership with secular organisations or should it focus on equipping local churches to carry out local-level advocacy?

The first scenario would have Tearfund draw on its Christian faith as the motivation for its work and retain its Christian culture of prayer and devotion, but would accept that its overseas relief and development work would be carried out in much the same way as secular development agencies. The second scenario would embed Christianity much more deeply in the organisation's overseas work and enable it to carry out relief and development activities *themselves* in a distinctly faith-based manner, combining evangelism and development into one integrated activity, drawing on beneficiaries' own faith to motivate them to change their behaviours, and using the power of the gospel to transform lives. Different parts of Tearfund were heading in different directions and tensions were running high. It became crucial to make high-level decisions about Tearfund's identity, purpose, and mode of working. In 2006 Matthew Frost came in as CEO and carried out a major strategic review in order to answer these questions. This was a major inflexion point in the history of Tearfund.

By this time there had been some significant changes in wider society, including what has been called a 'global resurgence of religion' (Falk 2003, Scott

2005). Religion seemed to be making a comeback and was gaining increasing prominence in the public sphere. Scholars were starting to talk about 'post-secular society' and the 'de-privatisation of religion' (Casanova 1994, Habermas 2008). This turn to religion was also influencing the relief and development field. During the 1990s there had been a rapid increase in the number of religiously inspired relief and development NGOs, the vast majority of them evangelical, and their presence and activities were getting noticed. In 1996 a new Welfare Reform Act had been passed in the US, which had enabled faith-based organisations to apply for federal funding for welfare projects, and in 2001 the Faith Based and Community Initiatives Act further enabled faith-based organisations also to apply for funding for overseas relief and development work (Clarke 2007: 82, Deacon and Tomalin 2015: 74). These initiatives led to funding to American FBOs almost doubling in the early 2000s, from 10.5 per cent of aid in 2001 to 19.9 per cent in 2005, with much of this increase going to evangelical Christian organisations (Occhipinti 2015: 332).

This turn towards religion was not only confined to the USA. Governments in the UK, Switzerland, the Netherlands, Denmark, and Sweden, as well as the World Bank, had also become interested in faith-based organisations. This was partly motivated by the World Bank's *Voices of the Poor* study, conducted in 1999, which had highlighted that many people in poor communities around the world were identified with a faith tradition and that religious institutions often played important roles in local rural communities, and the subsequent series of discussions and conferences about the possible role of religion in development initiated by then President of the World Bank, James Wolfensohn. The 9/11 attack on the World Trade Center in New York and the ensuing 'war on terror' had also led to various governments proactively engaging with religion in their development strategies. Thus for a variety of reasons many governments had started to channel more funding to faith-based organisations for both domestic and international projects (Marshall 2001, Jones and Petersen 2011, Clarke, 2013, Haustein and Tomalin 2017).

By the early 2000s the term 'faith-based organisation', along with the acronym 'FBO', had emerged and become widely used in relief and development circles, and by the mid-2000s FBOs had become recognised as significant players in the relief and development sectors (Ferris 2011). It has been estimated that at this time around 30 per cent of the $8.5 billion per year that was given to development NGOs worldwide was channelled through explicitly Christian NGOs, both Catholic and Protestant (Ferris 2005: 312, Ferris 2011: 611–12).

Their confidence buoyed by this turn of events, many FBOs had started to claim that they actually offered specific advantages, compared with secular relief and development NGOs. Most of these claims centred on their access to networks of religious institutions embedded in local communities and their purported ability to engage with beneficiaries more deeply because of their shared religious beliefs (Olivier 2016). At this time many in the development world were looking for new ideas and alternatives to the harsh economic approaches of IMF Structural Adjustment Programs, and there was an openness to more holistic approaches. Thus donors began to be interested in engaging with FBOs as specifically religious actors, which were seen to offer different benefits from secular NGOs (Deacon and Tomalin 2015).

This change in external context clearly influenced Frost's decision regarding which direction to take Tearfund. He decided to foreground Tearfund's Christian nature and to orient its work in this direction. He decided that Tearfund should not simply be 'Christians doing development', but should 'do Christian development'. The decision to focus on the Christian, faith-based nature of Tearfund's work had major implications for all of its work in the areas of development, humanitarian relief, and advocacy. It was decided to put the local church explicitly at the centre of Tearfund's work and a new unified high-level vision for the coming ten years was created in which Tearfund would seek to support a worldwide network of 100,000 local churches to 'release 50 million people from material and spiritual poverty' (Tearfund 2006).

Whereas people had been talking about the local church before, it could actually mean different things to different people, as discussed in Chapter 5 – a large denomination, a village church, or even Christian NGOs. In the 2006 strategy review Tearfund defined 'church' as 'a community that is Christ-centred, loving, accessible to the poor and sustainable'. In this definition it was clear that a Christian NGO or the development wing of a denomination was not a church – as they were not accessible to the poor – and that instead a church was a community-level group of people, organised and acting in a certain way. It is what I have called the local 'village church', and from 2006 onwards the new strategy was to embed development, humanitarian, and advocacy approaches centred on the local village church throughout as much of Tearfund's work as possible. Tearfund's new emphasis on the local village church fit in nicely with discussions in the wider development sector about the need to work more closely with local actors and institutions. As Matthew Frost recalls:

> At that time every organisation in development that I knew was dealing with the issue of how you create and sustain change at the local level. How do you get local level ownership of an agenda to tackle poverty and injustice and how do you create local ownership to create sustainability so that the momentum for tackling poverty and injustice at the local level is sustained and a momentum is built? Of course, what you need is some kind of local level organisation that has the kind of values that are passionate about tackling poverty and tackling injustice – all that is of course the local church.*

Frost's new strategy marked the beginning of an important shift in Tearfund's work and its identity – having just transformed itself from quasi-missionary agency into major relief and development NGO, it was now going to morph again into an evangelical FBDO, which carried out relief and development in a distinctive faith-based way.

In order to try to achieve its new vision Tearfund clarified four areas of work: community development, disaster response, policy change, and 'church

116 *Becoming an FBO*

envisioning'. Since the church was the centrepiece of this vision, a necessary element of Tearfund's work would become 'envisioning' the church. This would essentially be a theological debate, encouraging the church to see mission as broad and integral and not just focussing on evangelism and spiritual matters. The idea was that, once churches were convinced, Tearfund would then give them practical advice and support so that they could begin to transform their communities as they outworked integral mission in their local context. Tearfund and its partners would thus serve churches, resource them, equip them, provide them with technical assistance, and help them to mobilise themselves at a local level. The aim was that churches would then carry out development projects with the community, respond to disasters, and engage in local- and national-level advocacy. For many this was an uplifting call.

> The vision is of an army of ordinary people; grassroots members in their millions, equipped and empowered to bring local transformation to their streets and workplaces. The world can be redeemed by small local action in every neighbourhood of the planet. The powerless, who sit at the back of our congregations by their millions, are our capacity for this dream to come true. If we can envision and empower the 99% in our members who we have taught to be passive consumers of privatised religion, the church will become the most powerful agent for transformation the world has ever seen.
> (Iszatt 2003: 1)

Over the next ten years Tearfund worked to fine-tune its overarching vision and theology, while the practical teams set to work shifting their respective departments to line up with this new vision. Across the development, humanitarian, and advocacy teams, staff tried to shift their work to centre on the local village church. This chapter will outline the ways that the different departments changed their work and the extent to which they succeeded in shifting to a faith-based, church-centred approach. Even while Frost had decided to foreground the faith-based approach, he still intended for Tearfund to stay part of the mainstream, to continue to grow and receive institutional funding, and to continue being signed up to international codes and standards. At this point in time this seemed more possible than it had ten years earlier, since now the mainstream was actively interested in FBDOs and apparently open to alternative, faith-based ways of working. However, as this chapter will show, things were not that straightforward and many of the tensions discussed in the previous three chapters remained.

Shifting to church-centred approaches

Refining and codifying CCM

The first two church-based approaches – CCM and the behaviour change work with faith leaders around HIV and sexual and gender-based violence – had emerged out of the development side of the organisation and much emphasis was now put on further refining these methodologies, codifying them, and trying to spread them out of Africa and into other parts of the world.

A whole suite of church-based development methodologies was developed and refined during this period. Along with CCM other methodologies included church mobilisation (CM), in which the local church identifies and responds to needs around it without the local community getting involved; church involvement (CI), in which a Christian NGO carries out the intervention but seeks to involve the local church in the process; envisioning for integral mission (EIM), in which Tearfund runs workshops, organises learning visits, or holds national conversations in order to help develop or strengthen an organisation's or church denomination's vision for integral mission; and establishing sustainable Christian communities (ESCC), for cases where there is no local church but the possibility of establishing one exists. A partner survey in 2006 suggested that around 30 per cent of Tearfund-supported development projects used one or other of these approaches. In 2008 Tearfund set a target to increase this to 67 per cent by 2014 and started to work together with the Micah Network to spread the CCM approach globally (Tearfund 2009: 3). While precise numbers are not available, there was certainly a very significant increase in CCM-type projects during this period.

CCM work was spreading rapidly in Africa and the early CCM projects in Kenya, Tanzania, and Uganda seemed to be progressing well. For many participants the CCM Bible studies brought about a major shift in attitude and in behaviour. In many respects it was rather like group coaching sessions in which individuals were encouraged to see their self-worth and their agency in their lives, and also to look at the environment around them with new eyes, seeing possibilities rather than problems. And since most of these communities were Christian, going through this process in a faith-based way and in the context of a church was profoundly meaningful for them. Often just the Bible studies used at the very beginning of the CCM process would lead to individuals changing their behaviour – planting more crops in their fields, starting to engage in petty trading, and improving their relationships with their families and neighbours. And very often they would start attending church more often. Sometimes new people would decide to join the church so that in many cases church membership began to grow.

Very often church members would start to tithe, or with their increased wealth would increase the amount that they gave to the church. In many cases the first project that a congregation would carry out would be to build a new church building (e.g. Tearfund 2015b: 24, 54, Tearfund 2015c: 16, Kenya field visit 2018). They would move out of their small church built of mud and construct a much bigger church with brick walls, concrete floors, and glass windows. Their increased tithes would further support the pastor and be channelled upwards in the denomination's hierarchy. Changes such as these helped local churches to grow and helped CCM to be viewed positively within several denominations. In many cases community projects with a more developmental focus would also be initiated, leading to new schools, clinics, irrigation systems, and so on.

Case study: church and community mobilisation in Kenya

Tearfund had been supporting the Anglican Development Services of Mount Kenya East (ADS-MKE), the development department of the diocese, for many years on a variety of conventional development projects. In 2002 Tearfund asked them to try out its newly developing CCM methodology. ADS-MKE initially chose seven churches to pilot the new approach. Like most of the rural Anglican churches in the country, these were small churches, often built of mud and straw, with a congregation of around 40–50 people. Most were located in communities with several churches of other denominations – including Roman Catholic, Methodist, Lutheran, and Pentecostal – as well as some people following the practices of the local traditional culture.

Over the next two years groups of 20–30 people in each of these seven church congregations met regularly to work through special Bible studies looking at God's purpose for Christians, considering how all people are valuable and should have agency in their lives, and looking at examples of biblical stories where God provided people with all the resources that they needed, and then encouraging church members to look creatively at their environment and see what resources they had that they had not 'seen' before.

The results were often extremely transformative. Just from working through the Bible studies church members began to see themselves differently and to act differently. Some people started planting more crops on land they hadn't utilised before, others started practices to increase their productivity per hectare, and yet others started to engage in petty trading. Many women became more self-confident, and previously shy people stepped up to take on roles within the church. People felt that the church was really helping them to improve their lives and as a result many started to attend church more often and many started to tithe to the church. Quite early most congregations decided that they should work together to build a new, more impressive church building, and they made extra donations to start construction work.

After the first two years members of these church congregations, now envisioned and inspired, organised meetings with the broader community and discussed with them their shared problems, their available resources, and how they might work together to improve things. These meetings were generally successful and six out of the seven communities started to plan and carry out community development projects – they built schools and dispensaries, they raised money to set up irrigation infrastructure for their agricultural fields, they created a community dairy cooperative, they set up dairy goat groups, and they established new market places.

The energy and determination of these communities was impressive as they worked together to try to improve their lives, rather than passively wait for others to help them. Nonetheless, many of these projects faced several problems. Setting up irrigation systems required lots of money. Not everyone could afford to contribute and those people that did not pay did not receive water to their fields. In one case the group worked with the local administrative offices to get a foreign contractor to pump water from a local source, lay pipes, and build a professional irrigation system. Community members paid the first instalment of their share of the cost but later defaulted on the subsequent payments, meaning that several of them are now in debt to the irrigation office. Those communities that had set up dispensaries had expected to be able to run them themselves as profit-making businesses and were then frustrated when they learnt that they had to be run by the government. Some of the dispensaries were handed over to the government and continue to work, while others closed down. Some communities that managed to increase their production of cash crops then found that there was no market and failed to sell them.

Nonetheless, in 2011 ADS-MKE and Tearfund wondered if it would be possible to scale this work up. They started to train vicars and archdeacons to facilitate CCM in their churches and parishes, and this way they spread CCM to a further 58 churches. However, while the Bible studies continued to be very successful and well received, the majority of this generation of CCM churches failed to mobilise the wider community. They called community meetings, but hardly anyone came. The reasons for this are not clear. However, some 48 out of these 58 churches failed to mobilise the community and thus failed to set up projects. Many people in the congregations who were envisioned by the Bible studies felt more empowered and changed their own practices and improved their livelihoods. Most congregations started to tithe and to build new church buildings. But the impact beyond the church was negligible.

However, in 2016 the Anglican Church of Kenya decided that it would take on ownership of CCM itself. Even without funding from Tearfund it would work to spread CCM around its churches. Julius Njogu, who leads the CCM work at ADS-MKE, explains why:

> Churches that have done CCM are different to other churches. Once they understand integral mission the giving in the churches increases, the numbers increase, the buildings improve. The diocese sees CCM as an excellent tool for mission, that's why they embrace it.

Spreading CCM to other continents and contexts

In order to help CCM to spread to other regions Tearfund staff created a manual setting out the process in a step-by-step manner, with Bible studies and group exercises. Taking its name from the Swahili word for 'togetherness', the *Umoja Manual* was published in 2009. In the following years the *Umoja Manual* was translated into about 20 languages by Tearfund partners as they adapted it for use in their countries. In this way CCM work spread from Africa into Asia (particularly to Nepal, Bangladesh, Cambodia, Myanmar, and India) and into Latin America and the Caribbean (particularly to Bolivia, Brazil, Peru, and Haiti). By 2014 CCM was taking place in 41 countries – 21 in Africa, ten in Latin America and the Caribbean, and ten in Asia and the Middle East (Bulmer *et al.* 2014: 3).

CCM had been developed in Africa in Christian majority communities. How would it work in the different contexts of Asia and Latin America? And how would it work in different religious contexts, where Christians were minorities or where there were sharp divisions between the Protestant and Catholic churches? How could Tearfund do CCM when there were no local churches?

CCM spread fairly easily among certain churches in Latin America. In fact, when Tearfund partners started to approach churches with the *Umoja Manual* to discuss CCM they quite often found that the churches were already doing something rather similar on their own initiative. This may have been the result of some of the earlier work carried out by René Padilla, who had been speaking at conferences and producing publications to spread the idea of 'misión integral' in Latin America since the 1970s and who had taken the original *Church Community Change* toolkit produced in the mid-1990s for Tearfund's work in the UK (see Chapter 5), translated it into Spanish, and distributed it around many churches in Argentina. Due to this pre-existing theological foundation it was easy for several of the churches to adopt and adapt the CCM methodology to their own needs.

CCM proved more challenging in Asia, however, where in many countries the majority of the population are Hindu or Muslim, and Christians are only a tiny minority. In many cases governments in these countries are resistant to international NGOs working with local churches and promoting evangelism, and they can refuse registration and permits if they find such work being carried out. Even in countries where governments are more open to NGOs working with churches, it is often the case that Christian communities are very small and very new and often somewhat marginalised by surrounding communities of other faiths. In these situations it can be very difficult for such churches to take a leading role in mobilising communities for joint activities. In other cases the pastors are so new and with so little theological training that they find it difficult to lead the Bible studies confidently. In yet other cases these new Christians feel that they should just focus on verbal evangelism and should help each other rather than seeking to help the broader community. And it must also be remembered that in very many poor communities across Asia there are no Christians and there is no local church. In such situations it is obviously not possible to use the CCM approach. So while there are examples of CCM working well in Asia and cases where it has actually helped to build bridges between Christians and those of other faiths, it faces more challenges and issues in this region than in any other.

Case study: CCM in a Hindu context

Tearfund started supporting projects in this country in the 1970s and since then it has worked with many Christian development NGOs, churches, and mission agencies in a wide range of community development work. This country is one of the poorest countries in Asia and there is widespread unemployment, low agricultural productivity, high levels of migration, and endemic corruption. The majority of the population are Hindus and the caste system is strong in many areas, often rendering low-caste groups and tribal populations marginalised and disenfranchised. Christians are only a tiny minority and there are restrictions on religious freedom and on the activities of Christian organisations. Local Christians sometimes face discrimination, disinheritance, and social exclusion. Because of the 'sensitivities' of this situation this case study will not reference the name of the country or mention the names of the partners or the specific locations of the projects discussed.

In recent years Tearfund has started to support its partners to use the CCM methodology in their community development work. In a country with few churches, this has posed particular challenges. To date four partners have envisioned about 100 local village churches around the country through the CCM process. Since most churches in this country typically focus only on evangelising, the first task has been to convince them that they should get involved in community development. The CCM process leads them through Bible studies to show them that they should be 'salt and light' to the world. It then looks at changes that can be made in their families, then in their churches, and finally in their communities.

Many of the churches have made progress in mobilising the congregation through these Bible studies, but fewer have been able to involve the wider community. Being a small minority in most communities, church congregations have often been rather isolated from their surrounding communities and many have thus not felt confident to try to initiate community activities. Nonetheless, a number of small-scale development projects have been carried out, sometimes by the church and sometimes by the church and the community together. Examples include provision of drinking water and of irrigation water; construction of latrines, bridges, and walking paths; provision of health, literacy, and numeracy education; and establishment of savings and credit groups.

However, CCM has also had some challenges. In particular it can only be used in communities where there actually is an existing local church. In a predominantly Hindu country this severely limits the communities in which Tearfund's partners can work using the CCM methodology. Furthermore, while Tearfund staff report that in some cases CCM has led to improved relations between the church and the wider community, in other cases there have been tensions when the community has pushed back, fearing that the church is trying to convert them.

Some Tearfund partners had been working for several years on the issue of anti-child trafficking, and with the introduction of the CCM methodology they decided to change their approach and try to integrate this work into a broader CCM programme. In the old approach the Tearfund partner organisation worked to raise awareness with the families and girls who were at risk of being trafficked. They organised women's groups, youth groups, and school clubs in order to tell people about the horrors of child trafficking and how they could keep their daughters safe. They also mobilised and strengthened the capacity of local government officials to combat against human trafficking and tackle child protection issues.

In the new approach they sought to base their work around local churches and have them raise awareness in the wider community through their CCM activities. This led to a number of challenges. In one case the partner chose to work in an area where there was very little incidence of child trafficking because there was a church there. In some cases interventions focussed on people who lived close to the local church and thus did not target the most marginalised and needy. And in the context of Christians being a religious minority with sometimes strained relations with the wider community, there were some cases in which pastors were afraid of confronting abuse in the community for fear that the community might turn against them.

Thus it seems that using CCM and working in a faith-based way in a largely non-Christian context is extremely difficult for Tearfund and its partners. There are specific challenges with designing and implementing appropriate and effective interventions through the local church when the local church is not present in many communities, and where Christians are often discriminated against and socially excluded.

Spreading CCM to other Christian FBOs

As well as spreading CCM around its network of partners Tearfund also decided to try to spread the approach more widely in the burgeoning Christian relief and development sector. It thus made the methodology open to any other organisation that was interested in using it. It sought to spread it to evangelical relief and development agencies in the Micah Network. And in order to try to spread it more widely, in 2011 Tearfund and the Council of Anglican Provinces in Africa (CAPA) organised a meeting in Kenya for interested organisations to go and see CCM in action. Richard Lister, Tearfund's Global Church and Development Lead, recalls:

> We gathered a whole series of Anglican Bishops, development workers and a few Archbishops along with people from Mothers' Union, TEAR Netherlands and the Anglican Alliance. We showed them CCM in the field and explained it to them in a workshop context. And, critically, we prayed. We soaked that meeting in prayer. People went away very inspired and there was a huge uptake after that.

In 2012 Tearfund set up the 'Friends of Umoja' network to strengthen and spread the CCM methodology by organising regular meetings for organisations to share their experiences of implementing CCM and to learn from each other. Members include a wide variety of development NGOs and missionary agencies from across the Protestant relief and development sector, including liberal, mainline organisations such as the Anglican Alliance, Mothers' Union, Christian Aid, and the United Society for the Propagation of the Gospel (USPG), alongside Tearfund's more usual evangelical interlocutors, such as Samaritan's Purse UK and TEAR Netherlands. This has helped CCM to spread widely in the Protestant relief and development sector and has led to organisations from both the evangelical and liberal wings of the church coming together for the first time in many years. Despite widely diverging theologies, histories, and institutional structures, many of these organisations have started to implement CCM with their partner churches. In many respects CCM is no longer 'owned' by Tearfund, but has become a methodology used extremely widely by very many Protestant FBOs.

Thus by 2016 Tearfund partners had envisioned over 400 denominations and trained around 130,000 local village churches in CCM. Around 10,000 (approximately 8 per cent) of these local churches had started working in and with their communities. Beyond this several other Protestant NGOs and mission agencies had also started to use CCM with thousands more churches.

Working with the church on behaviour change

This strand of work built on Tearfund's earlier experience of starting to work with the church in Africa in the response to HIV and AIDS and massively expanded in this period. There had been a huge expansion of funds for HIV and AIDS programmes since 2002, with the creation of the Global Fund to Fight HIV-AIDS, Tuberculosis, and Malaria and the American Presidential Emergency Plan for AIDS Relief (PEPFAR), and in the early 2000s antiretroviral drugs had started to be rolled out in Africa. Many Christian organisations had stepped up their work on education, counselling, and care for AIDS patients and in AIDS treatment programmes (Burchardt 2009, Kalofonos 2008, Nguyen 2009, Olivier and Smith 2016, Prince 2009). By this time it was widely recognised that religion had an important role in framing people's understandings of the AIDS epidemic and in shaping their responses to it (Becker and Geissler 2009). There was a new-found interest in the role of faith in shaping health-related behaviour and this led to an 'open door opportunity' for those who believed that religion needed to be taken more seriously in development practice (Olivier 2016: 3). FBOs advocated strongly that they could bring a better and more effective response, and many government donors and some UN agencies, such as the United Nations Population Fund, became interested in supporting their work (Karam 2010, UNFPA 2008).

In this context Tearfund had placed a growing emphasis on HIV and AIDS and by 2005 25 per cent of all Tearfund-supported projects actively addressed HIV (Tearfund 2005a: 4). Later that year Tearfund made responding to HIV and AIDS one of its official corporate priorities and in 2006 it launched an ambitious ten-year plan to stop the spread of HIV and reverse the impact of AIDS in all of the communities where its partners were working. Substantial grants for HIV work were received from the World Bank and from the US and Irish governments, and over the next few years the proportion of Tearfund-supported projects addressing HIV and AIDS increased to 34 per cent (Tearfund 2007: 4).

In much of Tearfund's HIV work the core of its approach was to try to change the church – from being part of the problem to becoming part of the solution. Thus it started to develop a new church-based approach for this area of work. Based on the earlier work it seemed that working with faith leaders could make a significant difference in attitudinal and behaviour change. So in

2006 Tearfund started a pilot project with two local Christian NGOs – Vigilance (in Burkina Faso) and Christian AIDS Taskforce (in Zimbabwe) – to work with local churches to address HIV and AIDS. The projects took a 'whole life approach' discussing gender inequality and HIV in the wider context of relationships, life skills, and Christian life. The partners organised training sessions to discuss the issues with local church leaders so as to embed the training within the church structure and to ensure consistent messaging. They also carried out teaching in churches and ran camps for young people looking at life skills, making positive choices, and goal setting. Most importantly they ran workshops for couples in which people reflected together on biblical passages about marriage, gender, and women. They also addressed some of the Bible passages commonly used to justify gender inequality and dealt with these head on. They discussed gender roles within the local culture and the different social expectations of men and women. In this way they gently suggested that gender roles were negotiable and that there were biblical bases for gender equality. They also sought to develop more open forms of communication between husbands and wives, and discussed issues such as safe and healthy sex, relationship skills, and parenting skills.

These workshops opened up an unusual space for discussion about very sensitive issues, all carried out within the space of the local church. While not everyone agreed, and there were even theological differences with some of the partner organisations, many participants were called to stop and think about their behaviour and to consider making different choices. For Tearfund, it was clear that addressing peoples' fundamental beliefs was central to bringing about behaviour change. And furthermore, by supporting local churches to carry out this work for themselves, a greater degree of local ownership was achieved. Veena O'Sullivan, who led this initiative, explains how faith was central in this work:

> The biggest excitement for us was that when you worked with faith it became their thing.... Once they were convinced they would carry on.... Their attitudes changed, their minds opened up.... There was a huge change in the church. Obviously it varied from place to place, but overall there was a very significant change in the church's attitude towards HIV.

As Veena developed the work on HIV she began to realise that many HIV-positive women were the victims of rape. Seeing that this was a widespread issue she commissioned some initial research to understand the context and issues around sexual and gender-based violence (SGBV) in Africa. The researchers were shocked to learn how many women had experienced rape, both within and outside the family, and to discover how widespread the problem was. The research, published as *Silent No More* (Le Roux 2011), also showed that Christian women wanted the church to be a safe and compassionate place for them to go, but that most of the time church leaders did not want to get involved or were even implicated in the violence themselves.

Indeed, in many cases faith communities were again part of the problem. They were often strongly patriarchal and legitimised gender inequality through texts from the Bible and other sacred books. This situation had motivated several other Christian FBDOs to start working on the issue of sexual and gender-based violence at this time (Le Roux et al. 2016). So in the early 2010s Tearfund developed a new, specifically faith-based methodology to address sexual violence, which it called *Transforming Masculinities* (Deepan 2017).[1] This intervention sought to create meaningful spaces for reflection for both faith leaders and communities in which they could challenge cultural practices that promoted gender inequality and justified gender-based violence and instead promote positive ideas and images of masculinity. In this approach the first step is to raise awareness among local and national faith leaders about SGBV, and gender inequality more broadly, based on a discussion of biblical texts and to equip them to provide leadership and support for the *Transforming Masculinities* process. The next step is for these faith leaders to select key male and female members of their community to be trained as 'gender champions'. These gender champions then organise weekly 'community dialogues' using a scripture-based curriculum in which they lead discussions on issues such as gender roles in daily life, power, status, and sexual violence, and the role of faith in sexual violence. In these dialogues people would come together to reflect on how their religious beliefs and their culture shape their ideas and practices and to think about how things could be different. The first five community dialogues are conducted in single-sex groups while in the sixth one men and women come together to share their views and to collectively envisage a future free of sexual violence.

To date this work has mainly been carried out in majority Christian contexts but there are also some examples of this approach being used in mixed religious contexts. Prabu Deepan, who leads the Protection and Gender Unit, explains:

> The scriptures in the curriculum are primarily from the Bible, but in mixed faith communities we also have suggestions for similar Qur'anic verses that facilitators can suggest to the groups. In these situations the facilitators are advised to use inclusive language – they would talk about 'holy texts' instead of 'scripture', 'places of worship' instead of 'churches', and so on. When it's time to reflect on the texts they would say, 'This is what the Bible says, and we would like Islamic participants to share verses from the Qur'an or hadith that resonate with this message.' If no-one comes forward, then we say, 'This is what previous participants have shared with us, what do you think?' Then we read the texts and reflect together.

Thus by 2015 Tearfund had expanded its faith-based, church-centred work on HIV and AIDS and developed new faith-based approaches to working on sexual and gender-based violence, such as *Transforming Masculinities*. At this point most of this work still took place in Africa and in majority Christian communities.

Disaster management work with churches

On the humanitarian side of the organisation Tearfund also made efforts to develop new, church-based approaches. In 2008 it produced a publication called *Engaging with the Local Church in its Response to Disasters* (Tearfund 2008), which analysed the role of the local village church in disaster preparedness and response and identified eight distinctive roles or niche areas for church involvement – it could act as a facilitator of community action, a connector with the wider world, an advocate on behalf of the poor and marginalised, a community peacemaker, a provider of relational care and support, an influencer and shaper of values, a provider of resources, and an immediate responder to sudden-onset disasters.

Tearfund sought to get churches involved in disaster work beyond just its network of partners, and thus later that year it met with representatives from the Micah Network, Integral Alliance, and the World Evangelical Alliance to hold a 'Strategic Conversation on Disaster Management', in which they discussed ways to build the disaster management capacity of local churches and Christian communities more widely.

Case study: church-based disaster response in Colombia

In the early 2000s one of Tearfund's partners in Colombia, the Corporation for Social Community Development (CORSOC), started to work with a local evangelical church, 'Iglesia Cristo el Rey' (Church of Christ the King), to assist people displaced by the violent struggle that had been taking place in parts of the country between armed rebel groups and the government and that had left over 220,000 people dead and a further 7.2 million displaced. When some of the internally displaced persons (IDPs) flooded into the small town of Tierralta, in the north of the country, church members immediately responded, giving them support and meeting their basic needs. As one church member recalls:

> Some weren't Christians but we welcomed them all. We all gave whatever we could ... little by little ... it all came together.

As they realised the scale of the emergency, the church reached out to Tearfund's local partner, CORSOC, to help them to help the IDPs. With Tearfund's technical support and financial resources, CORSOC started to build the capacity of Iglesia Cristo el Rey in disaster response and longer-term rehabilitation projects. Initially, Tearfund/CORSOC provided the church with resources to help the displaced families rebuild their lives by securing new lands, building shelters and community kitchens, and starting new livelihood projects. Together, they turned wastelands into small community dwellings, with houses for each family, and built communal structures, including a church, a primary school, roads, and a water tank. The new community was named 'Nueva Esperanza' – 'New Hope' – as a symbol of a fresh beginning.

After the emergency phase, CORSOC used Tearfund's technical guides to encourage the church and the community to work together on development projects, through the CCM process. They started working on joint initiatives such as 'health brigades' and work to improve sanitation facilities. CORSOC also delivered advocacy training to educate the church and community on how to draw down government resources. Many of the former IDPs are now members of Iglesia Cristo el Rey and are helping other, more recently displaced, families.

The members of Iglesia Cristo el Rey developed a good knowledge of disaster response procedures and increased technical knowledge about building techniques, advocacy tools, and psychosocial support. They are now prepared to be a first responder in crisis situations. They have helped many more internally displaced persons through rehabilitation and community development projects. And in the process they have brought people to Christ, facilitated 'whole life transformation', and grown their congregation.

In order to help churches to start to engage practically Tearfund published a handbook for church leaders in 2011, which explained what they could do in the event of a disaster and beforehand – *Disasters and the Local Church: Guidelines for Church Leaders in Disaster Prone Areas* (Tearfund 2011). The handbook explained what disasters were and outlined practical ways that church leaders could be prepared, could help mitigate disasters, and if necessary, could respond. It explained how to set up disaster committees and volunteer teams, and how to conduct needs, risks, and capacity assessments. There are sections on floods, landslides, earthquakes, and various other kinds of natural disaster. Each section was backed up by Bible studies, giving a biblical basis for the church's involvement in this activity. This resource, known internally as 'Pastors in disasters', has proved extremely popular. It has been translated into ten languages and used by partner organisations and churches in some 20 countries around the world.[2]

An example of the type of activity that this resource brought about was the work of Tearfund's partner International Care Ministries (ICM) in the Philippines. ICM trained 28 church leaders and 128 volunteer pastors using the *Disasters and the Local Church* resource. These faith leaders then trained pastors in over 2,500 local churches, who then trained their communities in preparing for disasters and what to do if a disaster occurred. This led to many pastors developing disaster contingency plans for their communities, forming disaster committees, and preparing quick-run bags. ICM also worked to ensure that local churches would be plugged into the country's early warning system. Thus it helped 200 pastors connect with their regional Barangay Disaster Risk Reduction and Management Council, and it also set up a bespoke early warning system network between churches, known as the Pastor Information Network, through which over 500 pastors receive timely information about disasters by SMS.

Ebola response

A few years later Tearfund realised that there were some special situations where getting faith leaders involved in responding to a disaster could be particularly important. These are situations in which attitude and behaviour change are important elements of the disaster response. This became clearly apparent during the humanitarian response to the Ebola epidemic in Sierra Leone and Liberia in 2014–2016.

At the beginning of the outbreak there was widespread ignorance about Ebola. Local people did not know what it was and many believed that it did not even exist. In this context many of their behaviours unwittingly spread the disease. When humanitarian agencies first started to work, their initial response to the outbreak was blind to the cultural and religious beliefs and practices of the local people. Dead bodies were removed by anonymous relief workers wearing protective clothing that fully covered their faces, making them appear like aliens. It was not explained to people where the bodies were taken to or what would happen to them. Rumours developed that Ebola was being spread by these relief teams and that they were using it as an excuse to kidnap people for cannibalistic purposes (Featherstone 2015: 25). This of course led to people hiding their sick and not taking them for treatment, thus leading to the epidemic spreading and getting worse.

Tearfund and other religious NGOs realised that to curb Ebola it would be necessary to find a way to persuade people to change their behaviour – to take their relatives for treatment, to refrain from touching the sick, to bury the dead in safe ways, and so on – but that it would not be brought about by the approaches of the government or the mainstream international organisations. Instead a culturally appropriate discussion needed to take place in order to convince local people of the reality of Ebola and of the ways that they needed to change their behaviour in order to stop it spreading. The vast majority of people in these countries were either Christian or Muslim and therefore Tearfund and other religious NGOs started to work with their local partner organisations to engage local faith leaders to spread health messages to people in a way that they would understand and trust.

Thus through the Ebola work and through the *Pastors in Disasters* resource, Tearfund's humanitarian team have managed to shift some of their work to more faith-based and church-centred approaches.

Case study: working with faith leaders to respond to Ebola in Liberia

Tearfund supported Ebola response work in both the predominantly Muslim Sierra Leone and the predominantly Christian Liberia. In Liberia it worked with the Association of Evangelicals of Liberia (AEL), an inter-denominational fellowship of evangelical churches that had experience working on food security and water sanitation and hygiene, and EQUIP, a Christian NGO with experience working in relief, health, social welfare, and community development, both of whom Tearfund had partnered with since 1996. Since these partners were already present on the ground they were able to begin emergency work very quickly, using their own funding and initial funds from Tearfund before large-scale appeal funding started to come in.

During the emergency phase the partners' initial response focussed on trying to stop the spread of Ebola, supporting people's immediate needs, and reducing their immediate pain and suffering. Much of the work focussed on distributing hygiene kits with soap and disinfectant, and food, clothes, and housing support. However, AEL's and EQUIP's main interventions focussed on non-material matters, such as education and behaviour change, and providing trauma counselling and psychosocial support.

Since ignorance of the disease and deeply entrenched cultural practices, especially around care for the sick and burial of the dead, were enabling the disease to spread rapidly, AEL and EQUIP set about disseminating information about Ebola through a wide variety of channels – through radio programmes, video shows, village meetings, and house-to-house visits. At this point several churches were part of the problem – telling people that Ebola was God's punishment because people were not following his ways, and preaching messages of doom. Some were also inadvertently contributing to the spread of the virus by laying hands on people for healing. In the face of this, AEL and EQUIP trained around 200 religious leaders about the causes of Ebola and how it was spread and then encouraged them to pass this information on from their pulpits. They delivered the messages in a culturally appropriate way, emphasising a compassionate God and giving people hope, while also explaining what they needed to do. Coming in a respectful and understandable form these messages were much more likely to be heard and accepted, and this led to behaviours beginning to change.

The messages explained what Ebola was and how it was transmitted. They also sought to convince people that certain cultural practices had to change in order to reduce its transmission. Traditional greetings were no longer appropriate, and traditional burial ceremonies and mourning practices needed to stop in order to stop the virus from spreading. Changing attitudes and behaviours related to deep-seated cultural practices was not an easy task, especially when people believed that if they were not buried and mourned properly then they would go to hell. But when local faith leaders testified to their own behaviour change by no longer laying on hands when praying for the sick and by themselves adopting new kinds of burial practices that would not lead to the spread of the virus, people started to listen and to follow them in changing their own practices.

Once the disease had subsided and the main emergency phase was over, AEL and EQUIP started to help families and communities put their lives back together. They continued to train local faith leaders to provide counselling and psychosocial support, and they sought to work with communities to reduce the stigmatisation and marginalisation that was faced by many survivors. Pastors and Imams were trained to offer psychosocial support to people in need through door-to-door visits and over the phone, and they sought to reduce the stigma surrounding Ebola survivors during their sermons.

Later on, when many of the international humanitarian teams had left the country, AEL and EQUIP continued to work with affected communities, now seeking to promote resilience by improving access to water, supporting Ebola orphans, and restoring livelihoods. They carried out a range of activities including rehabilitating old wells and building new ones so that people would have access to safe drinking water; giving grants to families that had taken in orphans to pay for their school fees; distributing improved seeds to farmers so that they could increase their yield; giving small grants to people to restart their businesses; training people in soap making; and offering cash support to the most needy.

Advocacy work with churches

The advocacy team also set about trying to move some of its work to a more church-based approach and started to put more emphasis on supporting partners, and in particular churches, to carry out advocacy at local and national levels. In 2006 only about ten of Tearfund's overseas partners had a significant advocacy capacity, and most of these were Christian NGOs, such as Mopawi and Paz y Esperanza, rather than church denominations or local village churches. Thus during this period Tearfund sought to deepen this part of its advocacy work and began to place more emphasis on building up the advocacy capacity of its partners, and where possible, of the local church. By 2015 the number of partner organisations that were regularly carrying out quality advocacy work had increased to 125.

Tearfund staff helped partners to develop their advocacy capacity in a number of ways – they developed a number of educational and training resources, took them to international conferences and summits, supported local advocacy facilitators from some partner organisations to help other partner organisations, and funded full-time advocacy staff in a number of partners. Tearfund also learnt from the advocacy experience of some of its partners, particularly Paz y Esperanza, and helped to share this learning with other partners in the region and more widely.

In 2002 it had produced the *Advocacy Toolkit*, which was translated into many languages and widely used by partners and others over many years. As well as providing a step-by-step guide to understanding what advocacy is, when it might be useful, and how it can be done, the *Advocacy Toolkit* also developed a theology of advocacy. It looked at the biblical basis for advocacy and the reasons why Christians should do it. And it dealt head on with arguments that Christians should not get involved in politics or advocacy, by carefully reading and interpreting Bible passages. In this way it sought to convince more conservative evangelicals around the world, many of whom still felt cautious about engaging in politics in any way, that advocacy for justice was something that Christians should do.

In around nine countries churches have been supported to include local-level advocacy within the framework of CCM, leading to local churches seeking to hold local governments accountable and to draw down more locally available resources (Flowers 2016). In other cases local Christian NGOs have supported churches to start advocacy. For example, Christian Community Services of Mount Kenya East (CCSMKE), a local Christian NGO, helped several churches in the district of Kerugoya to lobby their MP for permission to repair a derelict government water system. When this failed CCSMKE helped them to get permission, and to access funding from the local authority, to build a new water system.

This work tends to be a 'localist' form of advocacy, focussing on small-scale local issues rather than system-changing matters of global concern. It thus cannot account for all of Tearfund's advocacy work, but during this period it began to expand in many of the countries where Tearfund's partners work.

Case study: human rights advocacy in Peru with Paz y Esperanza

Tearfund had been supporting the evangelical human rights NGO Paz y Esperanza (PyE) – 'Peace and Hope' – since the 1990s. The organisation had been set up in 1984 by the National Evangelical Church of Peru (CONEP) as a truth commission to promote peace and justice when the country was suffering the outbreak of internal armed conflict between government forces and rebel groups, such as the 'Shining Path'. During the conflict human rights abuses were committed by both the government and the rebels and an estimated 70,000 people were killed, while a further 1.5 million were displaced from their homes and thousands of innocent people were unfairly imprisoned to cover up for crimes committed by others.

Paz y Esperanza focussed on investigating war crimes and providing legal defence to those falsely imprisoned. It also worked with church leaders to educate communities about their human rights. PyE was run by a group of evangelical legal graduates who were passionate about combining their faith and vocation to bring justice, but who had very little experience or example to follow as it was the first evangelical human rights organisation in Latin America. This was a time when the language of human rights was very new, and for many Christians it was extremely controversial. For Tearfund itself the notion of human rights was rather contentious at this time, as was the notion that evangelical Christians should be politically engaged. These concerns were shared by many conservative Christians in Peru, who saw this work as risky and did not consider it the responsibility of the church to be involved in political matters.

Tearfund was PyE's first external funder and with their support PyE's work has grown considerably. They lobbied for the creation of a commission that reviewed the sentences of innocent prisoners and led to the release of more than 1,000 people who were falsely imprisoned. They also led an advocacy campaign for the creation of the Truth and Reconciliation Commission in 2001. This raised awareness across the country about the true causes of the violence and identity of the victims who had been falsely imprisoned and led to institutional reforms to prevent such conflict happening again.

Tearfund also played an important role in connecting the UK church with the work of PyE and raising awareness of the injustices in Peru. Over the years

Tearfund supporters have written letters to prisoners who were being defended by PyE, and to the UK embassy and Peruvian government calling for fair trials. Juan Mallea was one such prisoner who received thousands of letters from Tearfund supporters during his time in prison. Eventually, Mallea was acquitted and his case became so high profile that it set a precedent for other innocent prisoners being set free. Today he runs his own church.

In the late 1990s and early 2000s, when Tearfund was ready to engage more deeply with advocacy work and wanted to develop a more strategic and theologically grounded approach to it, the organisation worked closely together with PyE to learn from each other and to develop a set of theological principles that went on to form the basis of the first advocacy toolkits used by both organisations. This work laid out the biblical motivations for advocacy work, and portrayed a Christian way of doing it. The role of faith in PyE's work is subtle and much of its work is the same as that which would be carried out by a secular organisation. Its staff pray before taking on new defence cases and seek to conduct themselves in a peaceful way in order to rebuild relationships. For the most part, however, faith acts as a motivator for their work and they do not use any specifically faith-based methodology.

Campaigning with the local church

The campaigning team also sought to focus more of its work around the local church. While UK campaigning had always been very faith based and centred around local churches, during this period Tearfund took its first steps towards mobilising churches around the world to campaign, through its initiation of and involvement with the Micah Challenge campaign.

During this period Tearfund developed its thinking about how campaigning could be a deeply religious activity and experienced as an outworking of people's faith. Most basically, demonstrations were always preceded by a church service and often there would be a workshop in a local church afterwards. More deeply, Tearfund sought to develop a distinctive focus on 'lifestyle', encouraging people to understand how their high-consumption lifestyle in the global North was fuelling climate change, natural disasters, and poverty in the South. Speaking in 2006, David Westlake explained:

> I think the challenge before us now is this personal lifestyle discipleship issue. It is not enough to campaign against global injustice if our lifestyles are actually contributing to injustice on a personal level and it is not enough to support Kyoto if we are driving cars or having lifestyles that pollute and contribute to global warming and those will be hard messages to say and I think Tearfund needs to say them because we have had a blind spot about what the Bible teaches about creation and stewardship and we need to expose that and also because it is the poor that suffer and it will be the poor that pay the price for our lifestyles.*

Lifestyle changes often helped activists to really feel the change they were making on a deep experiential level and they also sent a clear signal to politicians that people were willing to accept changes to their lifestyle for the sake of the global good. Tearfund encouraged its supporters to make sacrifices for the general good as it framed this as a kind of religious activity. For several years, for example, Tearfund organised a 'Carbon Fast' during Lent in which supporters were offered biblical reflections, lifestyle guides, and simple actions to reduce their carbon usage – turning the heating down, switching to clean energy providers, walking rather than taking the car, and so on.

Tearfund spoke about campaigns at churches and at Christian festivals and in this way, using existing church networks and emphasising the faith perspective, was sometimes able to mobilise tens of thousands of campaigners. This was often its largest contribution to joint campaigns and coalitions. While other NGOs might lead on the policy and lobbying side of things, Tearfund came to be known and respected for its ability to inspire and mobilise thousands of people. Ben Niblett, then Head of the Campaigns Team, reflects:

> In Tearfund you can go to supporters through the churches. You've got the structure there, and the community. The community is really important. Having worked for organisations that didn't have that, I now see how valuable that is. Because there's a bunch of people who know each other, who meet regularly, who are committed to each other.... And that's a really powerful thing.

At this time Tearfund also started to move towards a bigger vision – to mobilise evangelicals around the world to engage in advocacy, beyond just Tearfund partners. To this end Tearfund was instrumental in the establishment of Micah Challenge, a global evangelical campaign in support of the Millennium Development Goals (MDGs), run by the WEA and Micah Network.

The campaign ran from 2004 to 2015, with national campaigns in 41 countries across the North and South and three global campaign moments in which everyone participated together (Edwards 2008, Winter and Woodhead 2014). A key part of the work of the campaign was to convince evangelical churches around the world that advocacy and campaigning for justice were deeply biblical and deeply religious, and it sought to mobilise local churches and local Christians to carry out advocacy and campaigning as part of their religious practice. As well as playing a key role in initiating the campaign, Tearfund supported it in a number of ways – it was its largest funder, it hosted the International Secretariat in its offices for several years, several of its staff served on the Board, and many of its partners supported and participated in the national campaigns. While the Micah Challenge was only partially successful, it played an important role in opening up a conversation with evangelical churches worldwide about whether they should be involved in political advocacy for the poor. Although many evangelical churches in the UK had become convinced of the biblical acceptability of advocacy during the Jubilee 2000 campaign, and in part because of the educational work of Tearfund, evangelical churches in many other countries remained cautious and sceptical about political involvement. The Micah Challenge campaign sought to convince them of the biblical basis of advocacy for the poor and to convert them to a justice-oriented form of evangelicalism (Freeman, in press).

Thus in all these ways Tearfund took very significant steps towards implementing its vision of working with the local church and carrying out a specifically Christian, faith-based, and church-centred form of development. However, the list of activities discussed above is actually rather short, and all of this work only constituted a tiny proportion of the relief, development, and advocacy work that Tearfund carried out during this period – a bit more on the development side of things, rather less on the humanitarian and advocacy sides. By far the majority of its work continued in much the same way as it had before – mainstream work, carried out by professional NGO partners, and in a manner much the same as the secular NGOs.

Mainstream work

In what follows I will give only a cursory overview of some of this more predominant mainstream work simply to give a sense of some of the issues that Tearfund worked on during this time. The main point is that, despite the increased rhetoric about faith-based development and working with the local church, the vast majority of Tearfund's work continued in a mainstream, secular manner.

On the development side of the organisation Tearfund staff found that many interventions required technical expertise that was simply not available in local churches and/or large-scale government funding that could not be used for work that included evangelism. Thus during this period it continued to support its network of professional Christian NGO partners to implement a wide range of projects. It developed significant technical expertise in five key areas – food security, livelihoods, water and sanitation, resilience, and HIV and AIDS – and this part of its work expanded considerably. Despite attempts to shift projects over to the new church-based approach, in very many cases this was just not possible. Some projects simply did not seem to have a faith-based component to them. Digging a well was digging a well. In the context of the new emphasis on faith-based approaches, this was a cause of some angst for several people in the team. Mike Wiggins, who heads the Technical Support team, explains:

> My team has really struggled with the question of what makes our work different from that of secular organisations. Sometimes it seems that others think that digging a well doesn't count because it isn't some holy activity, it isn't faith-based.

On the humanitarian side of the organisation these dynamics were even more pronounced. Tearfund continued to respond to disasters with its operational teams and through its partners. Tearfund operational teams were on the ground in a number of countries, including South Sudan, the Democratic Republic of the Congo, the Central African Republic, and Iraq. They responded to the Kashmir earthquake in Pakistan and the drought in Northern Kenya. Partners responded to a wide range of disasters including the Nepal earthquake, the Philippines cyclone, and the Haiti earthquake, among many others. They distributed food, built shelters, provided water and sanitation facilities, and so on.

While this work was often technically excellent, there was very little, if anything, that was distinctively faith based about it. Again, this was a cause for much concern and much debate in these years. While Tearfund could put its work in a biblical frame and foreground its Christian values with staff, it essentially carried out much the same actions on the ground as secular agencies.[3] According to Peter Grant, International Director from 2005 to 2010:

> We were accessing a lot of institutional funding for this work and doing the humanitarian work on the basis of need, so I think it is a slightly different kind of Christian witness. The holistic vision that was coming out of the strategy review – the gospel and social engagement – wouldn't really apply on the humanitarian side. It would be very much following international codes of conduct and doing things according to need, but from a Christian perspective.

For the most part, international standards and global norms continued to guide Tearfund's humanitarian work, and this meant that humanitarian relief and evangelism often had to be separated and kept clearly distinct. In fact, during this period the number of international standards grew phenomenally and as a significant actor in the field Tearfund signed up to most of them. So alongside the SPHERE Guidelines and the Red Cross Code of Conduct, it also signed up to the HAP Standard in Humanitarian Accountability and Quality Management, the Humanitarian Charter and Minimum Standards in Disaster Response, the People in Aid Code of Good Practice in the Management and Support of Aid Personnel, the Code of Good Practice for NGOs Responding to HIV, the Keeping Children Safe Coalition standards, and the UN Statement of Commitment on Eliminating Sexual Exploitation and Abuse by UN and non-UN Personnel, among others. Implementing all these standards and ensuring compliance by field staff began to become a serious issue.

In order to streamline this process in 2009 Tearfund made a synthesis of all the international standards that it had signed up to and created its own internal 'Quality Standards'. These Quality Standards were initially rolled out in the humanitarian section of Tearfund, and then a few years later they were mainstreamed throughout the whole organisation, and also sent to all its partners. In this way a whole set of external, secular standards came to be incorporated into all of Tearfund's work and into that of the churches and Christian organisations that were its Southern partners, in this way subjectifying a wide range of religious actors to (secular) global norms. Moreover, Tearfund also worked with

Integral Alliance to develop 'Integral Standards', very much based on Tearfund's Quality Standards, and thus further spread these international humanitarian standards throughout much of the evangelical relief sector. Even though most of the codes sought to keep religion and humanitarian work firmly separate and put limitations on certain types of evangelism, there were very few people in Tearfund in the 2010s who were resistant to them. At this point in time, in contrast to the late 1990s, there was a broad consensus that Tearfund should adopt and incorporate best practice standards. Even when the Board reviewed the risk register and discussed the risk of Tearfund secularising, it did not object to the development and roll out of the Quality Standards.

Case study: Tearfund's humanitarian response in Iraq

In 2014, when Islamic State (IS) had captured significant portions of Iraqi territory, triggering mass displacement, extreme violence, and severe humanitarian needs, Tearfund decided to respond, even though it was a country in which it was not working at the time. There were only a very small number of local churches – Orthodox and evangelical – and they did not have the capacity to carry out a large-scale humanitarian response, and so Tearfund decided that it would work through its own Operational Teams.

Tearfund initially collaborated with two other evangelical organisations – MedAir and Mission East – who were also part of Integral Alliance. They carried out their scoping work together and shared assets and assessments. Then each organisation set up its own separate project. Tearfund set up an office in Erbil, in the Kurdish region of Northern Iraq, and set about making a plan and recruiting a team. It hired around 60 staff – roughly a quarter were international staff who were Christians and roughly three-quarters were local staff who were predominantly Muslim.

They focussed on helping the huge civilian population that had been displaced by the IS occupation. Over two million people had fled from their homes and were now living in temporary dwellings in formal and informal internally displaced persons (IDP) camps. Some were in tents, while others resided in partially constructed apartment blocks that were only a concrete shell with no doors, windows, or sanitation facilities. Since many other organisations were providing humanitarian support in the formal IDP camps, Tearfund decided to focus on the informal camps. These were in many ways more vulnerable, having no protection and registration from the UN and often not even a perimeter fence. Most of the people who came to these informal camps were ethnic and religious minorities, such as Yazidis, Turkmen, Assyrian Christians, and others.

Tearfund's emergency response was built around improving shelter, setting up water and sanitation systems, and providing cash and essential non-food items. It helped to improve shelters in the informal camps and for those living in unfinished buildings it provided 'sealing off kits', which included a range of items such as wood planks, wood beams, plastic sheeting, and a variety of tools, enabling people to secure and weather-proof the concrete shells in which they were living. Tearfund also distributed kitchen sets, winter clothing, and heaters, along with jerry cans, hygiene kits, and other items. In certain cases it gave out cash so that people themselves could purchase what they needed. The water team set up household water facilities, installing water tanks and extending pipelines. In the camps it mobilised people to dig latrines, and it trucked in water and arranged hand-washing and bathing facilities.

Since Tearfund had signed up to many international humanitarian standards that require religion and humanitarian work to be kept separate, it was careful not to evangelise or to discriminate positively towards Christians in any way. For the most part, therefore, Tearfund's operational teams carried out their work in much the same way as secular organisations. The only way that beneficiaries would even know that they were Christians was because it was briefly mentioned in the fliers that the teams distributed to inform people about the water and sanitation work or about the resources that could be made available to them. And even here all it said was, 'Tearfund is a Christian relief and development organisation.' Nothing more.

Tearfund's Christian faith thus had very little influence on the way that the organisation went about its work. Staff followed Tearfund's code of conduct and sought to work in accordance with their Christian values. International staff would take part in Christian fellowship and prayer with members of other Christian NGOs and they would start their work day with devotion in the office. But for the most part there was nothing distinctively 'faith based' about Tearfund's response and little to distinguish its work in this context from that of secular organisations.

On the advocacy side of the organisation, again, most of the work that Tearfund carried out was resoundingly mainstream. By 2006 Tearfund had one of the largest advocacy capacities in the evangelical development world. Between 2005 and 2014 Tearfund carried out high-level advocacy work on four major issues at any one time and campaigned on two of them. It sought to influence the development policy of the UK government, and also carried out lobbying and advocacy work in major intergovernmental forums at the European and global levels. It worked on climate change, disaster risk reduction, water and sanitation, governance and corruption, trade, HIV, and food security. Staff from the advocacy team were active members of the Trade Justice Movement, the Publish What You Pay coalition, the Climate Coalition, and several other broad-based advocacy networks. Alongside other organisations they advocated for the UK government to take a stronger position on good governance and corruption, resulting in the UK government passing the Bribery Act in 2010; lobbied the EU to consider the interests of poorer countries during the negotiation of trade agreements; pushed for the EU to adopt laws requiring extractive companies to publish publicly all payments that they made to governments in any country; and so on. As will be clear, all this work was much the same as the work of secular NGOs, and indeed was often carried out in collaboration with them.

One of the topics on which Tearfund advocated and campaigned most actively in this period was climate change. In 2005 it appointed a dedicated Climate

Change Officer and in the following years it produced reports showing how climate change was affecting poor communities, lobbied about climate mitigation at the annual Conference of Parties (COP) of the United Nations Framework Convention on Climate Change (UNFCCC), and in collaboration with others persuaded the UK government to instigate the world's first national Climate Change Act in 2008. All this was much the same as the work of secular NGOs. However, as an evangelical organisation advocating on climate change Tearfund could not ignore the fact that one of the largest and most influential communities arguing *against* climate change was in fact the right-wing evangelical community in the US. Tearfund began to think that this was an area in which it had a particular faith-based opportunity to have a very distinctive and very important influence. With a shared faith background Tearfund was uniquely positioned to reach out to US evangelicals and try to start a meaningful discussion about climate change. As Paul Cook, co-leader of the Advocacy Team, explains:

> We can go into the Bible Belt heartland. We're evangelical Christians talking a similar language so we've got an in with them that other groups are never going to have. So it's amazing to be able to sit with those guys and try to bring them round, through the theology, through the science.

In 2006 Tearfund started to quietly engage with US evangelicals on climate change. It held meetings with key people and helped to bring religious leaders over to the UK to meet evangelical scientists, theologians, and businessmen working in the green economy. It took a group of well-known Christian singer–songwriters to the Paris climate talks in 2015 and produced short films about the event, which these worship leaders could then use to catalyse discussions in many churches and communities. As a result of this work several prominent Christians publicly changed their position about climate change.

However, for the most part, the only way that Tearfund's evangelical faith influenced its advocacy work was by leading it to avoid some of the more radical advocacy agendas that some secular NGOs were pioneering, such as highlighting human rights abuses by transnational corporations, lobbying for a global tax body, or calling for population control. As Ben Niblett, co-leader of the Advocacy Team, puts it: 'Our DNA is less radical than many, and the biggest reason for that is our supporter base.'

Conclusion

During the years 2006 to 2015 Tearfund worked towards bringing together its many divergent parts to focus on one common vision – to release 50 million people from material and spiritual poverty through a worldwide network of 100,000 local churches. In this way it sought to align its various parts to take on a more shared and coherent way of working.[4] A central feature of this was the focus on the local village church as the central actor in community development, disaster management, and advocacy. The three major departments thus developed new areas of work that focussed on envisioning and equipping local village churches to act in these ways.

This chapter has discussed these new methodologies in some detail, showing how Tearfund sought to codify and spread CCM, to work with local village churches to change attitudes and behaviours about sensitive issues such as HIV and AIDS and sexual and gender-based violence. And it has shown how Tearfund started to train local churches in disaster management and in advocacy and tried to get them involved in campaigning on justice issues. In all these areas Tearfund led the way in devising specifically faith-based forms of development.

However, it has also become clear that the vast majority of Tearfund's work, across the development, humanitarian, and advocacy teams, remained stubbornly secular. As Tearfund sought to implement faith-based approaches while also remaining part of the mainstream, it found that many of the tensions of the previous years continued to be present. While the mainstream development sector's new-found interest in religion and FBOs had seemed to offer an opportunity to bring faith-based approaches into the mainstream, this proved much more difficult in practice. The mainstream was mainly interested in instrumentalising religious actors to carry out secular development activities, and still showed considerable concern and even antipathy towards faith-based approaches that combined evangelism with development. Institutional funding could not be used for the small-scale specifically faith-based types of work. International standards and codes of conduct proliferated during this period and all of them sought to impose a separation between religious and developmental or humanitarian action. Thus as Tearfund sought to reposition itself as an FBO it found it difficult to shift very much of its work to the new faith-based methodologies.

Furthermore, in many cases Tearfund found that development work was simply fundamentally secular in nature. There was no specifically Christian way to dig a well or to devise effective disaster response strategies or to lobby members of parliament. Pure and simple, these were not religious matters. This rather calls into question several assumptions in the academic literature about FBDOs, specifically that they inherently offer alternative visions of development or that they carry out development in a different, specifically faith-based way. Rather, this chapter has shown that, even though Tearfund put considerable time and effort into developing specifically faith-based 'transformationalist' approaches, it found it difficult to implement these approaches in its work in other than relatively few areas. For the most part it was difficult to see how faith had a serious impact on the way that Tearfund and its partners carried out most of their work, or how their faith led to any particular 'comparative advantage' in their overseas activities. This was a cause for concern for many within Tearfund and, as the next chapter will show, led to renewed efforts going forward to try to find ways to expand the faith-based parts of its work and to try to bring them into the mainstream.

Notes

1 Tearfund also mobilised other Christian organisations, including Christian Aid, the Anglican Communion, and Restored, to launch an international Christian coalition to end sexual and gender-based violence in 2011. This coalition grew rapidly and became the *We Will Speak Out* network, a global coalition of Christian-based NGOs, churches, and organisations, supported by an alliance of individuals, who together commit themselves to see the end of sexual violence across communities around the world. In 2014 Tearfund started to support partners in 15 countries across Africa, Asia, and Latin America to mobilise faith leaders to respond to sexual violence and to grow a movement of survivors who would shape strategy and policy based on their priorities and experiences (Swart 2017).
2 For an independent review of this work see Tanner and Komuhangi 2018.
3 It could be argued that, while Tearfund's faith did not much affect *how* it carried out its humanitarian work, it did in some cases influence the type of work that it foregrounded or the type of approach that it favoured. Thus, for example, Tearfund decided to put a lot of emphasis on disaster risk reduction and resilience, rather than just disaster response, as it felt that this fitted with its 'whole life' perspective. And it was one of the first agencies to champion the importance of 'beneficiary accountability' in disaster response work – the idea that humanitarian responders should be accountable to the beneficiaries whom they serve – because it resonated with its Christian understanding of the value of the individual. But these were both mainstream approaches that were widely taken up in the wider humanitarian sector and Tearfund was far from unique in thinking these issues important.
4 In the latter part of this period Tearfund also decided to bring a number of workstreams to an end, including the UK Action Programme and Tearcraft. The UK Action Programme was ended because Tearfund wanted to focus more specifically on the poorest of the poor and felt that this group did not live in the UK. Tearcraft had been struggling for several years. In 2008 its name was changed to 'Created' and more focus was placed on internet sales. However, since performance was consistently low it was finally decided that Tearfund should focus on other areas. Created stopped operations in 2014 and was handed over to Traidcraft.

8 Mainstreaming faith-based development, 2015 onwards

Introduction

In 2015 Nigel Harris came in as Tearfund's new CEO. He produced a new strategy and clarified that Tearfund's vision was 'to see people freed from poverty, living transformed lives and reaching their God-given potential' (Harris 2017: 1). He decided to focus on three corporate priorities: church and community transformation (CCT),[1] humanitarian work in fragile states (FS), and environmental and economic sustainability (EES). While there were several new buzzwords and phrases, Harris very much chose to continue taking Tearfund along the path that had been set by Matthew Frost. With the wider development sector still apparently very much interested in religion and the potentials of faith-based development, Harris wanted Tearfund to further expand CCM and its other specifically faith-based methodologies and to try to bring them more into the mainstream. In other words, the aim was for Tearfund to consolidate itself as an FBO.

Harris wanted to continue spreading CCM throughout Tearfund and throughout the Christian development sector. He also wondered if there was a potential for it to spread even more widely and to become a methodology that could be accepted and respected by mainstream development actors and so could perhaps even be funded by mainstream donors. Thus in this period Tearfund put considerable effort into trying to turn CCM into a mainstreamable development approach. This would involve further formalising the methodology, linking it to a coherent theory of change, and developing quantifiable indicators of impact.

Tearfund also started to work on developing new faith-based methodologies so that more of its work could become 'faith based'. And it sought to think through how the apparently non-faith-based parts of its work could nonetheless still have some faith impact. This chapter sketches out the early phases of these three aspects of Tearfund's work and looks at some of the dynamics and challenges in trying to mainstream faith-based approaches to development.

Mainstreaming CCM into the wider development sector

Measuring holistic change

In order to turn CCM from being a small, niche-area type of project in which Tearfund works with local churches into a serious development modality that could be mainstreamed, Tearfund put considerable effort into formalising its approach and making it fit with the interests of the wider development sector. This required clarifying what the desired outcome of CCM actually was, working out how to measure to what extent this outcome had been achieved, and then using these measurements to try to 'prove' that CCM was an effective development methodology. Thus Tearfund is trying to bring the small-scale, messy CCM process into the framework of professional development work, with indicators, a theory of change, and, hopefully, evidence of impact.

Tearfund had started to think about what the desired outcome of 'Christian development' was back in the early 2000s when it had started to work on the *Overcoming Poverty* document. Over the next ten years, as CCM had become the dominant methodology for doing 'Christian development' (or 'integral mission'), it had put considerable effort into ironing out the problems with the original formulation and developing it further. In 2012 it had published a new document called *Overcoming Poverty Together*, which had two main innovations. First, it managed to integrate the different scales of analysis that had sat next to each other rather uncomfortably in the earlier formulations and clarified that in order to bring about transformation it was necessary to restore relationships at local, national, and international levels by using CCM and church-led campaigning and advocacy. Second, and rather fundamentally, it had clarified what it saw as the end point of 'transformation'. It defined the outcome that it wanted to see as 'human flourishing' (Tearfund 2012: 4).

For Tearfund 'human flourishing' is fundamentally about restoring broken relationships. It explains:

> This includes freedom from oppressive structures and a relationship with God which brings forgiveness and hope. Through seeing themselves as being made in the 'image of God', people discover their inherent self-worth, but also their capacity for creativity, stewardship of creation, relationships and generosity. Whole-life transformation is marked by adherence to a set of values (and hence lifestyles) which are often different to those of the world around us, not least solidarity with the poor and marginalised.
>
> (Tearfund 2016c: 2)

But what does it mean, for different people in different contexts, to flourish? And what does whole-life transformation look like in practical terms? Tearfund thus began to think through the different components of 'flourishing'. And it also started to think about how to develop indicators so that it could track and measure change in different life areas to get an overall picture of the newly conceived-of journey of 'whole life transformation'. At around this time Tearfund had recruited Catriona Dejean to lead its work on impact and evaluation and to begin to think about how to measure the kind of holistic change that Tearfund was seeking to bring about through its CCM work.

Up to this point Tearfund had not been very strong on measuring the impact of its work. The church and missionary world was much less concerned with these types of measurement than the secular development sector and it was taking a while for Tearfund to adapt to this new way of working. Project monitoring was rather weak and there was a tendency for partner reports to rely on anecdotal stories of transformational change in individual lives, rather than on providing solid data regarding reach and impact. Dejean recalls that when she first came to Tearfund there was very little rigorous monitoring of project outcomes:

> People were scared about monitoring and evaluation. They thought it was something done by an expert.... There were also a lot of assumptions that, 'We know we are doing a good job so why do we need to measure it?' There was a sense that this is God's work so why do we have to measure it? So we had to go through quite a culture change.

In the following years Tearfund had begun to place more resources into developing monitoring systems, carrying out more rigorous qualitative and quantitative project evaluations, and starting to think more critically about the nature of the change that it was trying to bring about. A key issue was to clarify the desired outcomes of CCM. Catriona Dejean recalls:

> When I came in people said, 'We do Umoja.' I asked, 'What change do you want to see?' And they just answered, 'Well, we do Umoja.' So we tried to unpack that, what do you want to achieve with that?

The challenge was that CCM, or Umoja, sought to bring about many different types of change. As well as material change, CCM also sought to bring about emotional and spiritual changes. How could these be measured?

Some years earlier Tearfund had tried to think about how it could measure spiritual change, but had reached a bit of a dead end. Tulo Raistrick, who led that work, explains:

> I was involved in a project to see whether we could measure transformation and what did spiritual transformation look like? Could you measure that? Ultimately, I think that's a very difficult thing to measure.... The initial thought was can we measure church attendance figures? ... I think the challenge was that to measure something like spiritual transformation in a way that was perceptive, rather than using a very blunt instrument [such as

church attendance figures] required a lot of questions and quite a lot of nuance. And to expect partners to do that just seemed excessive.... There was also a hesitation that what you measure begins to drive what you do.... In CCM if the church grew that was a wonderful by-product, but it couldn't be the purpose of the process. I think there was a fear that if we measured whether church numbers had grown that would set an expectation that that was what it was about.... There was an on-going debate about how you could best do it.

This work had petered out by 2010 and when Catriona came in she took a different approach. She started by looking outside to see what other academics and practitioners were doing in this area and was particularly influenced by some new work on development and wellbeing that was taking place at the University of Bath, work on spiritual metrics that was evolving at Eastern University in the USA, and a methodology called Outcome Stars that had been developed by Triangle Consulting Social Enterprise, a mission-led organisation that exists to help people reach their highest potential in the context of social disadvantage, trauma, disability, or illness. She also drew on work that Tearfund had carried out with Theos, a public theology think tank, and CAFOD, the Catholic relief and development agency, to begin to think through what 'Wholly Living' might look like in practice (Theos 2010). And in 2013 she commissioned research consultancy Gamos to try to assess the impact of CCM work in Tanzania over a wide range of areas including agricultural productivity, empowerment, sense of self-worth, church attendance, and church growth (Scott *et al.* 2014).[2] Based on all this work, in 2014 Catriona and her team produced the 'Light Wheel' – a new tool to measure the kind of holistic change that Tearfund is trying to bring about through CCM.

The Light Wheel sets out nine domains that have an influence over an individual's or community's ability to live well, flourish, and be resilient. Since Tearfund's theology of poverty emphasises the importance of restored relationships (between self, others, God, and the environment), there is a focus on measuring changes in these kinds of relationships. The nine areas form the nine 'spokes' of the Wheel – including social connections, personal relationships, living faith, emotional and mental wellbeing, physical health, stewardship of the environment, material assets and resources, participation and influence, and capabilities. By considering each spoke, a holistic view can be taken that brings together physical, social, economic, and spiritual wellbeing.

On each spoke there are five levels, with the lowest score being one and the highest score being five. By looking at the criteria for scoring five on each spoke we can understand Tearfund's vision of what human flourishing looks like and the outcome it seeks from its work. Its 'Light Wheel Maturity Model' suggests that a flourishing community is one that has the characteristics set out in the box below (adapted from Tearfund 2015a).

In a flourishing community:

- Cross-community dialogue and community action are the norm, with different elements of society working together for communal benefit. Differences are valued and respected and all elements of society are included in community activities. (Social connections)
- People demonstrate a commitment to building and sustaining loving, equitable, and affirming relationships, and are capable of managing conflict constructively to ensure and enable the common good. (Personal relationships)
- Christians from across denominations continue to work together as salt and light to achieve positive change not only in their own communities but also more widely. They work with other Christians to influence and impact society at the national as well as local levels. They continue to draw people, through love, to faith in Christ. (Living faith)
- People are at peace with the past and with hope for the future. They are able to share concerns and have the emotional resilience to withstand and adapt to shocks, stresses, and uncertainty. (Emotional and mental wellbeing)
- All groups show continually improving physical health indicators, particularly the most vulnerable, with equal access to resources for physical health. (Physical health)
- People actively engage with others who access natural resources both to understand how natural resource systems operate and to ensure their sustainable use for the common good. (Stewardship of the environment)
- All people can responsibly access and utilise the material resources they need to sustain their livelihoods and all are resilient to shocks. (Material assets and resources)
- The views of all groups are represented and considered in a way that means their views influence decision making about their future. (Participation and influence)
- Individuals plan creatively, learn, and adapt in response to changing needs and contexts to effect change collaboratively and achieve a shared vision. (Capabilities)

And by looking at the descriptions of the different levels on each spoke we can get an idea of the journey on which Tearfund would like communities to travel. For example, the desired journey regarding 'social connections' is from a situation where groups are separated by issues such as caste, ethnicity, tribe, or faith group, and in which there is little positive engagement between groups such that each group tends to distrust people from other groups, to a situation where cross-community dialogue and community action are the norm, with different elements of society working together for communal benefit, and in which differences are valued and respected and all elements of society are included in community activities. The journey for 'material assets and resources' would be from a situation where community members have few reserves and levels of vulnerability are high, with physical assets being limited, mostly controlled by a dominant few, or not recognised due to the context or environment, to a situation in which all people can responsibly access and utilise the material resources they need to sustain their livelihoods and thus all are resilient to shocks.

Where the Light Wheel is more innovative is in its consideration of more holistic matters, such as personal relationships and emotional and mental well-being. These are elements that many secular NGOs do not take into account in their programming. The journeys described here are thus a little different and potentially add some new perspectives. For example, the desired journey regarding 'personal relationships' is from a situation where personal relationships are often abusive and based on power, where powerful individuals are not accountable to others, where difficult issues are avoided, grievances are held, and forgiveness is uncommon, to a situation where people demonstrate a commitment to building and sustaining loving, equitable, and affirming relationships, where conflict is managed constructively and where people work together for the common good. And the desired journey for 'emotional and mental well-being' is from a situation in which many people feel isolated and alone, painful issues are hidden, and many feel bitter and resentful towards those who may have wronged them in the past, to a situation in which people are supportive of each other, are at peace with the past, and have the emotional resilience to withstand and adapt to shocks, stresses, and uncertainty (adapted from Tearfund 2015a). These types of changes are off the radar for most secular development NGOs, which tend to focus on economic and material change. Tearfund believes that its more holistic, more spiritual, church-based approaches can facilitate these types of changes.

Things get a little more complicated, however, when it comes to looking at 'spiritual development' and the area of 'living faith'. Here the desired journey is from a situation in which people may claim a Christian faith but it remains largely nominal, there is little time dedicated to personal prayer or Bible study, and divisions exist between churches, to a situation in which Christians from different denominations work together to influence society and to draw people to faith in Christ. What would the secular development world make of this journey? Furthermore, these indicators only deal with Christianity and apply to Christians, yet Tearfund seeks to help people of all faiths and none. What would the 'living faith' indicators look like when applied to a mixed community or a community of Muslims or Hindus? Is its goal to help people of other faiths develop a more profound connection with their own religious tradition or is it to help them become Christians? Tearfund's theology would suggest the latter, but this is not yet explicitly addressed and worked out in the Light Wheel. Clarifying and measuring this type of spiritual development may yet prove challenging and controversial.

By 2018 Tearfund had developed a methodology for measuring holistic change and a set of indicators to quantify the impact of CCM work, which it now sought to pilot. In this way it was seeking to turn CCM into a serious development modality whose impacts could be measured in accordance with the demands of the wider sector. The idea was to prove that CCM was a development methodology that could bring about beneficial impacts in local communities, and thus for it to gain legitimacy as a development approach that could be used and perhaps funded by the wider mainstream development sector.[3]

Nonetheless, the issue of how to measure 'spiritual development' will likely emerge as a controversial issue. Despite the development sector's apparent openness to faith-based development it is still widely seen that any attempt to convert beneficiaries to another religion is unacceptable. While the Light Wheel could perhaps meet the development sector's demands for measurement and impact, the fundamental desire to combine evangelism and development that is central to CCM still clashes with general development norms.

Challenges to mainstreaming CCM

As more and more Tearfund partners started to implement CCM, a number of other issues began to emerge, which presented further challenges for CCM to be brought into the mainstream.

The most pressing concern was how well CCM works in the complex religious contexts that characterise many communities. While Tearfund's reports and internal documents often talk about 'the church and the community' as if there were one central church in a religiously homogenous community, the reality on the ground is generally far more complex. Even in predominantly Christian communities there will often be a number of different Christian denominations, with major theological and organisational differences, often competing for followers. And in many parts of the world communities consist of people from different religions and there may be a variety of churches, mosques, temples, and so on. What happens in these contexts when you centre development interventions on one particular church?

From a review of the largely anecdotal reports and documents that Tearfund has produced to date it seems that CCM can sometimes work well in mixed religious contexts, or in contexts where there are two or more different church communities, for example Orthodox and evangelical, or Catholic and Protestant, and can lead to evangelicals changing their attitudes towards those of other faiths or other denominations such that these communities work more together and improve their relations (e.g. James 2018, Tearfund 2017b). However, in other cases there can be tensions and challenges.

In contexts where there are several different churches CCM can exacerbate tensions between the churches or the pre-existing tensions can lead to certain churches not taking up CCM because it is also being done by certain other churches (e.g. Tearfund 2018c). In some cases community members from other churches sometimes push back against the idea that project activities should be carried out in the evangelical church. They fear that that church is trying to convert them and they argue that meetings and activities should take place in a more neutral location, such as in a community meeting place or in someone's house. For example, when a CCM project started in a Southern Ethiopian town in which there were tensions between Orthodox Christians and evangelicals, the Orthodox participants refused to take part if the meetings were held in the evangelical church. After long discussions it was eventually agreed to hold the meetings in the house of a respected local woman, who was Orthodox, and then the rest of the project proceeded smoothly. So in this case the community actively tried to take the church out from the centre of CCM.

In mixed religious communities, where Christians live alongside Muslims or Hindus or Buddhists, the tensions are sometimes even more difficult. In some cases non-Christians are wary of participating in community projects organised by the church and accuse the church of trying to convert them (e.g. Diaz 2008: 10). In other cases the project is again removed from the church into more neutral ground. In this way people try to directly resist the evangelistic possibilities that Tearfund and its partners seek to bring about through CCM. A further challenge in communities where Christians only represent a small minority is that church members can find it difficult to enter into the community and to mobilise people for communal development work (e.g. Brown and Rokhum 2012: 9).

When looked at through the lens of 'transformation', these tensions and local disagreements may be seen as an uncomfortable but largely necessary stage to go through as people leave other religions and come to embrace the Christian faith. It is well known that this often causes conflicts within and between families, as sons or daughters, brothers or sisters, take on new ideas and practices and stop taking part in traditional rituals and activities alongside their families and communities (e.g. Freeman 2013). Thus from this perspective they would not be a major cause for concern. However, looking through a mainstream development lens would more likely lead to a conclusion that CCM can be a divisive methodology, exacerbating religious tensions and causing conflict in mixed religious communities. Viewed from this perspective, these issues would be a major cause for concern and would need to be resolved before CCM could be used widely as a community development methodology. As Tearfund seeks to mainstream CCM, they become issues with which it now needs to engage.

Another set of concerns springs from the current emphasis of the mainstream development community on working with 'the poorest of the poor' and 'leaving no-one behind'. To become a mainstream methodology in the late 2010s it is necessary to show that your approach targets the very poor. Does CCM do this? Experience so far has showed that CCM often tends to help the local middle classes rather than the poorest of the poor and the marginalised (e.g. Tearfund 2018c: 17). The sick, destitute, and very poorest sometimes do not come to church and are often unable to participate in the community activities that CCM initiates. For example, a CCM project in Kenya mobilised the community to set up an irrigation system for their agricultural fields. In order for the pipes to come to a person's fields they had to pay $70 at the start of the project and a further $70 at the end. The poorest of the poor could not afford this and thus did not receive irrigation to their fields. In another CCM project in Kenya the community set up a dairy so that they could sell milk to local traders. But the poorest of the poor did not have any cows and thus were unable to benefit from this intervention. So even in these rather successful projects, where many in the community did benefit, the poorest of the poor did not.

In order to respond to this challenge so that CCM can be accepted as a mainstream methodology, Tearfund is currently working to develop some revised CCM methodologies that aim to enhance 'inclusion' so that the marginalised and the poorest of the poor are more involved in activities. For example, Tearfund is currently commissioning some research in Rwanda to look at how to increase the inclusion of the elderly in CCM. In Zimbabwe, Chad, and Central America Tearfund is planning pilot projects that will put intentional focus on inclusion of marginalised groups within CCM. And in Kenya Tearfund is piloting a new approach in which the envisioned church is encouraged to target the poorest of the poor in their communities and organise them into self-help groups (SHGs) so that they can save money together and slowly build up their assets and begin to start small businesses or petty trading.[4] In this adapted methodology the church congregation will be envisioned and trained to help others and they would not see any material benefits themselves. This is quite a significant change from the original CCM methodology and it remains to be seen whether or not church members find it appealing.

Tearfund is still very much at work trying to refine CCM and turn it into a methodology that can be accepted and respected in the wider development sector. At the same time it is finding that it also needs to convince evangelical churches that CCM should be a core part of their activities. Thus it is also working to mainstream CCM into the wider evangelical world.

Mainstreaming CCM among evangelical churches

As Tearfund has sought to encourage Southern evangelical churches to start doing CCM it has come up against a different set of issues, some practical and some theological.

In some cases pastors can find it quite challenging to implement CCM because it is a long and time-consuming process and it can be difficult for busy pastors to find time to organise all the meetings and Bible studies. They are often busy with weddings, funerals, and other matters, simply do not have the time to work with the community on development projects, or do not see it as their priority. They are busy 'doing church' and do not want to turn themselves into some kind of development NGO.

In other cases churches may not be convinced of the theological basis for engaging in CCM and matters of material development. Tearfund's response to this is mainly to try to convince church leaders that helping their congregants to meet their material needs is part of the overall mission of the church and thus should be seen as a central part of their work, on a par with organising weddings and funerals. This, indeed, is the fundamental tenet of the 'integral mission' approach that Tearfund seeks to spread among the churches. Thus going forward Tearfund sees one of its key roles to be influencing evangelical churches around the world to carry out integral mission.

In 2016 Tearfund formed a new team working on 'Theology and Network Engagement', which seeks to share learning between churches that are already practising integral mission and to spread the approach more widely. There are team members in each region who map out the situation of the evangelical church in that part of the world and consider appropriate ways to influence it. In Africa and Latin America, for example, Tearfund is thinking about how it can equip pastors to introduce integral mission theology into their churches and Bible Colleges and it is organising a number of high-profile 'Thinking Theology' conferences to further mainstream the integral mission approach. In doing so, Tearfund staff and partners often find themselves arguing against the currently popular 'prosperity gospel', with its focus on individual gain and miraculous ways, which has been sweeping across much of Africa and Latin America since the late 1980s (e.g. Gifford 1990, Hasu 2012, Heuser 2015).

While there are continuities with some aspects of the work carried out by the former Evangelism and Christian Education Department, Tearfund is now engaging theologically with the churches in a much more conscious way, in a two-way dialogue, and as a particular part of a larger aim – to transform evangelical churches around the world into active civil society organisations that will work for the betterment of their communities. These activities can lead Tearfund into some complex discussions as some might argue that it is not the role of a relief and development agency to influence theology in churches. But as Tearfund morphs from being an NGO into being an FBO it is beginning to find that this is indeed its role. As Nigel Harris explains:

> We're not just another agency doing relief and development work. I see Tearfund as the technical advisor and facilitator to the church to help them carry out integral mission.

Mainstreaming the church?

As Tearfund tries to mainstream the church – to draw it into the mainstream development field so that it can be recognised as a legitimate and effective development actor – it is finding that it has to work hard to convince both church leaders and the wider development sector that this is a good idea. Fundamentally, the development sector is interested in material matters, while the churches are interested in spiritual matters. But both sides see a potential in instrumentalising the other side for their own purposes. The church (or missionaries) have a long history of trying to utilise development activities for evangelistic purposes. And more recently, the development sector has become interested in utilising the church for development purposes. Tearfund believes that a balanced middle ground can be found where the objectives of both sides can be met.

However, this middle ground is a very unstable place and organisations that have sought to occupy it before have tended to fall in one direction or the other, most often secularising. Nineteenth-century Christian charities and humanitarian societies were largely replaced by secular organisations, and the mainline liberal missionaries largely gave way to, or turned into, secular development NGOs. Despite the continually recurring desire of Christian organisations to combine evangelism with aid or charity, the demands of the post-enlightenment world seem to impose an almost entropic force, seeing these activities as two very different kinds of intervention and forcing them apart.

Tearfund, and other evangelical FBDOs like it, are the latest group seeking to occupy this middle ground, and Tearfund hopes that its CCM methodology can stabilise this area and enable evangelism and development to be carried out together in one integrated activity that meets the standards of development best practice and which also helps churches to grow and thrive. Some of the mainline liberal missionary organisations are also seeing CCM as a way back to this middle ground that they used to occupy, and this explains why it is being taken up so widely by Northern church and missionary organisations from across the evangelical and liberal wings of the Protestant church. The response of the Southern evangelical churches and the mainstream development sector remain to be seen.

Faith-based approaches to humanitarian relief

Tearfund has also been trying to develop more faith-based ways of working on the humanitarian side of the organisation and to mainstream them into the wider humanitarian sector. As before, this is proving far more difficult than on the development side of the organisation. Nonetheless, Tearfund is working to develop faith-based methodologies that will lead to behaviour change and is seeking to influence the wider humanitarian sector to work more closely with local churches.

Peacebuilding

In 2016 Tearfund decided that going forward it would place particular emphasis on working in fragile states in which humanitarian crises are often linked to complex political situations, and in which development gains are at risk of being undone by violent conflict. Tearfund is therefore developing analyses of what it thinks are the root causes of the problems and devising interventions to try to restore long-term stability. Given that faith-based work seems to have particular potential when it comes to behaviour change, Tearfund is beginning to develop new faith-based methodologies in the area of peacebuilding.

This work is being pioneered by Veena O'Sullivan and seeks to build on the approaches of the behaviour change work around HIV/AIDS, gender-based violence, and the Ebola response. In contexts where there is inter-ethnic or inter-religious conflict Tearfund will seek to establish a network of peacemakers and to work with these individuals to heal their trauma so that they can move from a 'revenge mindset' to a 'reconciliation mindset'. The idea is that then they will be able to work with local communities to bridge gaps and move forward together.

Tearfund has also started to work with community leaders and faith leaders to model new forms of leadership and integrity. And it seeks to develop more work with youth, equipping them with livelihood skills and encouraging them to engage in advocacy to constructively drive social change within their communities. This work is all focussed on changing individuals so that they can then change their communities. Where possible it will work through local churches to create safe spaces and bring about varieties of 'whole life transformation'.

At the time of writing this work is still in very early stages. Since most fragile states are in Muslim majority countries, much of this work will be carried out with Muslims. Trying to use Christian faith-based approaches in Muslim contexts is a new departure for Tearfund and the results remain to be seen.

Influencing the humanitarian system to work with local churches

In recent years there has been a trend in the wider humanitarian sector towards international funding being channelled directly to local organisations. This has become known as the 'localisation agenda' and is currently being discussed and debated widely in the sector (ICVA 2016, McKechnie and Davies 2013, ODI 2013). Tearfund and its networks have been involved in regional consultations about the localisation agenda and have been strongly supportive. In particular, they are advocating that local churches should be included and that international humanitarian funding should be channelled to them directly. In 2013 they collaborated with Christian Aid, CAFOD, Oxfam GB, and ActionAid to commission research looking at the case for strengthening partnerships with local organisations – NGOs and churches – in disaster management. The study, *Missed Opportunities: The Case for Strengthening National and Local Partnership-Based Humanitarian Responses* (Ramalingam *et al.* 2013), made the case that working with local partners could significantly increase the relevance and appropriateness of disaster response.

In 2015, in the run-up to the World Humanitarian Summit, a number of commitments were made towards the localisation agenda. One was the Charter for Change, which called for increased direct funding to Southern-based NGOs for humanitarian action. Another was the Grand Bargain between the UN and donors in which donors committed to make funding more accessible, longer term, and more localised, in return for greater efficiencies and greater accountability when the UN delivers aid. They set a target for local NGOs to get 25 per cent of international humanitarian funding by 2020, a big jump up from the then 0.4 per cent. At the same time Tearfund and many other faith-based organisations developed the Charter for Faith-Based Humanitarian Action, which was launched at the Summit, calling for more funding to be channelled to churches and other faith-based organisations. However, this has so far not proved successful and no formal commitments were made about working more closely with faith-based organisations.

Doing 'integral mission' in Muslim contexts

Many of the countries that are classified as 'fragile states' are countries with no religious freedom, often Muslim. In these restricted contexts there are no churches and no evangelical partners on the ground, so Tearfund has to choose between responding through an operational team or not responding at all. Tearfund decided to respond to the recent Iraq crisis by setting up an in-country operational team, while it took the decision not to respond at the start of the crises in Yemen and Somalia. If Tearfund is going to focus its humanitarian work on fragile states then it means that going forward it will be working increasingly in Muslim contexts. Thus Tearfund has started thinking again about what it means to do integral mission in its operational work in these contexts.

One idea is that Tearfund's long-term presence and its intentionality of demonstrating Christian values can build trusting relationships and break down negative perceptions about Christians and the Christian faith in these countries. Sarah Newnham, who is leading on developing Tearfund's thinking about working in such restricted contexts, explains:

> We will work according to particular principles which we believe will contribute to holistic transformation.... Long-term vision, presence, solidarity, building trust. It's not about 'reaping the harvest' or even 'sowing the seeds', it's more like clearing the stones from the field, before the seeds can even be planted. It's about breaking down negative perceptions about Christians.... It's about living with integrity and Kingdom values and bearing witness to Christ through who we are and how we behave. And of course, contributing in many ways to improving their quality of life.

Another suggestion, building on some of Tearfund's work in Muslim-majority countries, has been that Tearfund's biggest missional impact in these situations will be with its non-Christian staff. As Oenone Chadburn, Head of Humanitarian Support since 2012, explains:

> I think that one of the potentials that we have in working in restricted locations is to create an enabling environment for Christianity to be more accepted. That gives the potential for the church to grow.... The indirect consequences of our work in Muslim countries has enormous potential.

As in previous years, finding ways to do faith-based work on the humanitarian side of the organisation continues to be much more difficult and contentious. For the time being, the vast majority of Tearfund's humanitarian work remains mainstream and not particularly 'faith based'.

Faith-based advocacy and campaigning

A global campaign for a restorative economy

In 2013 the advocacy team changed their strategy and decided to focus all their work on just one major issue – the unsustainable high-carbon economy and its damaging environmental impacts. As Paul Cook, one of the leaders of the Advocacy Team, explains:

> Our analysis was that the world has made enormous progress on lifting people out of extreme poverty in the nearly 50 years since Tearfund was founded. The proportion of people in every continent lacking food, water, sanitation, a good job, safe housing, education, healthcare etc. have all declined significantly. This is overwhelmingly the result of the expansion of the global economy. However, during the same period all the environmental trends such as climate change, biodiversity loss, and so on, were all heading dramatically in the opposite direction. The tragic irony being that the same economy that has lifted so many out of poverty is driven by high carbon energy, and high-consumption of limited natural resources and that continuing this form of progress along 'business as usual' lines will undo all that progress and drive the world off a cliff.

While partner-led in-country advocacy would continue to focus on local and national priority issues, Tearfund felt that it had a particular contribution to make to the global issue of green and fair economies, based on its ability as a faith-based organisation to discuss worldviews, beliefs, and values, and on its strength of bringing about behaviour change.

Tearfund decided that the key was to change the views of the public, not just in the UK but in several key G20 countries, and it decided to shift to a movement-building approach in order to try to build a groundswell of support for broad social and cultural change, which could then lead to the transformation of social norms, policies, and systems in order to deliver environmentally and economically sustainable development outcomes. Thus Tearfund set out to build a grassroots movement in a number of countries, with the church playing a central role.

In 2015 Tearfund published a major paper called *The Restorative Economy: Completing our Unfinished Millennium Jubilee*, which outlined its analysis of the problem and its suggestions for the future. The restorative economy concept built on the biblical notion of jubilee, which it saw as something wider than just the cancellation of debts that was highlighted in the Jubilee 2000 campaign. Going back to the Bible Tearfund noted that the jubilee year was also a time of environmental restoration, when land was left fallow; a time of liberty, when slaves were freed; and a time for wealth redistribution, when land ownership was reset. The report states:

> Jubilees, and the closely linked idea of sabbaths (every seven days and every seven years), set out concrete procedures for how to correct economic,

social and environmental imbalances – in effect, providing an instruction manual for how to build and maintain a *restorative economy*.

(Evans and Gower 2015: 7, emphasis in original)

Tearfund asked, 'What might it look like to organise our 21st-century economy around the idea of jubilee?' The answer focussed around three key themes – living within our environmental limits, ensuring that everyone can meet their basic needs, and keeping inequality within reasonable limits.

On the policy and advocacy side Tearfund has sought to become a thought leader on the topics of decentralised clean energy and circular economy interventions for developing countries. It has published several reports on these topics and has had its work featured by the World Economic Forum, Chatham House, and other leading players. Regarding UK policy change it has worked on issues such as food waste and plastics. So far it has called for seven out of the UK's top ten supermarkets to commit to halving their food waste by 2030, and it has also persuaded the UK government to invest more in waste management systems in middle-income countries, among other things.

However, the main emphasis is now on grassroots campaigning and organising, building on Tearfund's faith-based strengths in these areas. The aim is to use mobilising, organising, and connecting to strengthen a global movement of Christians around the world, who will collectively shape a widespread change in social norms, values, and lifestyles, and call on political and government actors for changes in unjust policies and practices (Global Advocacy Team 2016).

In 2015 Tearfund launched the Ordinary Heroes campaign, which aimed to shift the church to be at the front of creating a more just and sustainable world and to encourage people to make small but significant changes in their lifestyles. The campaign sought to encourage a grassroots movement of people to take responsibility for bringing about change, and was part of the international campaigning pressure for the 2015 Paris Agreement on climate change. In 2016 Tearfund launched the Big Church Switch campaign, in collaboration with Christian Aid and the Church of England, which sought to persuade church members to switch both their own home energy supply and the supply of the church building to 100 per cent renewable energy. In 2017 it co-founded and launched the Renew Our World campaign starting in ten strategic countries, including Australia, Brazil, Nigeria, the UK, and the US, mobilising local Christians to call on their governments to deliver on their commitments in the Paris climate change agreements. And in November 2018 it hosted the first UK Justice Conference, in which it sought to help evangelical churches to understand their own agency and become more active and compassionate.

Conclusion

This chapter has shown how Tearfund is seeking to consolidate itself as an FBO that implements a specifically faith-based approach to development. A major part of this is trying to bring its CCM work into the mainstream development sector by refining it and developing new indicators and forms of measurement in order to 'prove' that it brings about positive change in the lives of beneficiaries. In this way Tearfund is trying to order and regularise what many in the mission world would see as the inherently messy and unpredictable matter of social and spiritual change. At a recent conference on religion and development where Tearfund presented some of its new measurement work, a member of one of the mainline missions commented to me:

> Look at all those indicators! There are dozens of them! That's such a Tearfund way to do things, so systemised and so complex.... It's like the Light Wheel – highly complex, way too many moving parts, but a highly systematic attempt to track things that are not always measurable.... They have such a professional edge, such a structured way of thinking about things and trying to monitor and evaluate things.... It's all highly polished and highly efficient. I have spent quite some time with them recently and I found it really striking. It's very different to our organisation or some of the other organisations that I know.

These other organisations are mainline, liberal missionary organisations that carry out quite a lot of development work but are not mainstreamed into the wider development sector. They do not access government funding, do not sign up to international standards or codes of conduct, and for the most part stay within the networks and discourse of the WCC and the mainline Protestant world. Having not become part of the mainstream development sector, these organisations have not professionalised and bureaucratised in the same way as the faith-based development NGOs. In this contrast we can see more clearly some of the differences between FBOs and mission organisations, and the influence that the mainstream development sector has on those religious organisations that enter it.

This chapter has also shown some of the ways that Tearfund is trying to mainstream CCM into the evangelical church sector by engaging church leaders in theological debates about the nature of mission and trying to convince them to adopt an understanding of mission that is 'integral'. Through all these efforts Tearfund is hoping to combine evangelism and development into one integrated activity that can ultimately be carried out by churches and perhaps funded by donors. At the time of writing this is still very much a work in progress.

And finally, this chapter has also discussed how Tearfund is working to further expand the other faith-based parts of its work, particularly by developing new faith-based methodologies regarding peacebuilding and by expanding its faith-based campaigning work with local churches.

However, despite all these activities, faith-based work still constitutes a fairly small – although growing – proportion of Tearfund's work. The majority of the development, humanitarian relief, and advocacy work continues to be carried out in a secular, mainstream manner by professional Christian NGO partners that, when they can, try to evangelise while doing so.

Thus as it reaches its fiftieth year, Tearfund is still grappling with many of the same questions that it faced in its early years – fundamental questions about how to effectively combine evangelism and development, whether it is possible to be a mainstream NGO and yet still retain an evangelical identity, and what it means to do faith-based development. Despite the enormous changes, the growth and professionalisation, and the creation of new faith-based methodologies, Tearfund still finds itself sitting somewhere between the evangelical missionary world and the mainstream development sector. Perhaps the main difference is that, while in the early years Tearfund occupied a rather lonely place in the middle, neither fully part of the missionary world nor fully part of the mainstream development sector, now it occupies a respectable place in both.

Notes

1 CCT is the umbrella term for the various church-based methodologies that have evolved from the original CCM approach. See p. 117.
2 The study sought to compare changes over a five-year period in communities that did CCM and communities that did not. After a number of interviews and focus group discussions, the research team created a household survey, which it administered to 757 households in 18 communities. The results suggested that those involved in CCM experienced an improved sense of self-worth and empowerment, improved relationships, and some increased agricultural productivity due to a 'more entrepreneurial' approach to farming. There was also a marked increase in church growth and church attendance in CCM communities (Scott *et al.* 2014).
3 For example, in 2016 Tearfund commissioned researchers at Bath Social & Development Research Ltd to try to assess the impact of CCM work in Uganda and to utilise the Light Wheel framework as part of their methodology. The study looked at predominantly Christian communities in which CCM had been running for four to five years. The researchers concluded that overall CCM had had a positive impact on people's lives, particularly in 'soft' areas such as increased feelings of empowerment, self-worth and confidence, improved relationships, and enhanced mental and emotional wellbeing. Impact on livelihoods and material assets, however, was harder to ascertain. But for Tearfund the key thing was to get external validation that CCM had a beneficial impact. For more information see Copestake *et al.* 2019.
4 This draws on the work that Tearfund and its partners have been developing in Ethiopia over the past 15 years, where SHGs have mainly been established directly, in a non-CCM framework (Tsegay *et al.* 2013).

Part IV
Paradoxes of faith-based development

9 Conclusion

This book has traced Tearfund's 50-year journey as it emerged in the 1960s as a new kind of missionary organisation, transformed itself into a major development NGO in the 1990s, and then began to re-orient itself as an FBO from the mid-2000s onwards. It has shown how Tearfund started out as a small evangelical charity making grants to evangelical missionaries to carry out relief and development projects and then started to work more with the development wings of overseas evangelical church denominations and other newly emerging local Christian NGOs in an attempt to construct a new form of mission that would be better suited to the realities of the post-colonial world. Then, in the 1990s, as neoliberal policies spread around the world and development NGOs grew rapidly in size and number as increased levels of government funding were made available to them, Tearfund saw the opportunity to transform itself into a development NGO and to scale up its work significantly. Over the course of a decade or so it completely restructured itself, implemented professional managerial and accounting systems, professionalised its overseas partners, signed up to international standards and codes of conduct, and joined the various networks of mainstream development and humanitarian NGOs. It emerged out of the introspective evangelical world and became recognised and respected as a major mainstream NGO. And it more than tripled in size.

Yet entering into the mainstream brought with it some secularising forces as international standards stipulated that religious matters and humanitarian matters should be kept apart, government donors insisted that their funds could not be used for activities that included evangelism, and the heavy weight of bureaucracy threatened to squash out spiritual passion. A revitalist counter-movement emerged as junior staff, closer to the field, often from the South and predominantly female, drew on the work of the theologians and developed alternative ways of doing development that sought to make local churches into development actors as they carried out a more 'integral' form of mission. Different parts of the organisation were pulling in different directions as the tensions between evangelical mission and mainstream development became increasingly evident.

However, by 2005 the mainstream development world had itself begun to change as the resurgence of religion into public life and the aftermath of the 9/11 terrorist attack had led many of the large government donors to become interested in the role of religion in development and the possibility of working with and funding faith-based organisations. In this new context Tearfund thought that it might be possible to carry out a more faith-based, missional, form of development while also staying part of the mainstream. It began to re-orient itself into an FBO and tried to institutionalise church-based forms of 'integral mission' as its main working modality. However, despite the apparent mainstream interest in FBOs, international standards continued to force apart religious and humanitarian matters and government donors continued to refuse to fund activities that included evangelism. Thus even as Tearfund foregrounded its identity as an FBO and sought to implement more faith-based approaches it found that these had to be limited to a rather small proportion of its work. As it reaches its fiftieth year Tearfund is seeking to consolidate itself as an FBO, to expand the proportion of its work that is faith based, and to bring its major church-based development modality into the mainstream.

In tracing out this history in detail it is possible to see a particular instantiation of the cycle of secularisation and revitalisation up close. This dynamic has recurred again and again in Protestant organisations since at least the nineteenth century. The practices of the modern world have a tendency to cause spiritually passionate organisations to secularise as they access government funding and subjectify themselves to modern bureaucratic systems and norms. But just when it seems that the original fire has been extinguished it suddenly pops up somewhere else. The mainline missionaries of the nineteenth century were initially 'spiritually hot', but as they accepted funding from the colonial government to carry out development in the early twentieth century they began to secularise. Spiritually hot evangelical organisations such as Tearfund emerged to take their place. But as they too began to accept government funds and enter the mainstream they also began to secularise. In the case of Tearfund the revitalist movement happened from inside, as a group of spiritually hot staff came to the fore and pushed for a faith-based way of doing things. Going forward, as Tearfund tries to mainstream its CCM methodology, loading it with indicators in order to provide evidence of its impact, it will be interesting to see if this approach also begins to secularise, and if so, what revitalising countermovement will emerge.

At the heart of the matter is the desire to combine evangelism with development, or as Tearfund would put it, to 'see development as part of mission'. In the modern world evangelism and development are seen as fundamentally different activities – religious and secular, sacred and profane, spiritual and material, private and public. Thus while evangelical organisations such as Tearfund seek to combine them, the norms and systems of the secular state seek to push them apart. This dance has taken place over the past 200 years. In today's post-secular world there are some new twists – while religious organisations have frequently tried to instrumentalise secular resources for evangelistic ends, today secular organisations have started to try to instrumentalise religious resources for development ends. The academic field of 'religion and development' has largely emerged out of this new reality and is, I would argue, still trying to find its feet and find an appropriate framework through which to analyse and understand faith-based development actors and initiatives.

As the detailed historical and contextual analysis of this book has shown, many of the questions and assumptions of this literature have little to do with the reality of actual faith-based development organisations. In the rest of this chapter I will return to the theoretical issues raised in the introduction and consider what this detailed case study of one FBDO contributes to these broader scholarly discussions.

From typologies to historical and contextual analysis

The analysis in this book has sought to position Tearfund within the field of Protestant development actors. It has shown that a major line of division exists between mainline and evangelical organisations, based on substantial differences in theology, objectives, and organisational structure. It has been shown that Christian FBOs are not all the same and that there are very major differences between mainline Protestant NGOs, such as Christian Aid, and evangelical Protestant NGOs, such as Tearfund.

The contextual and historical approach has further highlighted the complicated repositioning of secular and Protestant organisations engaged in development activities during the second part of the twentieth century and into the twenty-first. In the 1960s the most important development actors in many respects were the mainline missionaries. They sat in a complex field between evangelical missionaries on one side, who were present in Africa and Asia but mainly engaged in verbal evangelism, and the newly emerging secular development NGOs in Europe and America, on the other, who were beginning to raise money and give it to local partners – often the mainline missionaries – to carry out development projects. While the mainline missionaries sought to combine development and evangelism, the stipulations of the secular development sector began to force a divide between these two activities.

By 2018 much has changed in both the mission and development worlds. Evangelical mission agencies and secular NGOs have both increased spectacularly, while the mainline mission agencies have gone into a major decline (Carpenter and Shenk 1990: xiii–xiv, Clarke 2007: 83, Hearn 2002: 40, Lewis and Kanji 2009: 2).[1] There has also been the emergence of a huge number of 'local NGOs' in the global South and most Northern development NGOs now give their grants to these organisations to carry out development projects. In this way the mainstream development field has become far more 'secularised' than it was in the 1960s. In parallel, the mission sector has expanded and become overwhelmingly evangelical, predominantly American, and increasingly fundamentalist (Hearn 2002: 40). While some evangelical mission agencies carry out some development work, the majority are committed to focussing only or mainly on the verbal proclamation of the gospel. In this new context, as the mainline missionaries have gone into decline, the evangelical FBDO sector has expanded to fill the middle ground that it once occupied – seeking again to combine evangelism and development.

Thus while Tearfund may see itself as positioned between the evangelical missionary sector and the secular development world, it actually has much in common with the mainline missionaries from the 1950s and 1960s. And indeed, several of these mainline missionary organisations are today beginning to collaborate with Tearfund and to use its CCM methodology. The Union Society for the Propagation of the Gospel (USPG), for example, a long-standing but now rather small mainline mission agency with a liberal theology, has recently joined Tearfund's 'Friends of Umoja' network and is presently supporting CCM projects in its partner churches.

As Tearfund has emerged into the mainstream development sector and started to accept government funding it has experienced many of the same secularising forces that affected the mainline missionaries decades earlier, and indeed the nineteenth-century Christian welfare charities decades before that. Balancing the support of 'contextually sensitive evangelism' with the growing pressures within the humanitarian and development sectors to keep evangelism and proselytism out of relief and development work has been an ongoing source of tension for Tearfund as it has striven to be *both* an evangelical organisation *and* an international development NGO. These tensions remain even in its current formulation as an FBO. When Tearfund is working operationally in contexts of restricted religious freedom, it does not evangelise. In all its work it ensures that it does not contravene any of the international standards to which it has signed up. But at the same time it has developed a new suite of working methods that seek to combine evangelism and development even more closely together and which can be used in appropriate contexts. Thus Tearfund's support of evangelism exists along a continuum and varies according to project, country, and context.

As the development and mission fields have changed, Tearfund has changed its identity – from a kind of missionary organisation to a development NGO and then to an FBO. It has also adapted its approach and working methods. But in all this it has retained its core purpose – to combine evangelism and development. Putting this all together, positioning Tearfund between 'mission' and 'development' is not a simple matter. For some people, including many Tearfund supporters, the fact that Tearfund supports evangelism means that even today Tearfund should be considered as a kind of missionary organisation. For others, including most Tearfund staff, Tearfund is better understood as a particular kind of development NGO. As Tearfund consolidates itself as an FBO and expands the faith-based part of its work in which it seeks to carry out 'integral mission', perhaps its staff will come to be thought of as 'integral missionaries'.

The role of faith in FBDOs

In contrast to literature suggesting that faith-based organisations have fundamentally different worldviews and ideas about development that emerge directly from their particular religious perspectives (e.g. Lunn 2009, Ter Haar 2011, Tyndale 2006), this study has shown that Tearfund has had to work incredibly hard to self-consciously *construct* a specifically faith-based approach to development. Moreover, the drive to construct this faith-based approach did not derive from a fundamentally different way of seeing the world, but rather from a desire to combine development with evangelism. Working out how to do this was not an easy process and took years of work and substantial internal debate and struggle.

Tearfund is a highly faith-permeated FBDO and is widely considered a leader in faith-based development, thus this insight calls into question some of the more fanciful claims being made in parts of the academic and practitioner literature about the 'alternative visions of development' that FBOs are supposed to offer. Despite claims of holistic worldviews, I would argue that most FBDOs, probably all of them, conceive of 'development' in much the same way as their secular peers, and then seek to combine this type of development with their faith motivations and beliefs. The separation between 'religion' and 'development' has been built into the FBDO sector, or at least the Christian FBDO sector, since the start.

Furthermore, even when Tearfund had succeeded in constructing a number of faith-based methodologies it found that it could not apply these approaches to all areas of its work. When it came to distributing food to disaster victims or digging wells or lobbying politicians, among other activities, it was difficult to find a specifically faith-based way of doing it. Despite a strong desire to work in a distinctly faith-based way, it was only possible to do so in certain contexts and in very specific areas of work. Tearfund would say that faith is part of their very DNA and therefore that all of their work is faith permeated. But they would also acknowledge that the influence of faith on their practical work is visible to different degrees in different contexts and in different projects. While Tearfund has made a considerable effort to develop and expand these more faith-based areas, across most of its teams the majority of work continues to be carried out in what I consider to be a standard, secular, non-faith-based way, by organisations who also carry out evangelism, much as in the early 'two wings of a bird' formulation.

This further calls into question the assumptions in the literature that FBDOs do development differently from secular NGOs. If a highly faith-permeated FBDO such as Tearfund finds that faith-based approaches can only be used in certain areas and that most of its work must be carried out in an essentially secular way, it is highly unlikely that other FBDOs do much differently. And indeed, several recent studies that have explored this question empirically at field level have similarly concluded that in most cases there are very few differences between the activities carried out by faith-based and secular organisations (Johnsen 2014, Leurs 2012, Occhipinti 2015).

The role of religion in development

The analysis in this book has had remarkably little to say about the broader question of the role of religion in the type of social and economic change that is generally called development. This is because, rather surprisingly, this question was not a matter of overt discussion among Tearfund staff and has not been a central question for Tearfund as an organisation.

Many scholars argue that, because most people in the world hold religious beliefs and are part of religious communities, it is important to engage with their religion when trying to bring about development, and therefore that FBDOs are uniquely positioned for this work (Ager and Ager 2011, Deneulin and Rakodi 2011, Noy 2009, Ter Haar 2011). Tearfund would argue that its theological reflections and writings, its hosting of discussion forums with theologians from around the world, and its work on faith literacy with the Joint Learning Initiative on Local Faith Communities constitute examples of its thinking about the role of religion in development. But what I am talking about here is something rather different. Does Tearfund actively think about the role of religion in social and economic change? Are its staff aware of the varieties of local religious understandings, including traditional beliefs and non-Christian ideas and practices? Do they devise different programmes of action in order to bring about contextually sensitive developmental change that will be socially, politically, and morally acceptable to their beneficiaries? I would argue that in the vast majority of Tearfund's work this is clearly not the case. And my experience in the wider FBDO sector leads me to conclude that Tearfund is not unique in this.

The exception is with regard to some of the faith-based behaviour change work around issues such as HIV/AIDS, sexual and gender-based violence, and Ebola. These areas of work focussed on situations where religious ideas were a major part of the problem – leading people to condemn those suffering from HIV, to condone gender-based violence, or to facilitate the spread of a dangerous infectious disease. In these cases, challenging these religious ideas was fundamental in order to change practice. And perhaps faith-based organisations coming from the same faith background were better placed to do this than secular actors.

However, in most other cases, Tearfund's work did not engage with local religious worldviews. At least from the vantage point of the head office, there was no discussion about how to deal with witchcraft accusations against those who had become successful in Africa, or how to deal with the occult forces that many people around the world believe arise alongside the expansion of capitalism and individualism. Instead, there were centralised strategies and methodologies to be applied in much the same way all over the world. For the most part, Tearfund approached its development work with a firmly modernist ontology, much the same as its secular peers. Thus it seems that, despite some of the claims in the literature, religious NGOs do not actually think very much about the role of religion in development.

The paradoxes of faith-based development

Taking an in-depth look at one FBDO and its evolution over a 50-year period has enabled a number of paradoxes of faith-based development to come more clearly into focus. These are unlikely to be unique to Tearfund, but are rather paradoxical characteristics of much of the so-called faith-based development sector. The first paradox is that, while claiming a 'comparative advantage' because of their 'faith distinctiveness', most of the work carried out by FBDOs is actually secular in nature and much the same as that carried out by their NGO peers. The second paradox is that, even when FBDOs do manage to create a specifically faith-based approach to development, this largely reflects an attempt to combine development with evangelism rather than a fundamentally alternative conceptualisation of development per se. And the third paradox is that FBDOs, for the most part, do not in fact think deeply about the role of religion in locally contextualised forms of development. Thus perhaps it is time for the academic and practitioner literature on FBDOs to step back from some of the more fanciful claims and to take a more careful and grounded look at the reality of faith-based development as it actually happens in practice.

The historical study presented here has allowed many dynamics of faith-based development to be seen more clearly. The analysis has shown how FBDOs are not only influenced by their religious ideas and theology, but also by changing ideas in the mainstream development and humanitarian sectors, opportunities to access new sources of funding, and wider changes in global policy and political economy. They exist between two different worlds with different discourses and different value systems. And as these two worlds themselves change over time, FBDOs find themselves constantly redefining themselves and renegotiating their position. In the current post-secular moment FBDOs such as Tearfund have been influenced by wider changes in public attitudes towards religion to begin to put *more* emphasis on their faith-based nature than they had in earlier times. Today Tearfund and other mainstream FBDOs are trying to expand the faith-based part of their work in order to distinguish themselves from their secular peers and claim a 'comparative advantage' in the competitive world of NGOs and donor funding. From being something that had to be 'left at the door', religion is now close to becoming an asset in the development world. And yet with all that, the quest to mainstream a truly faith-based development still remains elusive.

Note

1 In contrast to ideas that missionaries are in decline, there has in fact been a massive increase in both missionaries and mission agencies throughout the twentieth century. While in 1900 there were some 600 mission agencies, which sent around 62,000 missionaries overseas, by 2000 this had increased to around 5,500 mission agencies, sending some 440,000 missionaries (Johnson *et al.* 2015: 31). Over the same period the annual income of global foreign missions increased from $200 million to $18 billion in 2000 (Johnson *et al.* 2018). Interestingly, the vast majority of these missionaries, both in 1900 and in 2000, were Catholics. Focussing only on Protestants, then, the numbers are significantly smaller – some 18,000 missionaries in 1900 and around 80,000 approaching the turn of the century (Hearn 2002: 37). Mainline Protestant missionaries have gone into decline while evangelical missionaries have expanded at a phenomenal rate. By 2000 the overwhelming majority of the 80,000 or so Northern Protestant missionaries were American evangelicals (Hearn 2002: 40).

Appendix
Tearfund's work with supporters in the UK

Tearfund has also carried out a lot of work with its supporters in the UK. While this book has mainly been concerned with its overseas relief and development work, for the sake of completion a brief overview of some of its UK activities is included here. A full analysis of Tearfund's engagement with its supporters and its place within UK evangelicalism would of course require another book.

The first 25 years

From its earliest years Tearfund considered that it had a joint mandate – to help the poor and needy overseas and to educate the UK church about the state of the world and the importance of Christian compassion. During the 1960s much of the evangelical church still considered it more important to focus on preaching the gospel and saving souls, and considered social action to be somewhat of a distraction. So Tearfund set about to change that attitude.

In 1969 the organisation launched its supporter publication, *Tear Times*, initially as a four-page supplement to go inside the *Church of England Newspaper* and the *Christian Record*. In 1978 Tearfund decided to go for a much more striking form of communication and started to produce a quality journal, first in black and white and later in colour. The journal told supporters about the situations in other countries and the challenges that poor people faced. And it told them about the work of Tearfund's partners and how they were trying to alleviate poverty and suffering. Tearfund was quite distinctive in the quality of its publications and was one of only a few organisations at the time that had a full-colour magazine with high-quality design and photographs from around the world.

Tearfund also made many audio-visual aids – first film strips and then videos. These were to be used by churches in mid-week Bible study and sought to bring the reality of life in developing countries to people in a very real and immediate way. The first one was *Down to Earth* in 1971, and in 1982 Tearfund made its first full-length film, with Cliff Richard.

In 1971 it started Tearfund Sunday – a specific Sunday for churches to speak about Tearfund and its work. Tearfund provided educational materials to church leaders, including videos, sermon notes, posters, and collection boxes. The first Sunday, on 25 April 1971, focussed on the needs of the developing world, and

Tearfund suggested that churches organise a very basic 'austerity lunch' to provide an opportunity for associating giving with sacrifice (Endersbee 1973: 117).

Also in 1971 Tearfund started to send volunteers abroad. That year it established summer work camps for young people in their early twenties. Between 1971 and 1985 over 500 young people took part in summer work teams in 15 countries, typically carrying out building and renovation or working in health and rural development programmes. In 1986 this work was expanded and teams were sent out throughout the year and not just in the summer. The name was changed to Task Force Teams and the age range was widened.

In 1976 Tearfund began to establish regional offices around the UK so that it could interact more closely with local churches and supporters. It also set up a network of church representatives who would be Tearfund's main contact point in local churches and would help integrate Tearfund into the life of the church. Tearfund staff and a network of ambassadors would go to churches on Sunday and talk about Tearfund and its work and place it all in a biblical context. Stephen Rand, who worked for Tearfund from 1979 to 2004, recalls:

> The appeal to support Tearfund should not be based on simply 'there are starving people in the world, isn't it sad, and we can do something about it', but it actually ought to be rooted in biblical teaching that caring for the poor is an essential part of what it means to be a Christian.... I always felt that the principle of Tearfund's communication should be to create an understanding of what it meant to be a Christian and an understanding of what was happening in the world, so it was that classic 'Bible in the one hand and newspaper in the other' thing.*

Many of Tearfund's early supporters would have been people associated with the Evangelical Alliance. Some would have been donating to mission societies and then learnt about relief and development through Tearfund; others would have been donating to secular NGOs such as Oxfam or War on Want and then decided that they would prefer to 'do good in the name of Jesus' when they heard about Tearfund. Still others would have been donating to Christian Aid and then decided to support Tearfund because it was the aid agency of the evangelical community. To this day, many Tearfund supporters continue to support a wide range of other development NGOs, mission societies, and charities.

In 1978 a special Youth and Student Section was formed, aiming to help young people know more about Tearfund. There were different clubs and publications for different age groups – *TearAways* (for 5–8-year-olds), *On Target* (for 11–13-year-olds), and *Well* (for 9–13-year-olds). They all provided information about Tearfund people and projects, along with quizzes and games, in an age-appropriate way.

During this period Tearfund also developed a network of Tearcraft representatives who would organise events in their homes and churches, introducing their friends and neighbours to Tearcraft and its products. Tearcraft often opened doors for Tearfund to get involved with new churches as they would organise a stall at the church fete and in many cases this provided an entrée for people to learn more about Tearfund and get more involved.

In all these ways Tearfund sought to educate UK evangelicals about poverty and suffering in developing countries and to encourage them to give money to Tearfund and to pray for its staff, partners, and beneficiaries.

From 1990s to mid-2000s

In the early 1990s Tearfund set up a dedicated Communications Department to take forward the work of educating UK evangelicals about justice and world poverty and to inspire them to get involved by supporting Tearfund. During this period Tearfund built up a network of some 3,000 church representatives who would be the organisation's contact point in their church, distributing Tearfund resources and materials, and organising events. On top of this Tearfund developed a network of about 150 accredited speakers who would travel around the country giving talks and presentations in local churches, while Tearfund Regional Coordinators would organise events, speak with Christian youth groups, and set up monthly prayer groups. Sometimes UK tours were organised for speakers to tour the country, visiting local churches, accompanied by evangelical music bands. Tearfund also set up a dedicated call centre so that supporters could call in and ask any questions that they might have about the organisation and its work. In all these ways Tearfund strove to build and nurture relationships with UK evangelicals through the already-existing church networks.

Tearfund also continued to reach out to new churches and new communities. It sought to win them over to the new idea of integral mission and convince them that it was biblically sound and indeed biblically mandated. Stephen Rand, who worked in the Communications Department for many years, explains:

> Our communications sought to bring about a particular kind of conversion experience. People needed to be converted to the idea that caring for the poor was an essential part of what it meant to be a Christian.*

Tearfund developed a good relationship with the then newly growing charismatic churches, particularly with New Wine, and was largely successful in winning them over to integral mission. However, while it was successful in reaching out to certain sections of the UK evangelical church there were other sections that were not interested or where the relationship did not gel. Some churches, particularly on the more conservative end of the spectrum, held different theological views and thought that spiritual evangelism was the most important thing to be doing and were not interested in supporting practical action. Other churches had different ideas about the best way to carry out integral mission, preferring to send their own missionaries overseas or to support direct church-to-church projects.[1] Tearfund was also less successful in reaching out to black-majority churches. The organisation thus reached a particular segment of the UK evangelical church and its supporters were predominantly white, middle-class evangelical Anglicans, Baptists, Charismatics, Independents, Methodists, and Presbyterians.

In terms of reach, around 52 per cent of UK evangelicals had heard of Tearfund in 2005 and some 20 per cent were supporters (Ashworth 2017). These numbers remained broadly similar in 2018. At the time of writing, there are Tearfund church representatives in approximately 3,000 UK churches, out of a total of about 25,000 evangelical churches (and 50,000 churches in total). This means that about 12 per cent of evangelical churches support Tearfund in one way or another. While some churches support Tearfund by simply raising money for the organisation in church collections every now and then, other churches support Tearfund in a deeper and 'whole life' manner that can be transformative for both individuals and congregations.

One feature of Tearfund's engagement with the UK church is the emphasis put on prayer. Since the very beginning Tearfund had sent out a prayer diary along with *Tear Times*, asking supporters to pray for specific projects and situations. In all communications, whether by telephone or email or more recently WhatsApp, supporters were and are always encouraged to pray for the poor. In 1992 Tearfund took this a step further and launched *World Watch Prayer Link*, which sent out detailed prayer items to churches each week so that they would be able to knowledgeably talk about world issues and current disasters and lead focussed prayers on these matters, rather than, in the words of one Tearfund staff member, 'Just say, "God bless Africa"'.

At this time Tearfund began to place more emphasis on working with youth and to reduce its work with children. In 1989 a youth magazine called *Third Track* was launched, and in 1990 Tearfund partnered with Youth for Christ to set up the 'Through Different Eyes' scheme, in which young UK Christians were taken to developing countries to study the gospel with local Christians (Symonds 1993: 33).

During the mid-1990s Tearfund started to engage with a number of Youth Ministries, such as Soul Survivor, The Message, Scripture Union, Youth for Christ, and others. It sought to inject a justice element into these ministries and shift their discipleship to be more shaped by integral mission. In this way Tearfund was able to influence many young people that action for the poor was an integral part of being a Christian. David Westlake, who was Youth Director from 1995 to 2005, explains:

> In the formative years of growing up people come to convictions and make value choices which will guide them for the rest of their lives. So it is a massive time to present the full gospel to young people so that that becomes their understanding for the rest of their lives.*

The relationship with Soul Survivor turned into a partnership called 'Soul Action'. Soul Action encourages young people to do something about issues of injustice and poverty and offers them several creative opportunities. One of these is 'Slum Survivor' – a simulation experience designed to help young people connect with the lives of some of the world's poorest. Young people are sponsored to spend a few days living in a temporary shelter, eating a limited diet and facing tough challenges to get a taste of what it might be like to be poor and live in a slum. They also take part in Bible studies about poverty and compassion. This can be a significant experiential process for young people, opening their heart to compassion for the poor. Money raised from this and other activities goes to partner projects overseas. Through these and other similar activities Tearfund has sought to shape contemporary evangelical Christianity in the direction of caring for distant others. As David Westlake puts it:

> We were part of establishing justice as a Christian essential for a new generation of Christians. There were young people growing up who could not imagine helping the poor and seeking justice not being part of their faith.

Tearfund also started to reach out to UK evangelicals at Christian festivals that take place across the UK. It had been attending the Keswick Convention since the 1960s and over the years had expanded into other festivals, such as Spring Harvest and New Wine. Tearfund's characteristic activity is to run a café – where it would provide catering alongside information about its projects and activities. It would often also have a seminar space and run seminars and after-hour events, bands, and comedy shows, with a strong Tearfund focus, as well as organising items on the main stage. Many supporters would volunteer at these events, helping to spread the word about Tearfund's work. During the late 1990s and early 2000s there was a big shift as Tearfund became more known and its message more understood and better received. Jennie Collins recalls:

> When I first went to New Wine which was probably around 1996, it was a struggle for Tearfund to even get an appointment with the organiser.... I remember about two years later we managed to get a stand and I and several others did some workshops on justice. In 2005 there wasn't a speaker that I went to at New Wine who didn't talk about our view of the poor and how much this is part of who we are as Christians, and global issues, climate change and how that affects us and our responsibility to the poor.*

During this period there was also a major growth in Tearfund's overseas volunteering programme, which expanded from about 100 people per year to over 500 people per year. Volunteers would spend a few weeks or a few months working on the ground with Tearfund partners in developing countries. There was a particular focus on young people and many volunteers came through the Soul Action programme, which Tearfund had set up with Soul Survivor.

Tearfund was clear that the main reason for running these volunteer programmes was for the impact on the volunteer – to get a deep and experiential understanding of poverty and injustice and to see a practical Christianity in action. The Soul Action website puts it like this:

> It's all about the journey.... We go not to change the world but to encounter God and be changed. By leaving our comfort, exposing ourselves to the poor and the amazing brothers and sisters who work in incredibly challenging situations our own sense of discipleship is transformed. We meet with God. Our duty is to work out this encounter in the rest of our lives. To come home and live differently in the light of what we experienced. You will not change the world by volunteering overseas with Tearfund. But the world you encounter and the God who meets you there will change you for the rest of your life.
>
> (Soul Action 2018)

It is very hard to measure the impact of these activities. Many young people come back inspired and aflame and get involved in activities supporting Tearfund. Some give talks about their experiences, others set up prayer groups, and others challenge their church or university to become Fairtrade. Many start raising money for Tearfund. And quite a few have ended up working for Tearfund!

Tim Malcolm, who now works in Tearfund's Connected Church team, first heard about the organisation at its café at Soul Survivor. He later volunteered with it and then just continued to be involved. He says:

> One of the things that drew me to Tearfund was that you're not just a charity that wants my money, you really care about what God says about how we should be living our lives. And you're saying that what Jesus wants for me is not just to be good. You know, when I was growing up the church was more in the place of, 'You believe in Jesus and then you commit your life to the Lord and then you are saved, and that is good and then you can go to heaven.' While Tearfund was, 'No, Jesus is great, he gives us this model of how to live your life and it's all about how you live your life not just what you believe.'

Tearfund raises a large proportion of its funds directly from its UK supporters. In the early days all its funding came from churches and individuals in the UK. In the 1990s Tearfund started to professionalise, both by accepting more institutional funding from the UK government and others, and also by employing fundraising professionals and starting to use telemarketing and other dedicated fundraising approaches. To this day supporter donations still amount to a high percentage of overall funding, proportionally higher than that received by many secular relief and development NGOs.

Tearfund's Christian identity and its faith-based approach to fundraising is fundamental in this. Most of Tearfund's supporters are evangelical Christians and are motivated by their faith in their approach to charitable giving (Harrison 2017). According to a survey by the Evangelical Alliance British evangelicals are generous givers to charitable causes, with some 60 per cent giving 10 per cent of their income as a tithe to their church and charities. Most prefer to give to Christian charities, although they also give generously to secular charities. In 2010, for example, 86 per cent of the sample had given money to Christian charities while only 57 per cent had given to secular charities (Green and Hewitt 2011: 12).

Tearfund places great emphasis on developing relationships with its supporters and building trust. As well as telling them about the work of its partners around the world, Tearfund seeks to inspire them about integral mission and 'God's heart for the poor'. This 'whole life' approach encourages them to see giving to Tearfund as part of their religious practice, alongside praying for the end of poverty, changing their lifestyle, and campaigning for justice. One of the outcomes of this faith-based approach is that Tearfund supporters are very loyal and very generous.

Receiving this high proportion of supporter donations also affects how Tearfund can work. About half of this money is 'unrestricted', meaning that it can be spent on whatever Tearfund thinks is best, within agreed boundaries. It is not tied to particular projects or to particular outputs. Having a relatively large amount of unrestricted funding gives Tearfund a much higher degree of flexibility and freedom than many other NGOs. This means that it can experiment in new areas and with new methodologies more easily. It was this unrestricted funding that initially enabled Tearfund to experiment with the CCM approach and led to the development of a whole new faith-based methodology that would go on to become central to Tearfund's work. And, indeed, it is the unrestricted funding from supporters that enables it to continue with CCM work and to scale it up. Thus having such a pool of committed, faith-inspired, UK supporters has been crucial in Tearfund developing its specific faith-based approach to development practice.

Mid-2000s onwards

From the mid-2000s onwards many Tearfund programmes with its UK supporters began to take a new shape. In 2008 Tearfund set up a new programme called Connected Church. This built on an earlier programme called Partners in Development, which had run in the 1980s and in which supporters gave regularly to a specific country and then received updates about development issues within that country. In the new Connected Church programme more effort was put into using new technologies to nurture a closer relationship between supporters and the projects and their beneficiaries and Tearfund created an online programme linking UK churches to overseas partners. Churches would sign up and agree to support a particular partner, and in return they would receive news and updates and be able to chat to the partner online. Sometimes church groups would even organise visits to the partner and see the work on the ground. This programme still runs today and there are currently about 200–300 UK churches taking part.

The volunteer programme also took a new shape as it continued to grow. First known as Transform and then as the International Volunteering Team, it now enables 18–30-year-olds to go on different types of volunteer placements, for two to four weeks or three to six months. Many evangelicals think of these as 'short-term mission' opportunities and they are often advertised as such in evangelical media. The programme now also organises family trips and group trips. In 2013 Tearfund was able to further scale up its volunteering programme by participating in the International Citizen Service programme, funded by DFID. In this programme young people aged 18 to 25 years are sent overseas for 10–12 weeks on a volunteer placement on a partner project, where they also work with volunteers from within that country. When they come back, they are encouraged to do an action at home. This has enabled a much broader group of young people to experience the benefits of volunteering overseas.

Tearfund also set up a new Specialist Volunteers team, which works with community fundraisers to organise fun and challenging activities that will raise money for the organisation. Volunteers might organise a sponsored bike ride, or skydive, or big bake. Or they might take part in activities such as the Mean Bean Challenge, whereby participants get sponsored to eat only rice and beans for five days. This team uses new digital technologies and is active on social media. In this way it is able to reach out to evangelical Christians outside the Sunday church framework. Thus as well as bringing in funds for overseas work, this team is helping Tearfund to reach new supporters in new ways.

Tearfund has also been working to help its supporters see that caring for the environment is closely linked to overcoming poverty and during the mid-2000s it began to focus much more on lifestyle issues. It encouraged its supporters to 'be the change' by shifting their lifestyles into low-consumption, more environmentally friendly directions. It placed more emphasis on campaigning work and developed numerous Bible studies and methodologies to get supporters to see how they could help poor communities around the world by campaigning for justice and to show them that this was a deeply religious activity. Supporters were encouraged to 'give, pray and act' in order to outwork integral mission in their lives. This approach proved extremely inspiring and motivating for many people and enabled Tearfund to mobilise tens of thousands of supporters to carry out huge numbers of campaign actions.

More recently Tearfund has begun to expand its focus outside the UK in order to influence US and other global evangelicals towards integral mission. In the last few years it has contributed a number of Bible studies about poverty, spiritual growth, and the global church to the YouVersion app, which had been developed by LIFE Church. The app enables Christians to do Bible study any time and any place, and thus extends Tearfund's reach beyond communicating in churches on Sundays. So far there have been around 500,000 downloads of these studies and several have been translated into other languages including Chinese, Dutch, and Swahili. In 2018 Tearfund opened an office in the USA and started to reach out more actively to US evangelicals.

Concluding thoughts

This appendix has given a brief overview of some of Tearfund's work with supporters in the UK. It has shown that during its first 25 years Tearfund carried out significant educational work with its predominantly evangelical supporters by developing relations with a network of churches and providing them with resources and materials to educate their congregations about the situation of people in developing countries and the importance of supporting social action. In its second 25 years Tearfund began to change the way that it worked with its supporters. It developed a more professional approach to fundraising and it began to shift the emphasis from educational work towards developing a specifically faith-based approach to mobilising its supporters to 'give, pray and act'. This approach centred on 'whole life response' in which donating to Tearfund, praying for the poor, making lifestyle changes, and campaigning for justice are seen as religious activities and an outworking of faith. This faith-based approach has been very inspiring for many UK evangelicals and enabled Tearfund to mobilise high numbers of donations and high numbers of campaign actions.

While most UK development NGOs, and indeed most mission agencies, seek to establish a network of supporters by providing them with information about overseas activities and organising local fundraising events, Tearfund has placed particular emphasis on combining the material and the spiritual into a specifically faith-based approach to outreach and fundraising. Connecting with the network of evangelical churches in the UK – in a community in which the majority still attend church most Sundays – Tearfund has been able to use this religious structure to reach a very large number of people. This has enabled them to be known within the development world as an organisation that can bring huge numbers of campaigners to rallies. When it comes to supporter-facing work, the combination of faith and development is much more straightforward.

Note

1 I am not aware of any in-depth studies of development carried out through direct church-to-church partnerships between evangelical churches, but for an excellent study of such projects carried out between Catholic congregations in the US and Haiti see Hefferan 2007.

Bibliography

Adeney, David. 2003. Project Caleb: Partner Verification Events. Interim Report for Tearfund.
Adeney, David. 1994. Memo to Executive Team. Internal Tearfund document.
Agensky, Jonathan. 2013. Dr Livingstone, I Presume? Evangelicals, Africa and Faith-Based Humanitarianism. *Global Society*, 27, 4: 454–74.
Ager, Alastair and Joey Ager. 2011. Faith and the Discourse of Secular Humanitarianism. *Journal of Refugee Studies*, 24, 3: 456–72.
Alkire, Sabina. 2005. *Valuing Freedoms: Sen's Capability Approach and Poverty Reduction*. Oxford: Oxford University Press.
Ashworth, Jacinta. 2017. Market Research Tracking Survey 2005–2017: Summary of Key Insights. Tearfund Awareness Monitor, Wave 10. Tearfund and Ashworth Research. Internal document.
Atherstone, Andrew. 2017. Evangelicals Exit their Ghetto. Church Times. Available at www.churchtimes.co.uk/articles/2017/31-march/features/features/evangelicals-exit-their-ghetto
Atkins, Andy. 2002. Corporate Advocacy Strategy, 2002–05. Tearfund.
Barnett, Michael. 2011. *Empire of Humanity: A History of Humanitarianism*. Ithaca, NY: Cornell University Press.
Barnett, Michael and Janice Stein. 2012. The Secularization and Sanctification of Humanitarianism. In *Sacred Aid: Faith and Humanitarianism*, edited by Michael Barnett and Janice Stein. Oxford: Oxford University Press.
Barrett, Marlene. 2000. *The World Will Never Be the Same Again*. London: Jubilee 2000 Coalition.
Bebbington, David. 1989. *Evangelicalism in Modern Britain: A History from the 1730s to the 1980s*. London: Routledge.
Becker, Felicitas and P. Wenzel Geissler (eds). 2009. *Aids and Religious Practice in Africa*. Leiden: Brill.
Bellah, Robert. 1963. Reflections on the Protestant Ethic Analogy in Asia. *Journal of Social Issues*, 19, 1: 52–60.
Bellah, Robert. 1957. *Tokugawa Religion: The Values of Pre-Industrial Japan*. Boston, MA: Beacon Press.
Benthall, Jonathan. 2012. 'Cultural Proximity' and the Conjuncture of Islam with Modern Humanitarianism. In *Sacred Aid: Faith and Humanitarianism*, edited by Michael Barnett and Janice Stein. Oxford: Oxford University Press.
Benthall, Jonathan and Jerome Bellion-Jourdan. 2003. *The Charitable Crescent: Politics of Aid in the Muslim World*. London: I. B. Tauris & Co Ltd.

Bibliography

Berger, Julia. 2003. Religious Nongovernmental Organizations: An Exploratory Analysis. *Voluntas: International Journal of Voluntary and Nonprofit Organizations*, 14, 1: 15–39.

Black, Maggie. 1992. *A Cause for Our Time: Oxfam, The First 50 Years*. Oxford: Oxfam Publishing.

Bocking-Welch, Anna. 2016. Youth Against Hunger: Service, Activism and the Mobilisation of Young Humanitarians in 1960s Britain. *European Review of History*, 23, 1–2: 154–70.

Boli, John and George Thomas. 1999. INGOs and the Organisation of World Culture. In *Constructing World Culture: International Nongovernmental Organizations since 1875*, edited by John Boli and George Thomas. Berkeley, CA: Stanford University Press.

Bornstein, Erica. 2003. *The Spirit of Development: Protestant NGOs, Morality and Economics in Zimbabwe*. New York: Routledge.

Bosch, David. 2011. *Transforming Mission: Paradigm Shifts in Theology of Mission*. New York: Orbis.

Bradbury, Steve. 2013. Missions, Missionaries, and Development. In *Handbook of Research on Development and Religion*, edited by Matthew Clarke. Cheltenham: Edward Elgar Publishing.

Bradley, Tamsin. 2009. A Call for Clarification and Critical Analysis of the Work of Faith-Based Development Organizations (FBDO). *Progress in Development Studies*, 9, 2: 101–14.

Bradley, Tamsin. 2006. Does Compassion Bring Results? A Critical Perspective on Faith and Development. *Culture and Religion*, 6, 3: 337–51.

British Council of Churches. 1966. *World Poverty and British Responsibility*. London: SCM Press.

Brown, Stephen and Lalbiakhlui (Kuki) Rokhum. 2012. Integral Mission Project Evaluation Report. Tearfund Nepal internal document.

Bulmer, Andrew, Jane Mackenzie, and Dadirai Chikwengo. 2014. CCM Investment Scoping Report. Tearfund internal report.

Burchardt, Marian. 2009. Subjects of Counselling: Religion, HIV/AIDS and the Management of Everyday Life in South Africa. In *Aids and Religious Practice in Africa*, edited by Felicitas Becker and P. Wenzel Geissler. Leiden: Brill.

Burkina Faso CCMP Evaluation 2017. Tearfund–CCMP Evaluation Report for 2010–2015. Tearfund internal evaluation report.

Byrne, Paul. 1997. *Social Movements in Britain*. London: Routledge.

Cabanes, Bruno. 2014. *The Great War and the Origins of Humanitarianism, 1918–1924*. Cambridge: Cambridge University Press.

Calhoun, Craig. 2008. The Imperative to Reduce Suffering: Charity, Progress, and Emergencies in the Field of Humanitarian Action. In *Humanitarianism in Question: Politics, Power, Ethics*, edited by Michael Barnett and Thomas Weiss. Ithaca, NY: Cornell University Press.

Canessa, Andrew 2000. Contesting Hybridity: Evangelistas and Kataristas in Highland Bolivia. *Journal of Latin American Studies* 32, 1: 115–44.

Cannell, Fenella (ed.). 2006. *The Anthropology of Christianity*. Durham, NC: Duke University Press.

Carpenter, Joel. 2014. What's New about the New Evangelical Social Engagement? In *The New Evangelical Social Engagement*, edited by Brian Steensland and Philip Goff. Oxford: Oxford University Press.

Carpenter, Joel and Wilbert Shenk. 1990. Preface. In *Earthen Vessels: American Evangelicals and Foreign Missions, 1880–1980*, edited by Joel Carpenter and Wilbert Shenk. Eugene, OR: Wipf and Stock.
Casanova, Jose. 1994. *Public Religions in the Modern World*. Chicago, IL: Chicago University Press.
Catalano, Roberto. 2014. Missionary Societies in the Evangelical Churches: Origins and Characteristics. *Annales Missiologici Posnanienses*, 19: 107–35.
Chambers, Robert and Gordon Conway. 1991. Sustainable Rural Livelihoods: Practical Concepts for the 21st Century. IDS discussion paper 296.
Chester, Tim. 2002. What Makes Christian Development Christian? Paper presented at Global Connections Relief and Development Forum. Available at www.global connections.org.uk/sites/newgc.localhost/files/papers/What%20makes%20Christian %20Development%20Christian%20-%20Tim%20Chester%20-%20May%2002.pdf
Chetri, Rupa. 2016. Church Strengthening and Mobilization Project Nepal: Evaluation Report. Tearfund internal document.
Clarke, Gerard. 2013. The Perils of Entanglement: Bilateral Donors, Faith-Based Organisations and International Development. In *International Development Policy: Religion and Development*, edited by Giles Carbonnier. Basingstoke: Palgrave Macmillan.
Clarke, Gerard. 2007. Agents of Transformation? Donors, Faith-Based Organisations and International Development. *Third World Quarterly*, 28, 1: 77–96.
Clarke, Gerard and Michael Jennings. 2008. *Development, Civil Society and Faith-Based Organizations: Bridging the Sacred and the Secular*. New York: Palgrave Macmillan.
Clarke, Matthew and Vicky-Anne Ware. 2015. Understanding Faith-Based Organizations: How FBOs are Contrasted with NGOs in International Development Literature. *Progress in Development Studies*, 15, 1: 37–48.
Clawson, Michael. 2012. Misión Integral and Progressive Evangelicalism: The Latin American Influence on the North American Emerging Church. *Religions*, 3: 790–807.
Cohen, David. 1993a. Policy Review of Evangelism and Christian Education. Report for Tearfund.
Cohen, David. 1993b. Scholarships Review. Report for Tearfund.
Cooper, Thia. 2007. *Controversies in Political Theology: Development or Liberation?* London: SCM Press.
Copestake, James, Michelle James, Marlies Morsink, and Charlotte Flowers. 2019. Faith-Based Rural Poverty Reduction in Uganda. In *Attributing Development Impact: The Qualitative Impact Protocol (QuIP) Case Book*, edited by James Copestake, Marlies Morsink, and Fiona Remnant. Rugby: Practical Action Publishing.
Crewe, Emma and Elizabeth Harrison. 1998. *Whose Development? An Ethnography of Aid*. London: Zed Books.
Dalelo, Aklilu. 2003. *The Church and Socio-Economic Transformation: The Impacts of the Community Development Services of the Ethiopian Kale Heywet Church*. Addis Abeba: Ethiopian Kale Heywet Church.
Deacon, Gerald and Emma Tomalin. 2015. A History of Faith-Based Aid and Development. In *The Routledge Handbook of Religions and Global Development*, edited by Emma Tomalin. London: Routledge.
Deepan, Prabu. 2017. Transforming Masculinities: A Training Manual for Gender Champions. Teddington: Tearfund.
Deneulin, Severine, with Masooda Bano. 2009. *Religion in Development; Rewriting the Secular Script*. London: Zed Books.

Deneulin, Severine and Carol Rakodi. 2011. Revisiting Religion: Development Studies Thirty Years On. *World Development*, 39, 1: 45–54.
Derham, Morgan. 1978. Springs Need No Pumps. *Third Way*, 2, 4: 8–9.
Diaz, Melvin. 2008. Cheas Ponleu/Shining Light Project, Cambodia: End Term Evaluation Report. Cambodia: Wholistic Development Organisation. Internal Evaluation sent to Tearfund.
Dromi, Shai. 2016. Soldiers of the Cross: Calvinism, Humanitarianism and the Genesis of Social Fields. *Sociological Theory*, 34, 3: 196–219.
Edwards. Joel. 2008. Micah Challenge: The Story So Far. In *Micah's Challenge: The Church's Responsibility to the Global Poor*, edited by Justin Thacker and Marijke Hoek. Milton Keynes: Paternoster.
Edwards, Michael and David Hulme. 1996. Too Close for Comfort? The Impact of Official Aid on Nongovernmental Organizations. *World Development*, 24, 6: 961–73.
Ellis, Stephen and Gerrie ter Haar. 1998. Religion and Politics in Sub-Saharan Africa. *The Journal of Modern African Studies*, 36, 2: 175–201.
Endersbee, Mary. 1973. *They Can't Eat Prayer: The Story of Tearfund*. London: Hodder & Stoughton.
Englund, Harri. 1996. Witchcraft, Modernity and the Person: The Morality of Accumulation in Central Malawi. *Critique of Anthropology*, 16, 3: 257–79.
Evans, Alex and Gower, Richard. 2015. The Restorative Economy: Completing our unfinished millennium jubilee. Teddington: Tearfund. Available at www.tearfund.org/~/media/Files/Main_Site/Campaigning/OrdinaryHeroes/Restorative_Economy_Full_Report.pdf
Eves, Richard and Miranda Forsyth. 2015. Developing Insecurity: Sorcery, Witchcraft and Melanesian Economic Development. Australian National University: SSGM Discussion Paper 2015/7.
Falk, Richard. 2003. A Worldwide Religious Resurgence in an Era of Globalization and Apocalyptic Terrorism. In *Religion in International Relations: Culture and Religion in International Relations*, edited by Pavlos Hatzopoulos and Fabio Petito. New York: Palgrave Macmillan.
Faught, Brad. 1994. Missionaries, Indirect Rule and the Changing Mandate of Mission in Colonial Northern Nigeria: The Case of Rowland Victor Bingham and the Sudan Interior Mission. *Canadian Society of Church History Historical Papers*, pp. 121–41.
Featherstone, Andy. 2015. Keeping the Faith: The Role of Faith Leaders in the Ebola Response. London: Christian Aid, CAFOD, Tearfund and Islamic Relief.
Ferris, Elizabeth. 2005. Faith-Based and Secular Humanitarian Organizations. *International Review of the Red Cross*, 87, 858: 311–25.
Ferris, Elizabeth. 2011. Faith and Humanitarianism: It's Complicated. *Journal of Refugee Studies*, 24, 3: 606–25.
Fiedler, Klaus. 2010. Edinburgh 1910, Africa 2010 and the Evangelicals. *Studia Historiae Ecclesiasticae*, 36, 2: 53–71.
Fiedler, Klaus. 1994. *The Story of Faith Missions*. Oxford: Regnum Books.
Fisiy, Cyprian and Peter Geschiere. 2001. Witchcraft, Development and Paranoia in Cameroon: Interactions between Popular, Academic and State Discourse. In *Magical Interpretations, Material Realities: Modernity, Witchcraft and the Occult in Postcolonial Africa*, edited by Henrietta Moore and Todd Sanders. London: Routledge.
Flowers, Charlotte. 2016. Bridging the Gap: The Role of Local Churches in Fostering Local-Level Social Accountability and Governance. Brighton: IDS and Tearfund.

Floyd, Richard. 2008. *Church, Chapel and Party: Religious Dissent and Political Modernization in Nineteenth-Century England*. Basingstoke: Palgrave Macmillan.
Forsythe, David. 2005. *The Humanitarians: The International Committee of the Red Cross*. Cambridge: Cambridge University Press.
Fountain, Philip. 2015. Proselytizing Development. In *The Routledge Handbook of Religions and Global Development*, edited by Emma Tomalin. London: Routledge.
Fountain, Philip. 2013. The Myth of Religious NGOs: Development Studies and the Return of Religion. In *International Development Policy: Religion and Development*, edited by Gilles Carbonnier. Basingstoke: Palgrave Macmillan.
Freeman, Dena. In press. Mobilising Evangelicals for Development Advocacy: Politics and Theology in the Micah Challenge Campaign for the Millennium Development Goals. In *Faith Based Organizations in Development Discourses and Practices*, edited by Jens Koehrsen and Andreas Heuser. London: Routledge.
Freeman, Dena. 2018. From 'Christians Doing Development' to 'Doing Christian Development': The Changing Role of Religion in the International Work of Tearfund. *Development in Practice*, 28, 2: 280–91.
Freeman, Dena. 2017. Affordances of Rupture and their Enactment: A Framework for Understanding Christian Change. *Journal of the Finnish Anthropological Society*, 42, 4: 3–24.
Freeman, Dena. 2015. Pentecostalism and Economic Development in Sub-Saharan Africa. In *The Routledge Handbook of Religions and Global Development*, edited by Emma Tomalin. London: Routledge.
Freeman, Dena. 2013. Pentecostalism in a Rural Context: Dynamics of Religion and Development in Southwest Ethiopia. *PentecoStudies* 12, 2: 231–49.
Freeman, Dena (ed.). 2012a. *Pentecostalism and Development: Churches, NGOs and Social Change in Africa*. Basingstoke: Palgrave Macmillan.
Freeman, Dena. 2012b. The Pentecostal Ethic and the Spirit of Development. In *Pentecostalism and Development: Churches, NGOs and Social Change in Africa*, edited by Dena Freeman. London: Palgrave Macmillan.
Freeman, Kathleen. 1965. *If Any Man Build: The History of the Save the Children Fund*. London: Hodder & Stoughton,
Friesen, Elizabeth. 2012. *Challenging Global Finance: Civil Society and Transnational Networks*. Basingstoke: Palgrave Macmillan.
Gailey, Charles and Howard Culbertson. 2007. *Discovering Missions*. Kansas City, KS: Beacon Hill Press.
Gardner, Katy and David Lewis. 1996. *Anthropology, Development and the Post-Modern Challenge*. London: Pluto Press.
Gasaway, Brantley. 2014. *Progressive Evangelicals and the Pursuit of Social Justice*. Chapel Hill, NC: University of North Carolina Press.
Geertz, Clifford. 1962. Social Change and Economic Modernization in Two Indonesian Towns: A Case in Point. In *On the Theory of Social Change*, edited by Everett Hagen. Homewood, IL: Dorsey.
Geertz, Clifford. 1956. Religious Belief and Economic Behaviour in a Central Javanese Town: Some Preliminary Considerations. *Economic Development and Cultural Change*, 4, 2: 134–58.
Gehman, Richard. 2004. The Africa Inland Mission: Aspects of Its Early History. *Africa Journal of Evangelical Theology*, 23, 2: 115–44.
Geschiere, Peter. 1997. *The Modernity of Witchcraft: Politics and the Occult in Postcolonial Africa*. Charlottesville, VA: University of Virginia Press.

Gifford, Paul. 1990. Prosperity: A New and Foreign Element in African Christianity. *Religion*, 20, 4: 373–88.

Global Advocacy Team. 2016. Movements for Change: Deep Dive Pre-Reading. Tearfund internal document.

Golooba-Mutebi, Frederick. 2005. Witchcraft, Social Cohesion and Participation in a South African Village. *Development and Change*, 36, 5: 937–58.

Gorsky, Martin. 1999. *Patterns of Philanthropy: Charity and Society in Nineteenth Century Bristol*. Woodbridge: Boydell Press.

Green, Phil and Benita Hewitt. 2011. 21st Century Evangelicals: A Snapshot of the Beliefs and Habits of Evangelical Christians in the UK. London: Evangelical Alliance.

Habermas, Jurgen. 2008. Notes on Post-Secular Society. *New Perspectives Quarterly*, 25, 4: 17–29.

Halvorson, Britt. 2018. *Conversionary Sites: Transforming Medical Aid and Global Christianity from Madagascar to Minnesota*. Chicago, IL: University of Chicago Press.

Hansford, Bob and Paul Venton. 2006. Reducing Disaster Risk in our Communities. Teddington: Tearfund.

Harris, Nigel. 2017. Business Plan Priorities 2018/19 Summary. Tearfund internal document.

Harrison, Katie. 2017. Joyful Givers. Teddington: Tearfund.

Hasu, Paivi. 2012. Prosperity Gospels and Enchanted World Views: Two Responses to Socio-Economic Transformations in Tanzanian Pentecostal–Charismatic Christianity. In *Pentecostalism and Development: Churches, NGOs and Social Change in Africa*, edited by Dena Freeman. Basingstoke: Palgrave Macmillan.

Haustein, Jorg and Emma Tomalin. 2017. Religion and Development in Africa and Asia. In *Routledge Handbook of Africa–Asia Relations*, edited by Pedro Amakasu Raposo, David Arase, and Scarlett Cornelissen. London: Routledge.

Hearn, Julie. 2002. The 'Invisible' NGO: US Evangelical Missions in Kenya. *Journal of Religion in Africa*, 32, 1: 32–60.

Hefferan, Tara. 2007. *Twinning Faith and Development: Catholic Parish Partnering in the US and Haiti*. Boulder, CO: Kumarian Press.

Helmstadter, Richard and Bernard Lightman (eds). 1990. *Victorian Faith in Crisis: Essays on Continuity and Change in Nineteenth Century Religious Belief*. Basingstoke: Macmillan.

Heuser, Andreas (ed.). 2015. *Pastures of Plenty: Tracing Religioscapes of Prosperity Gospel in Africa and Beyond*. Berlin: Peter Lang.

Hickel, Jason. 2014. Xenophobia in South Africa: Order, Chaos, and the Moral Economy of Witchcraft. *Cultural Anthropology*, 29, 1: 103–27.

Hilton, Matthew. 2012. International Aid and Development NGOs in Britain and Human Rights since 1945. *Humanity*, 3, 3: 449–72.

Hilton, Matthew, Nick Crowson, Jean-François Mouhout and James McKay. 2012. *A Historical Guide to NGOs in Britain: Charities, Civil Society and the Voluntary Sector since 1945*. Basingstoke: Palgrave Macmillan.

Hirsch, Eric 2008. God or Tidibe? Melanesian Christianity and the Problem of Wholes. *Ethnos* 73, 2: 141–62.

Hofer, Katharina. 2003. The Role of Evangelical NGOs in International Development: A Comparative Case Study of Kenya and Uganda. *Afrika Spectrum*, 38, 3: 375–98.

Hollow, Mike. 2008. *A Future and a Hope: The Story of Tearfund and Why God Wants the Church to Change the World*. Oxford: Monarch Books

Hopgood, Stephen. 2006. *Keepers of the Flame: Understanding Amnesty International*. Ithaca, NY: Cornell University Press.

Hopgood, Stephen and Leslie Vinjamuri. 2012. Faith in Markets. In *Sacred Aid: Faith and Humanitarianism*, edited by Michael Barnett and Janice Gross Stein. Oxford: Oxford University Press.

Hovland, Ingie. 2012. 'What Do You Call the Heathen These Days?': For and Against Renewal in the Norwegian Mission Society. In *Multi-Sited Ethnography: Problems and Possibilities in the Translocation of Research Methods*, edited by Simon Coleman and Pauline von Hellermann. London: Routledge.

Hovland, Ingie. 2008. Who's Afraid of Religion? Tensions between 'Mission' and 'Development' in the Norwegian Mission Society. In *Development, Civil Society and Faith-Based Organizations: Bridging the Sacred and the Secular*, edited by Gerard Clarke and Michael Jennings. New York: Palgrave Macmillan.

Howard, Roland. 1993. Tearfund Silver Jubilee. *Third Way*, 16, 8: 9–10. Available at www.icrc.org/eng/resources/documents/article/other/code-of-conduct-290296.htm

Hughes, Dewi. 2003. Proselytism Policy Statement. Tearfund internal document.

Hughes, Rebecca. 2013. 'Science in the Hands of Love': British Evangelical Missionaries and Colonial Development in Africa, c.1940–60. *Journal of Imperial and Commonwealth History*, 41, 5: 823–42.

Hylson-Smith, Kennet. 2011. Evangelical Missionary Alliance. In *Religion Past and Present*, edited by Hans Dieter Betz, Don Browning, Bernd Janowski, and Eberhard Jüngel. Leiden: Brill.

ICRC. 1994. The Code of Conduct for the International Red Cross and Red Crescent Movement and NGOs in Disaster Relief. Available at www.icrc.org/en/doc/assets/files/publications/icrc-002-1067.pdf

ICVA. 2016. Localisation in Humanitarian Practice. Geneva: International Council of Voluntary Agencies.

Iqbal, Shaukat, Sarah Dilloway, and Eleanor Tuck. 2008. Accountability to Beneficiaries in Kashmir. Teddington: Tearfund.

Iriye, Akira. 2002. *Global Community: The Role of International Organisations in the Making of the Contemporary World*. Los Angeles, CA: California University Press.

Iszatt, Phillip. 2003. Can the Nation be Changed – by the Church? Paper presented at the Global Connections Relief and Development Forum. Available at www.globalconnections.org.uk/sites/newgc.localhost/files/papers/Can%20a%20nation%20be%20changed%20-%20by%20the%20church%20-%20Philip%20Iszatt%20-%20Aug%2002.pdf

James, Michelle. 2018. QuIP Report on Tearfund's Church & Community Mobilisation (CCM): Western Urban Area & Bo, Sierra Leone. Teddington: Tearfund.

James, Michelle. 2016. QuIP Report on Tearfund's Church and Community Mobilisation (CCM): Kitgum and Soroti Region, Uganda. Bath Social and Development Research Ltd.

Jeavons, Thomas. 1998. Identifying Characteristics of 'Religious' Organizations: An Exploratory Proposal. In *Sacred Companies: Organizational Aspects of Religion and Religious Aspects of Organizations*, edited by N.J. Demerath, Peter Hall, Terry Schmitt, and Rhys Williams. New York: Oxford University Press.

Johnsen, Sarah. 2014. Where's the 'Faith' in 'Faith-Based' Organisations? The Evolution and Practice of Faith-Based Homelessness Services in the UK. *Journal of Social Policy*, 43, 2: 413–30.

Johnson, Todd, Gina Zurlo, and Albert Hickman. 2015. Status of Global Christianity, 2015, in the Context of 1900–2050. *International Bulletin of Missionary Research*, 39, 1: 30–1.

Johnson, Todd, Gina Zurlo, Albert Hickman, and Peter Crossing. 2018. Christianity 2018: More African Christians and Counting Martyrs. *International Bulletin of Mission Research*, 42, 1: 20–8.

Bibliography

Jones, Andrew. 2014. British Humanitarian NGOs and the Disaster Relief Industry, 1942–1985. PhD dissertation, Department of History, University of Birmingham.
Jones, Ben and Marie Juul Petersen. 2011. Instrumental, Narrow, Normative? Reviewing Recent Work on Religion and Development. *Third World Quarterly*, 32, 7: 1291–306.
Kalofonos, Ippolytos. 2008. Prayer is Medicine: HIV Evangelization in Central Mozambique. Paper presented to the workshop Religious Engagements with Disease, Past and Present, Copenhagen.
Karam, Azza. 2010. The United Nations Population Fund's Legacy of Engaging Faith-Based Organisations as Cultural Agents of Change. *CrossCurrents*, 60, 3; 432–50.
Khanal, Durga. 2016. Sagoal Evaluation Report. United Mission to Nepal internal evaluation report.
Kim, Kirsteen. 2007. Concepts of Development in the Christian Traditions: A Religions and Development Background Paper. Working Paper No. 16. Birmingham: Religions and Development Research Programme, University of Birmingham.
Krause, Monika. 2014. *The Good Project: Humanitarian Relief NGOs and the Fragmentation of Reason*. Chicago, IL: University of Chicago Press.
Krause, Monika. 2009. The Logic of Relief: Humanitarian NGOs and Global Governance. PhD dissertation, Department of Sociology, New York University.
Lawford, John. 1990. Memo to Management. Internal Tearfund document.
Le Roux, Elisabet. 2015. A Scoping Study on the Role of Faith Communities and Organisations in Prevention and Response to Sexual and Gender-Based Violence: Implications for Policy and Practice. Stellenbosch University: Unit for Religion and Development Research. Available at https://jliflc.com/wp-content/uploads/2015/10/Le-Roux_SGBVFaith-scoping-study_REPORT_30Sept15.pdf
Le Roux, Elisabet. 2011. Silent No More: The Untapped Potential of the Church in Addressing Sexual Violence. Teddington: Tearfund.
Le Roux, Elisabet, Neil Kramm, Nigel Scott, Maggie Sandilands, Lizle Loots, Jill Olivier, Diana Arango, and Veena O'Sullivan. 2016. Getting Dirty: Working with Faith Leaders to Prevent and Respond to Gender-Based Violence. *The Review of Faith and International Affairs*, 14, 3: 22–35.
Leurs, Robert. 2012. Are Faith-Based Organisations Distinctive? Comparing Religious and Secular NGOs in Nigeria. *Development in Practice*, 22, 5–6: 704–20.
Lewis, David. 1998. Development NGOs and the Challenge of Partnership: Changing Relations between North and South. *Social Policy and Administration*, 32, 5: 501–12.
Lewis, David and Nazneen Kanji. 2009. *Non-Governmental Organisations and Development*. London: Routledge.
Luetchford, Mark and Peter Burns. 2003. *Waging the War on Want: 50 Years of Campaigning Against World Poverty*. London: War on Want.
Lunn, Jenny. 2009. The Role of Religion, Spirituality and Faith in Development: A Critical Theory Approach. *Third World Quarterly*, 30, 5: 937–51.
Lynch, Cecilia and Tanya Schwarz. 2016. Humanitarianism's Proselytism Problem. *International Studies Quarterly*, 60: 636–46.
Manji, Firoze. 2002. The Missionary Position: NGOs and Development in Africa. *International Affairs*, 78, 3: 567–83.
Marshall, Katherine. 2001. Development and Religion: A Different Lens on Development Debates. *Peabody Journal of Education*, 76, 3–4: 339–75.
Marshall, Mandy and Nigel Taylor. 2006. Tackling HIV and AIDS with Faith-Based Communities: Learning from Attitudes on Gender Relations and Sexual Rights within

Local Evangelical Churches in Burkina Faso, Zimbabwe, and South Africa. *Gender and Development*, 14, 3: 363–74.

McKechnie, Alastair and Fiona Davies. 2013. Localising Aid: Is it Worth the Risk? London: Overseas Development Institute.

McLeary, Rachel and Robert Barro. 2008. Private Voluntary Organizations Engaged in International Assistance, 1939–2004. *Nonprofit and Voluntary Quarterly*, 37, 3: 512–36.

Micah Network. 2001. Micah Network Declaration on Integral Mission. Available at www.micahnetwork.org/sites/default/files/doc/page/mn_integral_mission_declaration_en.pdf

Moberg, David. 1972. *The Great Reversal: Evangelism versus Social Concern*. Nashville, TN: Holman.

Morris, Robert. 1983. Voluntary Societies and British Urban Elites, 1780–1950. *The Historical Journal*, 26, 1: 95–118.

Mounstephen, Philip. 2014. Our Story: The DNA of CMS. Available at https://churchmissionsociety.org/our-stories/our-story-dna-cms

Mulley, Clare. 2009. *The Woman Who Saved the Children: A Biography of Eglantyne Jebb, Founder of Save the Children*. Oxford: Oneworld.

Myers, Bryant. 2015. Progressive Pentecostalism, Development, and Christian Development NGOs: A Challenge and an Opportunity. *International Bulletin of Missionary Research*, 39, 3: 115–20.

Myers, Bryant. 1999. *Walking with the Poor: Principles and Practices of Transformational Development*. New York: Orbis Books.

Nash, Manning. 1965. *The Golden Road to Modernity: Village Life in Contemporary Burma*. New York: Wiley & Sons.

Nguyen, Vinh-Kim. 2009. Therapeutic Evangelism: Confessional Technologies, Antiretrovirals and Biospiritual Transformation in the Fight against AIDS in West Africa. In *Aids and Religious Practice in Africa*, edited by Felicitas Becker and P. Wenzel Geissler. Leiden: Brill.

Noy, Darren. 2009. Material and Spiritual Conceptions of Development: A Framework of Ideal Types. *Journal of Developing Societies*, 25: 275–307.

O'Connor, Daniel. 2000. *Three Centuries of Mission: The United Society for the Propagation of the Gospel, 1701–2000*. London: Continuum.

Occhipinti, Laurie. 2015. Faith-Based Organizations and Development. In *The Routledge Handbook of Religions and Global Development*, edited by Emma Tomalin. London: Routledge.

Occhipinti, Laurie. 2005. *Acting on Faith: Religious Development Organizations in Northwestern Argentina*. Oxford: Lexington.

ODI. 2013. Localising Aid: Sustaining Change in the Public, Private and Civil Society Sectors. London: Overseas Development Institute.

Offutt, Stephen. 2011. The Role of Short-Term Mission Teams in the New Centers of Global Christianity. *Journal for the Scientific Study of Religion*, 50, 4: 796–811.

Ogrizek, Michel. 2008. The Media-Driven Humanitarian Response: Public Perceptions and Humanitarian Realities as Two Faces of the Same Coin. In *Humanitarian Response Index 2007: Measuring Commitment to Best Practice*, edited by Augusto López-Claros and Silvia Hidalgo. Basingstoke: Palgrave Macmillan.

Oliver, Ernest. 1985. The Challenge of Mission Today. *Christian Brethren Review*, 36: 21–9.

Bibliography

Olivier, Jill. 2016. Hoist by Our Own Petard: Backing Slowly Out of Religion and Development Advocacy. *HTS Theological Studies*, 72, 4: 1–11.

Olivier, Jill and Sally Smith. 2016. Innovative Faith-Community Responses to HIV and AIDS: Summative Lessons from Over Two Decades of Work. *The Review of Faith and International Affairs*, 14, 3: 5–21.

Padilla, René. 2002. Integral Mission and Its Historical Development. In *Justice, Mercy & Humility: Integral Mission and the Poor*, edited by Tim Chester. Carlisle: Paternoster Press.

Paras, Andrea. 2014. Between Missions and Development: Christian NGOs in the Canadian Development Sector. *Canadian Journal of Development Studies*, 35, 3: 439–57.

Paulmann, Johannes. 2013. Conjunctures in the History of International Humanitarian Aid during the Twentieth Century. *Humanity*, 4, 2: 215–38.

Pelkmans, Mathijs. 2009. The 'Transparency' of Christian Proselytizing in Kyrgyzstan. *Anthropological Quarterly*, 82, 2: 423–45.

Pew Research Center. 2012. The Global Religious Landscape: A Report on the Size and Distribution of the World's Major Religious Groups as of 2010. Washington D.C.: Pew Research Center Forum on Religion & Public Life.

Piot, Charles. 2012. Pentecostal and Development Imaginaries in West Africa. In *Pentecostalism and Development: Churches, NGOs and Social Change in Africa*, edited by Dena Freeman. Basingstoke: Palgrave Macmillan.

Porter, Andrew. 2004. *Religion Versus Empire? British Protestant Missionaries and Overseas Expansion, 1700–1914*. Manchester: Manchester University Press.

Priest, Robert and Joseph Priest. 2008. 'They See Everything, and Understand Nothing': Short-Term Missions and Service Learning. *Missiology*, 36, 1: 53–73.

Prince, Ruth, with Denis Philippe and Rijk van Dijk. 2009. Engaging Christianities: Negotiating HIV/AIDS, Health, and Social Relations in East and Southern Africa. *Africa Today*, 56, 1: v–xviii.

Prochaska, Frank. 2006. *Christianity and Social Service in Modern Britain: The Disinherited Spirit*. Oxford: Oxford University Press.

Rakodi, Carole. 2012. A Framework for Analysing the Links between Religion and Development. *Development in Practice*, 22, 5–6: 634–50.

Ramalingam, Ben, Bill Gray, and Georgia Cerruti. 2013. Missed Opportunities: The Case for Strengthening National and Local Partnership-Based Humanitarian Responses. Research Report for Christian Aid, CAFOD, Tearfund, Oxfam GB, and ActionAid.

Rand, Stephen. 1991. Plans to Widen Tearfund's Profile Among Evangelicals in Britain and Ireland: A Consultative Document. Tearfund internal document.

Randall, Ian. 2004. Evangelicals, Ecumenism and Unity: A Case Study of the Evangelical Alliance. *Evangel*, 22, 3: 62–70.

Randall, Ian and David Hilborn. 2001. *One Body in Christ*. Carlisle: Paternoster Press.

Redfield, Peter. 2013. *Life in Crisis: The Ethical Journey of Doctors Without Borders*. Berkeley, CA: University of California Press.

Reid, Fiona and Sharif Gemie. 2013. The Friends Relief Service and Displaced People in Europe After the Second World War, 1945–48. *Quaker Studies*, 17, 2: 223–43.

Reitan, Ruth. 2007. *Global Activism*. London: Routledge.

Rhodes, José. 2002. Footsteps Readership Survey 2002. Report for Tearfund.

Rist, Gilbert. 1997. *The History of Development: From Western Origins to Global Faith*. London: Zed Books.

Robbins, Joel. 2004. *Becoming Sinners: Christianity and Moral Torment in a Papua New Guinea Society*. Berkeley, CA: University of California Press.

Robert, Dana. 1990. The Crisis of Missions: Premillennial Mission Theory and the Origins of Independent Evangelical Missions. In *Earthen Vessels: American Evangelicals and Foreign Missions, 1880–1980*, edited by Joel Carpenter and Wilbert Shenk. Eugene, OR: Wipf and Stock.

Rogers, J. 1989. Review of Tearfund's Overseas Evangelism and Christian Education Department. Report for Tearfund.

Rosen, Nicola. 2018. An Exploration into the Role of Faith within Tearfund's Campaigning. BA dissertation, Department of Religious Studies, University of Leeds.

Salemink, Oscar. 2015. The Purification, Sacralisation and Instrumentalisation of Development as a Religious Enterprise. In *Religion and the Politics of Development*, edited by Philip Fountain, Robin Bush, and Michael Feener. London: Palgrave Macmillan.

Saunders, Clare. 2009. British Humanitarian, Aid and Development NGOs, 1949–Present. In *NGOs in Contemporary Britain*, edited by Nick Crowson, Matthew Hilton, and James McKay. Basingstoke: Palgrave Macmillan.

Scoones, Ian. 1998. Sustainable Rural Livelihoods: A Framework for Analysis. IDS Working Paper 72.

Scott, Nigel. 2015. Longer Term Sustainability of the CCM programme. Tearfund and Gamos internal document.

Scott, Thomas. 2005. *The Global Resurgence of Religion and the Transformation of International Relations: The Struggle for the Soul of the Twenty-First Century*. Basingstoke: Palgrave Macmillan.

Scott, N., A. Foley, C. Dejean, A. Brooks, and S. Batchelor. 2014. An Evidence-Based Study of the Impact of Church and Community Mobilisation in Tanzania. London: Tearfund and Gamos.

Sen, Amartya. 1999. *Development as Freedom*. Oxford: Oxford University Press.

Sider, Ronald. 1978. *Rich Christians in an Age of Hunger*. Sevenoaks: Hodder & Stoughton.

Sider, Ronald and Unruh, Heidi. 2004. Typology of Religious Characteristics of Social Service and Educational Organizations and Programs. *Nonprofit and Voluntary Sector Quarterly*, 33, 1: 109–34.

Smith, Christian. 2002. *Christian America? What Evangelicals Really Want*. Berkeley, CA: University of California Press.

Smith, James. 2012. Saving Development: Secular NGOs, the Pentecostal Revolution and the Search for a Purified Political Space in the Taita Hills, Kenya. In *Pentecostalism and Development: Churches, NGOs and Social Change in Africa*, edited by Dena Freeman. Basingstoke: Palgrave Macmillan.

Smith, James. 2008. *Bewitching Development: Witchcraft and the Reinvention of Development in Neoliberal Kenya*. Chicago, IL: University of Chicago Press.

Smith, Jonathan. 2017. Positioning Missionaries in Development Studies, Policy, and Practice. *World Development*, 90: 63–76.

Soul Action. 2018. www.soulaction.org/mission/transform/

Spiro, Melford. 1966. Buddhism and Economic Action in Burma. *American Anthropologist*, NS, 68, 5: 1163–73.

Stamatov, Peter. 2013. *The Origins of Global Humanitarianism: Religion, Empires, and Advocacy*. Cambridge: Cambridge University Press.

Stamatov, Peter. 2010. Activist Religion, Empire, and the Emergence of Modern Long-Distance Advocacy Networks. *American Sociological Review*, 75, 4: 607–28.

Stanley, Brian. 2013. *The Global Diffusion of Evangelicalism: The Age of Billy Graham and John Stott*. Downers Grove, IL: InterVarsity Press.

Stanley, Brian. 2003. Where Have Our Mission Structures Come From? *Transformation*, 20, 1: 39–46.

Stanley, Brian. 1983. 'Commerce and Christianity': Providence Theory, the Missionary Movement, and the Imperialism of Free Trade, 1842–1860. *Historical Journal*, 26, 1: 71–94.

Steensland, Brian and Philip Goff. 2014. The New Evangelical Social Engagement. In *The New Evangelical Social Engagement*, edited by Brian Steensland and Philip Goff. Oxford: Oxford University Press.

Stone, Russell. 1974. Religious Ethic and the Spirit of Capitalism in Tunisia. *International Journal of Middle East Studies*, 5, 3: 260–73.

Stuart, John. 2008. Overseas Mission, Voluntary Service and Aid to Africa: Max Warren, the Church Missionary Society and Kenya, 1945–63. *The Journal of Imperial and Commonwealth History*, 36, 3: 527–43.

Swart, Gary. 2017. Phephisa Survivor Movement (Pilot Phase): Evaluation Report. Tearfund internal document.

Symonds, Melanie. 1993. *Love in Action: Celebrating 25 Years of Tear Fund*. Guildford: Eagle Press.

Tanner, Lydia and Komuhangi, Catherine. 2018. Review of Tearfund's Guidelines for 'Disasters and the Local Church'. The Research People. External Review.

Taussig, Michael. 1980. *The Devil and Commodity Fetishism in South America*. Chapel Hill, NC: University of North Carolina Press.

Tear Times, 1989. Issue 44.

Tearfund. 2018a. Annual Report and Accounts 2017/18. Teddington: Tearfund.

Tearfund. 2018b. Catalytic Country Operating Model Proposal. Tearfund internal document.

Tearfund. 2018c. Zimbabwe CCMP Review. Tearfund internal evaluation report.

Tearfund. 2017a. Liberia and Chad CCM Review Report. Tearfund internal document.

Tearfund. 2017b. Nigeria CCMP Review. Tearfund internal evaluation report.

Tearfund. 2016a. Tearfund's Theology of Mission. Tearfund internal document.

Tearfund. 2016b. Policy on Sharing our Faith. Tearfund internal document.

Tearfund. 2016c. Theological Underpinning of Church and Community Transformation. Tearfund internal document.

Tearfund. 2015a. Light Wheel Maturity Model. Teddington: Tearfund.

Tearfund. 2015b. Mozambique CCMP Evaluation. Tearfund internal document.

Tearfund. 2015c. Nigeria CCMP Review: Evaluation Report of the Church and Community Mobilisation Process of Church of Christ in Nations (COCIN) Community Development Programme (CDP) 2008–2014. Tearfund internal document.

Tearfund. 2013. Annual Report and Financial Statements: Year Ended 31 March 2013. Teddington: Tearfund.

Tearfund. 2012. Overcoming Poverty Together. Tearfund internal document.

Tearfund. 2011. Disasters and the Local Church: Guidelines for Church Leaders in Disaster Prone Areas. Teddington: Tearfund.

Tearfund. 2009. Annual Report and Accounts 2008–9. Teddington: Tearfund.

Tearfund. 2008. Engaging with the Local Church in Its Response to Disasters. Teddington: Tearfund.

Tearfund. 2007. Annual Report and Accounts 2006–7. Teddington: Tearfund.

Tearfund. 2006. Annual Report and Accounts 2005–6. Teddington: Tearfund.

Tearfund. 2005a. Annual Report and Accounts 2004–5. Teddington: Tearfund.

Tearfund. 2005b. Dried Up, Drowned Out: Voices from Poor Communities on a Changing Climate. Teddington: Tearfund.

Tearfund. 2004. Overcoming Poverty: Tearfund's Understanding. Teddington: Tearfund.
Tearfund. 2003. Paths out of Poverty. Revised June 2003. Teddington: Tearfund.
Tearfund. 2002. Paths out of Poverty. A Tearfund Discussion Paper. Teddington: Tearfund.
Tearfund. 1996. Tearfund: Mission, Beliefs, Values. Teddington: Tearfund.
Tennant, Bob. 2013. *Corporate Holiness: Public Preaching and the Church of England Missionary Societies, 1760–1870*. Oxford: Oxford University Press.
Ter Haar, Gerrie. 2011. Religion and Development: Introducing a New Debate. In *Religion and Development: Ways of Transforming the World*, edited by Gerrie Ter Haar. Oxford: Oxford University Press.
Thacker, Justin. 2015. From Charity to Justice Revisited. *Transformation: International Journal of Holistic Mission Studies*, 32, 2: 112–27.
Thaut, Laura. 2009. The Role of Faith in Christian Faith-Based Humanitarian Agencies: Constructing the Taxonomy. *Voluntas*, 20: 319–50.
Theos. 2010. Wholly Living: A New Perspective on International Development. London: Theos (in partnership with CAFOD and Tearfund).
Tiplady, Richard. 2005. The Legacy of Ernest Oliver. *International Bulletin of Missionary Research*, 29, 1: 38–41.
Tizon, Al. 2010. Precursors and Tensions in Holistic Mission: An Historical Overview. In *Holistic Mission: God's Plan for God's People*, edited by Brian Woolnough and Wonsuk Ma. Oxford: Regnum Books.
Tomalin, Emma. 2012. Thinking about Faith-Based Organisations in Development: Where Have We Got To and What Next? *Development in Practice*, 22, 5–6: 689–703.
Tsegay, Ephraim, Mulugeta Dejenu, Tadesse Dadi, Keith Etherington, and Courtenay Cabot Venton. 2013. Partnerships for Change: A Cost Benefit Analysis of Self Help Groups in Ethiopia. Tearfund internal document.
Turner, Bryan. 2019. The Cosmopolitanism of the Sacred. In *Routledge International Handbook of Cosmopolitanism Studies: 2nd Edition*, edited by Gerard Delanty. Abingdon: Routledge.
Tvedt, Terje. 2006. Understanding the History of the International Aid System and the Development Research Tradition: The Case of the Disappearing Religious NGOs. *Forum for Development Studies*, 33, 2: 341–66.
Tyndale, Wendy (ed.). 2006. *Visions of Development: Faith Based Initiatives*. London: Routledge.
Twigg, John. 2007. Characteristics of a Disaster Resilient Community: A Guidance Note. London: Aon Benfield UCL Hazard Research Centre.
UNFPA. 2008. Culture Matters: A Legacy of Engaging Faith-Based Organizations. New York: United Nations Population Fund.
Vallaeys, Anne. 2004. *Médecins Sans Frontières: La Biographie*. Paris: Fayard.
Van Ufford, Philip and Matthew Schoffeleers. 1988. *Religion and Development: Towards an Integrated Approach*. Amsterdam: Free University Press.
Venton, Courtney Cabot and Jules Siedenburg. 2010. Investing in Communities: The Benefits and Costs of Building Resilience for Food Security in Malawi. Teddington: Tearfund. Available at www.tearfund.org/~/media/files/tilz/research/investing_in_communities_web.pdf
Venton, Paul and Sarah La Trobe. 2008. Linking Disaster Risk Reduction and Climate Change Adaptation. Teddington: Tearfund.
Vilaça, Aparecida and Robin Wright (eds). 2009. *Native Christians: Modes and Effects of Christianity among Indigenous Peoples of the Americas*. Farnham: Ashgate.

Visser t'Hooft, Willem. 2004. The General Ecumenical Development since 1948. In *A History of the Ecumenical Movement, 1948–68*, edited by Harold Fey. Eugene, OR: Wipf & Stock.

Walker, Peter. 2005. Cracking the Code: The Genesis, Use and Future of the Code of Conduct. *Disasters*, 29, 4: 323–36.

Ward, Kevin. 2000. Taking Stock: The Church Missionary Society and Its Historians. In *The Church Mission Society and World Christianity 1799–1999*, edited by Kevin Ward and Brian Stanley. Grand Rapids, MI: Eerdmans.

Watts, Michael. 2015. *The Dissenters: The Crisis and Conscience of Nonconformity*. Oxford: Oxford University Press.

Weber, Max. 2008 [1904]. *The Protestant Ethic and the Spirit of Capitalism*. Translated by Talcott Parsons. Miami, FL: BN Publishing.

Weller, Robert. 1994. Capitalism, Community and the Rise of Amoral Cults. In *Asian Visions of Authority: Religion and the Modern States of East and Southeast Asia*, edited by Charles Keyes, Laurel Kendall, and Helen Hardacre. Honolulu, HI: University of Hawaii Press.

Whitaker, Ben. 1983. *A Bridge of People: A Personal View of Oxfam's First Forty Years*. London: Heinemann.

Williams, Daniel. 2010. *God's Own Party: The Making of the Christian Right*. Oxford: Oxford University Press.

Wilson, Francesca. 1967. *Rebel Daughter of a Country House: The Life of Eglantyne Jebb, Founder of Save the Children Fund*. Crows Nest: Allen & Unwin.

Winter, Emily and Linda Woodhead. 2014. Micah Challenge: An Evangelical Experiment in Development Advocacy. Evaluation Report.

World Bank. 2001. Attacking Poverty: Opportunity, Empowerment, and Security. World Development Report 2000/2001. Available at https://openknowledge.worldbank.org/bitstream/handle/10986/11856/9780195211290_overview.pdf

World Evangelical Fellowship. 1983. Transformation: The Church in Response to Human Need. Statement of the Wheaton Consultation. Available at www.lausanne.org/content/statement/transformation-the-church-in-response-to-human-need

Index

10/40 Window 61

abolition 22–3
accountability 56, 64, 72, 74, 82, 87, 152
accounting 64, 66–7, 73, 79, 83, 161
accumulation 9, 10
ActionAid 85, 152
Active Learning Network for Accountability and Performance (ALNAP) 11, 74, 75
Adams, Richard 48
Adeney, David 55, 58, 72, 88
advocacy 98–9, 104–6, 130–2, 133–4, 137, 155
advocacy toolkit 130, 132
advocacy work with churches 130–2
Afghanistan 58, 72, 76, 77, 78
Africa 9, 10, 20, 23, 26, 30, 46, 54, 61, 90–6, 101, 118–19, 122, 123–5, 166, 171
Africa Inland Church 91
Africa Inland Mission (AIM) 24, 44, 46
agriculture 26, 46, 67
All Nations Bible College 27
American Presidential Emergency Fund for AIDS Relief (PEPFAR) 123
Amnesty International 2
Anglican 12, 29, 30, 35, 37, 43, 46, 91, 93, 118–19, 122, 140, 171
Anglican Alliance 122
Anglican Development Services of Mount Kenya East (ADS-MKE) 118–19
Anti-Slavery International 37
Argentina 2, 43, 44, 47, 62, 120
Armenia 71
Asia 20, 23, 30, 46, 61, 65, 119–22, 163
Association for World Peace 30
Association of Evangelicals of Liberia (AEL) 128–30

Australia 6, 155
Austria 29
awakening 18, 20, 24, 28

Balfour, Doug 62–7, 73
Bangladesh 47–8, 51, 119
Baptist 12, 21, 37, 103, 171
Baptist Missionary Society (BMS) 21, 22
Basel Evangelical Missionary Society 21
behaviour change 10, 56, 116, 123–5, 128–9, 151, 166
beneficiaries 3, 8, 113, 114, 137, 140, 147, 156, 166, 174
beneficiary accountability 140
Bible belt 138
Bible colleges 51, 150
Bible Societies 19
Bible study 93, 117–19, 121, 127, 146, 149, 172, 175
Big Church Switch 155
Black, Maggie 1, 31
black-majority churches 170
Board 12, 27, 43, 45, 50, 62, 78, 80, 101, 103, 136
Bolivia 119
boreholes 9, 52
Bornstein, Erica 2, 9
Brazil 119, 155
British and Foreign Bible Society (BFBS) 21
British Council of Churches (BCC) 25, 29, 33, 36
British Evangelical Council (BEC) 35
British Overseas NGOs for Development (BOND) 11, 65
Buddhist 4
bureaucratisation 24, 161
Burkina Faso 124
Burundi 72

192 *Index*

Buxton, Dorothy 28

café 172–3
CAFOD 32, 36, 57, 58, 144, 152
Caleb process 63, 68
Calver, Clive 100
Calvinists 23, 28, 37
Cambodia 119
campaigning 98–101, 105–7, 132–4, 154–5, 174, 175
campaigning with the local church 132–4
capitalism 10, 108, 166
Carbon Fast 133
Carey, William 21
Caritas 74
Carter, Isabel 101, 109
Catholic 2, 4, 29, 32, 36, 57, 74, 94, 114, 118, 120, 144, 147, 176
Center for Faith-Based and Community Initiatives 6, 114
Central African Republic 46, 135
Central America 149
Chad 149
charismatic 12, 170, 171
charity 5, 13, 20, 31, 45, 58, 62, 107, 151
Charity Commission 78, 102
charity law 99
Charter for Change 152
Charter for Faith-Based Humanitarian Action 152
child sponsorship 47–9, 64
children 20, 26, 29, 48–9, 57, 64, 69, 91, 92, 135, 171
China 22
China Inland Mission 24, 46; *see also* Overseas Missionary Fellowship
Christian Aid 14, 25, 29, 30, 32, 33, 36, 41, 44, 46, 54, 57, 63, 65, 72, 75, 85, 99, 102, 122, 140, 152, 155, 163, 169
Christian Community Services of Mount Kenya East (CCSMKE) 131
Christian development 53–4, 81–5, 87–93, 106, 115, 142
Christian ghetto 15, 75, 79, 96
Christian Perspectives on Disaster Management 70
Christian Reconstruction in Europe Committee 29
Christian Right 61
Church and Community Mobilisation (CCM) 90–4, 96, 116–23, 127, 130, 141–51, 164
Church and community transformation (CCT) 141

church building 117–19, 155
Church Community Change 93, 120
church growth 51, 52, 144, 157
church involvement 117, 126
church leaders 50, 56, 93, 95, 104, 106, 113, 124, 127, 131, 149, 150, 156, 168
Church Missionary Society (CMS) 21, 24, 26, 31, 37, 46
church mobilisation 67, 117
Church of England 35–6, 37, 99, 155, 168
church representatives 12, 169, 170, 171
circular economy 155
classical missionary societies 24, 33
Climate Coalition 107, 137
clinics 41, 52, 57, 94, 117; *see also* hospitals
Collins, John 30
Colombia 126–7
Colonial Development and Welfare Act 26
commerce and Christianity 23–5
Communications Department 170
comparative advantage 1, 26, 61, 139, 167
Compassion 6, 37, 48, 65
conflict 69, 71, 131, 146; religious 148, 151; spiritual 82
Connected Church 173–4
conservative and liberal Protestants 25–7, 35, 37
construction 44, 46, 118, 121
Corporation for Social Community Development (CORSOC) 126–7
corruption 120, 137
cosmopolitanism 18, 23
Council of Anglican Provinces in Africa 122
Council of British Societies for Relief Abroad (COBSRA) 29
Council of Voluntary Societies for the Relief of Suffering and for Aiding Social Recovery 29
Country Offices 65–8, 79
creation 34, 81, 132
creation care 107
cross 13
crusades 42
cultural imperialism 10
cultural proximity 8, 11
cycle of secularisation and revitalisation 162

Debt Crisis Network 102
decentralisation 67, 68

Index

decentralised clean energy 155
Democratic Republic of Congo 135; *see also* Republic of Congo
Dent, Michael 101–2
Department for International Development (DFID) 6, 7, 63, 73, 96, 105; *see also* Ministry of Overseas Development
Derham, Morgan 35, 42, 45, 50–1
desk officer 64, 66, 68, 90, 94
development wing 54, 56, 66, 70, 76, 82, 115, 161
dichotomy between material and spiritual 6, 15, 54, 55, 58, 83, 88
Disaster Management Development Programme 77
disaster management work with churches 126–7
Disaster Response Team 70–5
disaster risk reduction 127, 137, 140
disasters 32, 46, 54, 70–1, 104, 116, 126–30, 134–8
Disasters and the Local Church 127
Disasters Emergency Committee (DEC) 11, 32, 72–3, 75
discourses 1, 8, 28, 167
dispensaries 24, 118–19
donors 4, 6–7, 10–11, 61, 64, 72–3, 93, 115, 123, 141, 152, 161–2, 167
Duffield, Mary-Jean 42, 98
Dunant, Jean-Henri 28

EAR Fund 43
earthquakes 12, 54, 71, 127, 135
Ebola 127–30, 166
ecumenical movement 25, 29, 33, 53, 84
Eden, Martyn 100
Edinburgh and Glasgow Missionary Society 21
Edinburgh Missionary Conference 25
eighteenth century 20–2, 37
emergency response 54, 56, 72, 75, 126–7, 128–9, 136
empowerment 10, 82, 86, 88, 144, 157
environment 69, 81, 105, 107
environmental and economic sustainability 141
envisioning 116–17, 139; for integral mission 117
EQUIP 128–30
Escobar, Samuel 34, 49, 62
Establishing sustainable Christian Communities 117
ethical tourism 105
Ethiopia 47, 55–7, 99, 147, 157

Europe 6, 8, 10, 13, 18, 20, 22, 27–30, 99, 137
evaluation 67, 73, 79, 92, 143–4
Evangelical Alliance 12, 17, 25, 35, 42–3, 50–1, 54, 98, 126, 169
Evangelical Alliance Refugee Fund 42
evangelical media 175
Evangelical Missionary Alliance 12, 27, 42, 51, 86; *see also* Global Connections
evangelical missionary sector 5, 20–7, 61–2, 86, 164
Evangelical Union of South America 44
Evangelicalism 10, 17, 35, 98, 134, 168
evangelism 6, 9, 20–7, 34, 41, 50–2, 57–8, 61–2, 75–7, 81–2, 87–8, 93–4, 106, 134, 151, 161–3
Evangelism and Christian Education Department 14, 41, 50–2, 64, 80, 88, 150
evangelism and social action 2, 6, 36, 49, 55, 83–5
exorcism 8
expatriate staff 22, 51, 64, 65, 69, 70, 77

Fairbairn, Graham 47, 50–2, 55, 57, 64
faith distinctiveness 167
faith missions 23, 24–5
faith-based organisations (FBOs) 1, 4–11, 36, 113–15, 164–5
Fall 81
famine 29, 43, 44, 55, 70, 99
festivals 133, 172
floods 48, 54, 71, 127
flourishing 142, 144–7
food security 69, 104, 128, 134, 137
Footsteps 101, 109
Forsythe, David 2
fragile states 141, 151–3
Freedom from Hunger campaign (FFH) 32
Friends Relief Service 29
Frost, Matthew 79, 115, 141
fundraising 42, 173, 176

gender inequality 124–5
Germany 21, 29
Gitau, Peter 92
Global Action Network 103
Global Connections 12, 85, 86; *see also* Evangelical Missionary Alliance
Global Justice Now 99; *see also* World Development Movement
global norms 67, 77, 135
Gollancz, Victor 30
good governance 69, 137

Index

Graham, Billy 42
Great Mandate 21
Greece 29

Haiti 12, 119, 135, 176
Halvorson, Britt 2
HAP Standard in Humanitarian Accountability and Quality Management 135
harmful traditional beliefs 9
Harris, Nigel 141, 150
healthcare 26, 27, 28, 54, 55, 69, 95, 121, 123, 127–8, 144–5, 154, 169
Hindu 4, 120; working in a Hindu context 120–2
HIV and AIDS 69, 94–6, 105, 123–4, 134, 137, 166
HIV Champions 95
Hoffman, George 42–6, 49
holistic development 5, 54, 83–4
Hollow, Mike 1, 3, 43, 44, 52, 104
Holy Spirit 17, 27, 90
Honduras 100
Hong Kong 42, 43
Hopgood, Stephen 2
hospitals 24, 46; *see also* clinics
human rights 2, 28, 30, 31, 85, 100, 104, 131, 138
Humanitarian Charter and Minimum Standards in Disaster Response 135
humanitarianism, emergence of 27–32

Imams 129
immorality 94
impact 10–11, 56, 57, 66, 69, 71, 119, 141, 142–7, 153, 157, 162
incarnational theology 26, 53
India 22, 23, 27, 43, 48, 88, 94, 119
indicators 141–7, 156, 162
indigenous churches 54, 57, 68
individual change 15, 98
individualism 10, 166
Indonesia 72
industrialisation 18–19, 27
inequality 18–19, 34, 98, 155
Iniciativa Cristiana 47
institutional funding 72–3, 79, 108, 116, 135, 139, 173
instrumentalisation 7, 162
Integral Alliance 11, 75, 126, 136
integral mission 34, 49, 52–3, 62, 83–6, 89, 116–19, 142, 149–50, 153, 162–4; *see also* misíon integral
integral missionaries 164

Inter-Church Aid and Refugee Service 29
International Care Ministries 127
international standards 15, 73–5, 135, 139, 156, 161
International Volunteering Team 174; *see also* Transform
Interserve 47, 86
Iraq 135, 136–7, 153
irrigation systems 93, 117, 118
Islamic State 136
Italy 29

Jackson-Cole, Cecil 29
Japan 103
Jebb, Eglantyne 28
Jewish 29, 30
joint campaigns and coalitions 107
Joint Learning Initiative on Local Faith Communities 12, 166
Jordan 43
Jordan process 62–3, 68
journal 26, 168
jubilee 13, 154–5; debt campaign 101–4, 107, 109, 133
Jubilee 2000 101–4, 133, 154
Justice Conference 155

Kale Heywet Church 55–7
Kenya 93, 94, 95, 109, 117, 118–19, 122, 131, 135, 148, 149
Keswick Convention 172
Kingdom theology 34, 53, 153

Labour movement 30
land rights 69, 100
Latin America 20, 34, 49, 54, 65, 82, 84, 88, 100, 120, 131–2, 150
Lausanne conference 49, 52, 61
League of Nations 28
Lent 133
liberation theology 34
Liberia 128–30
lifestyle 20, 100, 132–3, 142, 155, 174–5
Light Wheel 144–7, 156, 157
literacy 21, 67, 69, 92, 121, 166
livelihoods 67, 69, 86, 105, 119, 130, 134, 146, 157
living faith 144–6
Livingstone Inland Mission 24
Lloyd-Jones, Martyn 35
lobbying 98–100, 104–7, 131, 133, 137, 138, 165
local church 11, 66, 68, 79, 82, 90–4, 95–6, 115, 116–34, 142, 152, 161, 169

local elites 54
local faith leaders 7, 128–9
local instantiations of Christianity 8
localisation agenda 152
logframes 64, 66, 83
London Missionary Society (LMS) 21, 22, 26
Luetchford, Mark 1, 30
Lutheran 2, 74, 118
Lutheran World Federation 74

Madagascar 2
mainstreaming the church 150–1
Make Poverty History 107
Malawi 95
material and spiritual poverty 115, 138
MedAir 136
Médecins San Frontiers 2
Methodist 12, 21, 37, 118, 171
Micah Challenge 132–4
Micah Declaration 85
Micah Network 11, 85–6, 117, 122, 126, 133
micro-finance 69
middle class 12, 19, 148, 171
Middle East 88, 119
Milford, Richard 29
Millennium Development Goals 133
Ministry of Overseas Development 32, 72; *see also* Department for International Development
misíon integral 34, 49, 82, 120; *see also* integral mission
mission agencies 3, 24, 27, 34, 45, 54, 61, 86, 163, 167
Mission East 136
missionaries 20–7, 30–1, 33–6, 42, 44–7, 51, 54, 55, 57, 162–4, 167; agricultural 47
missionary networks 46
modernist ontology 166
Mopawi 100, 130
morality 3, 9, 10, 18, 33, 71, 88
Mothers' Union 122
Mukarji, Daleep 65
Muslim 4, 79, 120, 125, 128, 152; working in Muslim countries 77–8, 136–7, 153
Myanmar 19

National Assembly of Evangelicals 35, 43
National Evangelical Anglican Congress 35
National Evangelical Church of Peru (CONEP) 131

Neech, Alan 45
neoliberal 10, 61, 161
Nepal 12, 27, 51, 58, 119, 135
new policy agenda 61
New Wine 170, 172
New Zealand 48
NGO-isation 33
NGOs 2–3, 5–7, 27–32, 46, 63, 72; Christian 46, 52, 57, 66, 67, 70, 114, 115, 124, 130, 156; evangelical development 2, 5, 65, 78, 85, 151
Nigeria 43, 95, 155
nineteenth century 18–25
Njeroge, Francis 92
nonconformists 19, 37
nurses 47

O'Sullivan, Veena 94–6, 124, 151
Occhipinti, Laurie 2, 114, 165
Oceania 9
Oliver, Ernest 27, 42–3, 45, 50–1, 58
Open Doors 27
operating principles 81–3, 86, 92, 106
operational work 65–8, 71–4, 77–9, 108, 113, 134–7, 153, 164
Ordinary Heroes 155
Orthodox 136, 147, 148
Overcoming Poverty 89, 142
Overseas Missionary Fellowship 46; *see also* China Inland Mission
overseas personnel (OPs) 41, 47, 55, 57, 64, 70, 109
Oxfam 1, 15, 29, 30, 32, 36, 42, 44, 46, 48, 50, 54, 61, 72, 85, 99, 152, 169

Pacific 22
Padilla, René 34, 49, 62, 69, 82, 84, 120
Pakistan 72, 77, 135
pamphlets 26
paradoxes of faith-based development 166–7
Paraguay 43
parliament 19, 99, 100, 101, 139
Participatory Evaluation Process (PEP) 91–3
Partner Panel 69
Partners in Childcare 48
Partners in Development 174
Pastor Information Network 127
Pastors 120, 122, 127, 129, 149–50
Pastors in disasters 127–8
Paths out of Poverty 86–90
Paz y Esperanza 100, 130, 131–2
Peace Societies 27

peacebuilding 151–2, 156
Pentecostal 10, 17, 93, 94, 118
Pentecostal Assemblies of God (PAG) 93
Peru 46, 67, 100, 119, 131–2
Peters, Bill 101
Pettifor, Ann 102
Plan International 29, 48
policy 43, 73, 76–7, 100–1, 104–7, 115, 133, 155
political 3, 19, 22, 30, 32, 34, 61, 71, 79, 89, 98–104, 131–4, 151, 155
post-colonial context 14, 30, 33–4, 41, 45, 51, 161
post-secular society 114
poverty 19, 31, 33, 63, 65, 81, 86–90, 98, 103, 108, 141, 142, 154
prayer 3, 5, 9, 12–13, 26, 43, 50, 78, 82, 100, 103, 106, 137, 146, 170–1
prayer diary 171
preaching 21, 41, 77, 92, 129, 168
premillennial dispensationalist theology 24, 27, 53
Presbyterian 12, 37, 171
proclamation of the gospel 27, 34, 45, 49, 85, 163
professional excellence 64, 72
professionalise 15, 28, 63, 65–9, 70–5, 86, 96, 156
project proposals 64, 93
proselytism 6, 10, 76, 164
prosperity gospel 150
Protestant church 4, 25, 33, 151
psychosocial work 69, 127, 129
Publish What You Pay coalition 137

Quakers 27, 29, 30, 37
Quality Standards 135–6
Qur'an 125

'reaping the harvest' 153
reconciliation 8, 82–3, 86, 131, 151
Red Cross 2, 28–9, 32, 37, 74–5, 135
Red Cross Code of Conduct 74–5, 135
redemption 81
Redfield, Peter 2
refugees 29, 30, 42
regional advisors 68
regional coordinators 170
Regions Beyond Mission Union 24, 27, 44
relationships 65, 66, 77, 81–2, 85–7, 92, 106, 142–6, 153; broken 81, 86
religion as a worldview 5
religious conversion 9
religious freedom 76, 121, 153, 164

Renew Our World 155
Republic of Congo 42, 135; *see also* Democratic Republic of Congo
resilience 130, 134, 140, 145, 146
restorative economy 154–5
resurgence in religion 16, 113–14
Richard, Cliff 44, 168
Rio Earth Summit 100
risk register 78, 136
role of religion in development 6, 8–11, 114, 162, 165–6
Rwanda 71, 73, 149

Salvation Army 29
Samaritan's Purse 122
Satan 9
Save Europe Now 30
Save the Children 15, 28, 29, 32, 48, 61, 63, 65, 75
saving souls 27, 53, 61, 168
Scholarship Fund 42
schools 4, 8, 22, 24, 32, 94, 117, 118
scripture 20, 25, 34, 125
Scripture Union 171
secularisation 28, 33, 36, 61, 73, 78, 79, 162
self-help groups 149
senior leadership 12, 49, 50, 58, 62–3, 66, 68, 71, 73, 82, 96, 101–2
separation of church and state 8
sexual and gender-based violence (SGBV) 124–5, 139, 140, 166
Shelter Now 76
short-term mission 47, 175
Sierra Leone 72, 128
sin 53, 86–9, 95
slavery 18, 22–3, 37
socialist 30
Somalia 153
Soul Action 171–3
Soul Survivor 171, 173
South Africa 95
South American Missionary Society (SAMS) 21, 43–7
South Sudan 135
'sowing the seeds' 153
Spain 29
specialist volunteers 175
SPHERE guidelines 74–6, 135
spiritual development 23, 146–7
spiritual metrics 144
spiritual passion 63, 64, 66, 72, 161
Spring Harvest 100, 172
staff induction 3, 12

staff prayers 3, 12
statement of faith 4, 12, 57, 78, 81
Stott, John 34, 35, 49, 62, 82
Structural Adjustment Programs 61, 114
Sudan 51, 72, 77, 94
Sudan Interior Mission (SIM) 24, 47, 55
Sudan United Mission 24, 44
summer work camps 169
supporters 12, 26, 45, 46, 47, 72, 93, 100, 102–5, 132, 133, 168–76
Sutton, Harry 45, 47
Switzerland 21, 114
systemic change 15, 98

Tanzania 91, 93, 94, 117, 144
Taylor, Hudson 24
Taylor, Michael 57
team meetings 3, 12
TEAR Netherlands 122
Tear Times 47, 99, 100, 102, 108, 168, 171
Tearcraft 48–9, 64, 140, 169
Tearfund Sunday 168
tensions 1, 6, 35, 63, 70, 96, 107, 113, 121, 139, 147–8, 161, 164
Thailand 46
The Message 171
theologian 34, 81, 89, 100
theological adviser 15, 80
theological committee 78
theology 24–7, 34, 49, 51, 53, 80–5, 86–90, 97, 130, 144, 149, 150, 163–7; and network engagement 149; of advocacy 130; of development 53, 80–3, 97
theory of change 141–2
Theos 144
'they can't eat prayer' 43, 50
Thinking Theology 150
Third Track 171
Third Way 57
'three wise men' 54
tithe 117–19, 173
Topping, Mark 57
trade 33, 89, 98, 100, 104–5, 107, 108, 137
Trade Justice Movement 107, 137
Traidcraft 48, 140
Transform 174–5; *see also* International Volunteering Team
transformation 53, 54, 81–5, 90, 94, 113, 142, 143, 148
Transforming Masculinities 125
transnational activism 22
transnational corporations 138
transnational networks 28

Truman, President 30
trust 7, 65, 128, 153, 174
'two blades of a pair of scissors' 49
'two wings of a bird' 49, 165
typologies 1, 4–5, 163–4

Uganda 91, 93, 94, 95, 117, 157
UK Action Programme 92, 140
Umoja manual 119–20
Unevangelised Fields Mission 44
United Mission to Nepal 27, 51, 58
United Nations 30, 32, 89, 123, 138; Framework Convention on Climate Change 138
United Society for the Propagation of the Gospel (USPG) 37, 122, 164
Universal Declaration of Human Rights 30
unreached peoples 24, 27, 61
unrestricted funding 93, 174
USA 2, 27, 29, 37, 61, 108, 114, 123, 138, 144, 155, 175
USAID 6, 7

very poorest 54, 148
Vietnam 42, 43
Voices of the Poor 114
Volf, Miroslav 81
voluntary associations 19–21, 27
Voluntary Committee on Overseas Aid and Development 32
Voluntary Services Overseas (VSO) 47
volunteers 19, 28, 32, 47, 55, 127, 169, 171–5

war 28–9, 34, 71
war charities 28, 30
war on terror 114
War on Want 1, 29–30, 32, 36, 42, 48, 85, 102, 169
Warmis 67
Warren, Max 31
Wathanga, Gladys 90–4
Weber, Max 10
Welfare Reform Act 114
welfare state 20, 31
wells 41, 52, 57, 81, 93, 130, 165
Wheaton 34, 52–3, 81, 84
whole life discipleship 77
whole life transformation 127, 142–3, 152
Wholly Living 144
Whose Earth? 100, 105
working culture 12
World Bank 86, 87, 89, 114, 123
World Congress on Evangelism 34

World Council of Churches (WCC) 25, 29, 33, 54, 74, 156
World Development Movement 99; *see also* Global Justice Now
World Evangelical Alliance (WEA) 126, 133; *see also* World Evangelical Fellowship
World Evangelical Fellowship 46, 52–3, 54; *see also* World Evangelical Alliance
World Humanitarian Summit 152
World Refugee Year 42
World Vision 6, 9, 17, 37, 48, 49, 65, 79, 91, 97
World Watch Prayer Link 100, 171
Worldwide Evangelization Crusade (WEC) 44, 46
worship 12, 13, 106, 138
Wycliffe Bible Translators 27

Yemen 153
youth 32, 93, 102, 121, 151, 169, 170, 171
Youth Against Hunger (YAH) 32
Youth for Christ 27, 100, 171
Youth with a Mission 27

Zaire 46
Zimbabwe 2, 9, 124, 149